Alexander Wynne is the Academic Head
Project, based at Wat Phra Dhammakay
paring a critical edition of the Pali ca
Richard Gombrich at the University of Oxford, he has lectured on Buddhism and Indian religion in Thailand (at Mahidol University) and India (at FLAME, Pune), and has written extensively on the early history of Indian Buddhism, including the book *The Origin of Buddhist Meditation* (2007).

'Most introductions to Buddhism list the earliest teachings and practices, outline a few major doctrinal developments, and maybe add a thumbnail sketch of how Buddhism spread across the globe. They find little space for more than a catalogue of factual information. Alexander Wynne has managed to select the salient facts, but also to go far further. His book is valuable and original because he analyzes the historical context of the developments he is describing, providing rich insights which situate Buddhism within world history. Wynne's book is a remarkable achievement.' – ***Richard F. Gombrich, Boden Professor of Sanskrit Emeritus, University of Oxford and Director, Oxford Centre for Buddhist Studies***

'An engaging introductory survey of Buddhism that is alert to scholarly debates and that includes a thought-provoking account of meditation in early Buddhism.' – ***B. Peter Harvey, Emeritus Professor of Buddhist Studies, University of Sunderland, and author of* An Introduction to Buddhism *(1990) and* An Introduction to Buddhist Ethics *(2000)***

'More than just an introduction, this book provides a stimulating engagement with the intellectual history of Buddhism from its origins down to its encounter with the contemporary West. Wynne does a remarkably good job of joining up the dots without getting sidetracked by irrelevant details. I recommend his book to anyone looking for a more thoughtful introduction to the Buddhist tradition than is offered by many titles currently available.' – ***Damien Keown, Professor of Buddhist Ethics, Goldsmiths, University of London***

I.B.TAURIS INTRODUCTIONS TO RELIGION

In recent years there has been a surge of interest in religion and in the motivations behind religious belief and commitment. Avoiding over-simplification, jargon or unhelpful stereotypes, I.B.Tauris Introductions to Religion embraces the opportunity to explore religious tradition in a sensitive, objective and nuanced manner. A specially commissioned series for undergraduate students, it offers concise, clearly written overviews, by leading experts in the field, of the world's major religious faiths, and of the challenges posed to all the religions by progress, globalization and diaspora. Covering the fundamentals of history, theology, ritual and worship, these books place an emphasis above all on the modern world, and on the lived faiths of contemporary believers. They explore, in a way that will engage followers and non-believers alike, the fascinating and sometimes difficult contradictions or reconciling ancient tradition with headlong cultural and technological change.

'I.B.Tauris Introductions to Religion offers students of religion something fresh, intelligent and accessible. Without dumbing down the issues, or making complex matters seem more simple than they need to be, the series manages to be both conceptually challenging while also providing beginning undergraduates with the complete portfolio of books that they need to grasp the fundamentals of each tradition. To be religious is in the end to be human. The I.B.Tauris series looks to be an ideal starting point for anyone interested in this vital and often elusive component of all our societies and cultures.' – ***John M. Hull, Emeritus Professor of Religious Education, University of Birmingham***

'The I.B.Tauris Introductions to Religion series promises to be just what busy teachers and students need: a batch of high-quality, highly accessible books by leading scholars that are thoroughly geared towards pedagogical needs and student course use. Achieving a proper understanding of the role of religion in the world is, more than ever, an urgent necessity. This attractive-looking series will contribute towards that vital task.' – ***Christopher Partridge, Professor of Religious Studies, Lancaster University***

'The I.B.Tauris series promises to offer more than the usual kind of humdrum introduction. The volumes will seek to explain and not merely to describe religions, will consider religions as ways of life and not merely as sets of beliefs and practices, and will explore differences as well as similarities among specific communities of adherents worldwide. Strongly recommended.' – ***Robert A. Segal, Professor of Religious Studies, University of Aberdeen***

Please see the back of the book for the full series list

I.B.TAURIS INTRODUCTIONS TO RELIGION

Buddhism

An Introduction

by

Alexander Wynne

I.B.TAURIS
LONDON · NEW YORK

Published in 2015 by I.B.Tauris & Co. Ltd
6 Salem Road, London W2 4BU
175 Fifth Avenue, New York NY 10010
www.ibtauris.com

Distributed in the United States and Canada Exclusively by Palgrave Macmillan
175 Fifth Avenue, New York NY 10010

ISBN: 978 1 84885 396 6 (HB)
ISBN: 978 1 84885 397 3 (PB)
eISBN: 978 0 85773 814 1

A full CIP record for this book is available from the British Library
A full CIP record is available from the Library of Congress

Library of Congress Catalog Card Number: available

Typeset by Initial Typesetting Services, Edinburgh
Printed and bound in Great Britain by T.J. International, Padstow, Cornwall

MIX
Paper from responsible sources
FSC www.fsc.org FSC® C013056

sarvadṛṣṭiprahāṇāya yaḥ saddharmam adeśayat
anukampām upādāya taṃ namasyāmi gautamam

I bow down to Gautama, who out of compassion
Taught the true Dharma for the abandonment of all views

Nāgārjuna, *Mūlamadhyamaka-kārikā XVII.30*

Contents

Linguistic Conventions and References

All Buddhist terms are cited in their Pali forms until Chapter V, partly because the Pali canon is the source of almost everything contained in this part of the book, but also because the Pali language is close to the dialects spoken by the Buddha and his followers in the period this part of the book covers. The section on Theravāda Buddhism in Chapter VIII also uses Pali where appropriate. For most of Chapter VI all terms are cited in Sanskrit, reflecting the linguistic shift which occurred in Indian Buddhism in the first few centuries AD, and which is especially associated with the emergence of Mahāyāna Buddhism.

In Chapter VII all Chinese terms are cited in their Pinyin forms; in Chapter VIII Korean terms are cited according to the revised Romanization system, Japanese terms are cited according to the Hepburn system, and Tibetan terms are cited in a simplified phonetic form based on the system used in Matthew Kapstein's *The Tibetans* (2006).

In order to avoid cluttering the text with an unwieldy system of citations, this book lacks a reference section and a detailed bibliography. For both of these a document is available online at www.ibtauris.com/buddhism/notes

Acknowledgements

This book would not have been written without the encouragement of Paul Williams, who first suggested the project, and would not have been completed without the support of Alex Wright at I.B.Tauris, who waited patiently while the book unfolded. To both I am grateful. As with all my work I am indebted to Richard Gombrich for his wise advice.

Many of the ideas contained in the book were devised while I taught at Mahidol University, Thailand, and then developed while I lectured at FLAME, Pune. I am grateful to the staff at both institutions, for their kind encouragement, and to the students who attended my classes, and responded enthusiastically (at least occasionally) to my ideas. I am especially grateful to the Dhammakaya temple, for providing a stimulating research environment in which I could gather my thoughts while working on the final phases of the book.

In the course of writing this book many friends and colleagues have provided valuable comments, encouragement and criticism. I would particularly like to thank Achim Beyer, Georges Dreyfus, Paul Dundas, Volkmar Enßlin, Gergely Hidas, Matthew Kosuta, Peter Masefield, Justin Meiland, Charles Muller, Kieko Obuse, Jeffrey Race, Joe Rotheray and Matthia Salvini.

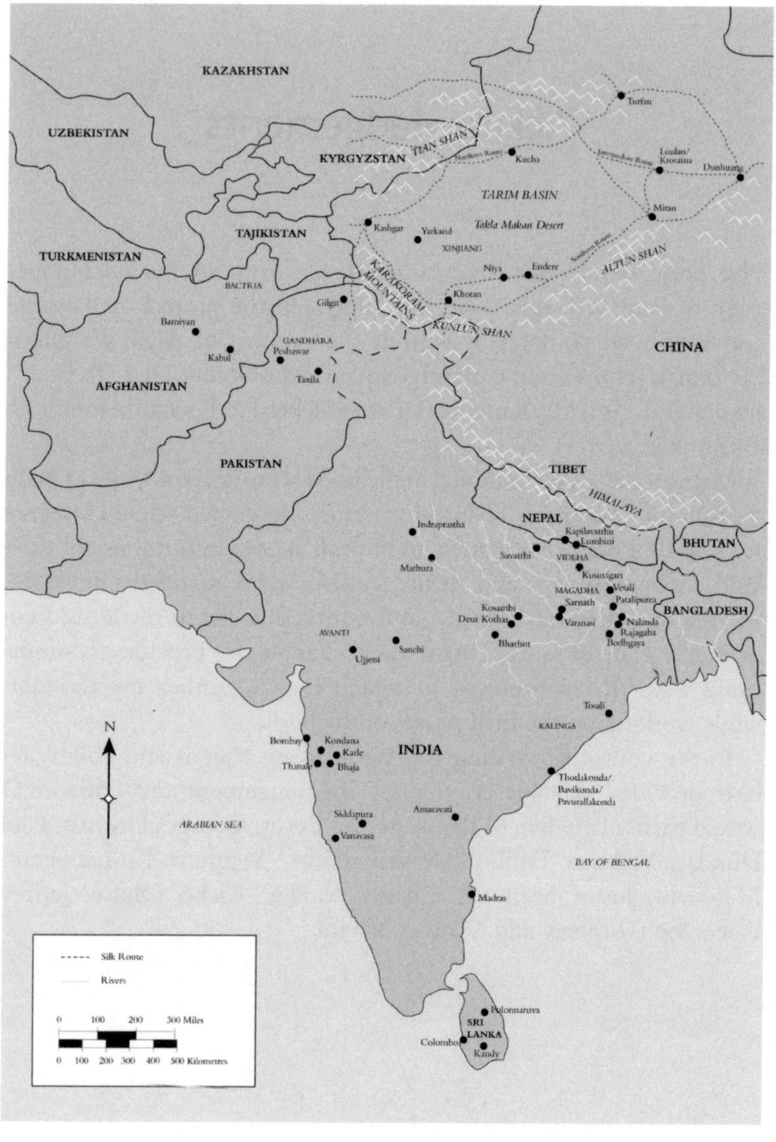

Map 1. Buddhist sites in South Asia

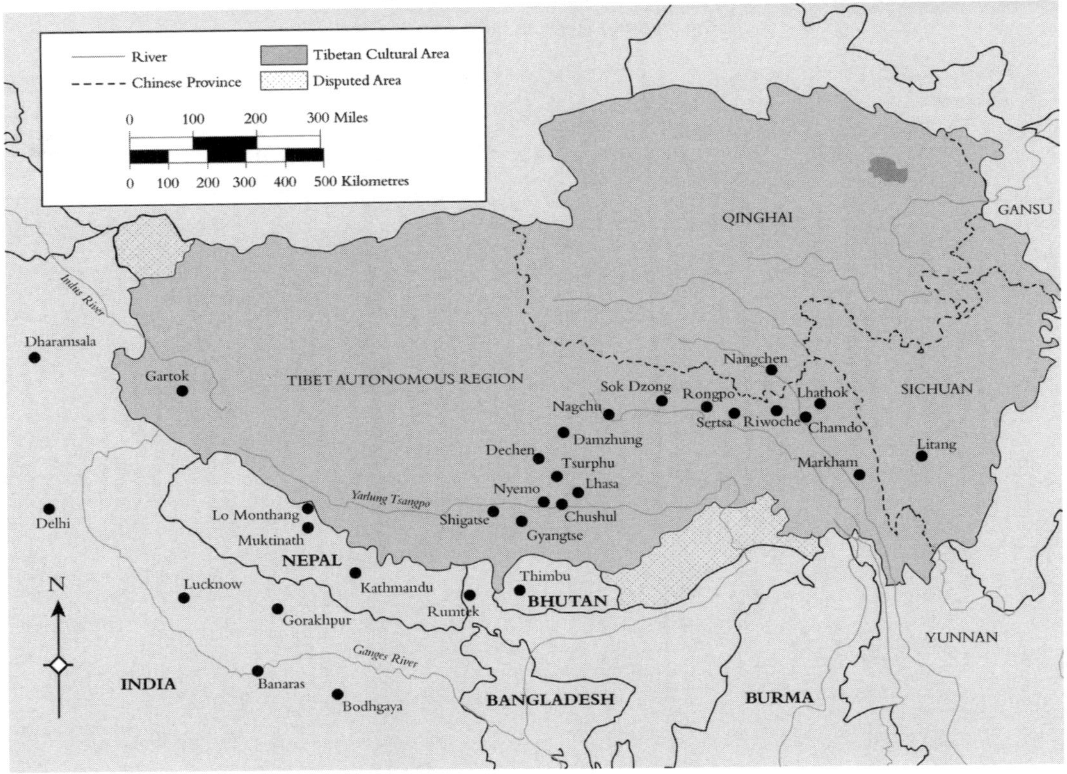

Map 2. Tibet, including Buddhist sites

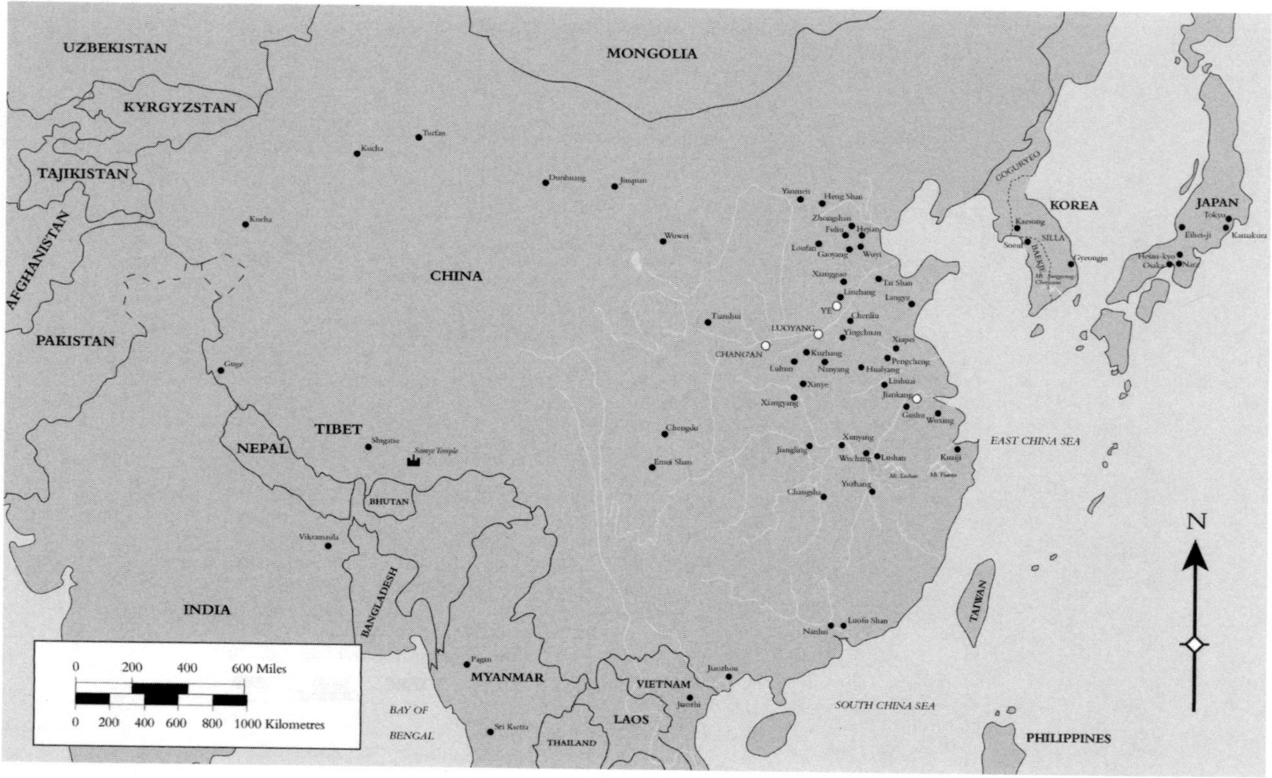

Map 3. East Asia, including Buddhist sites

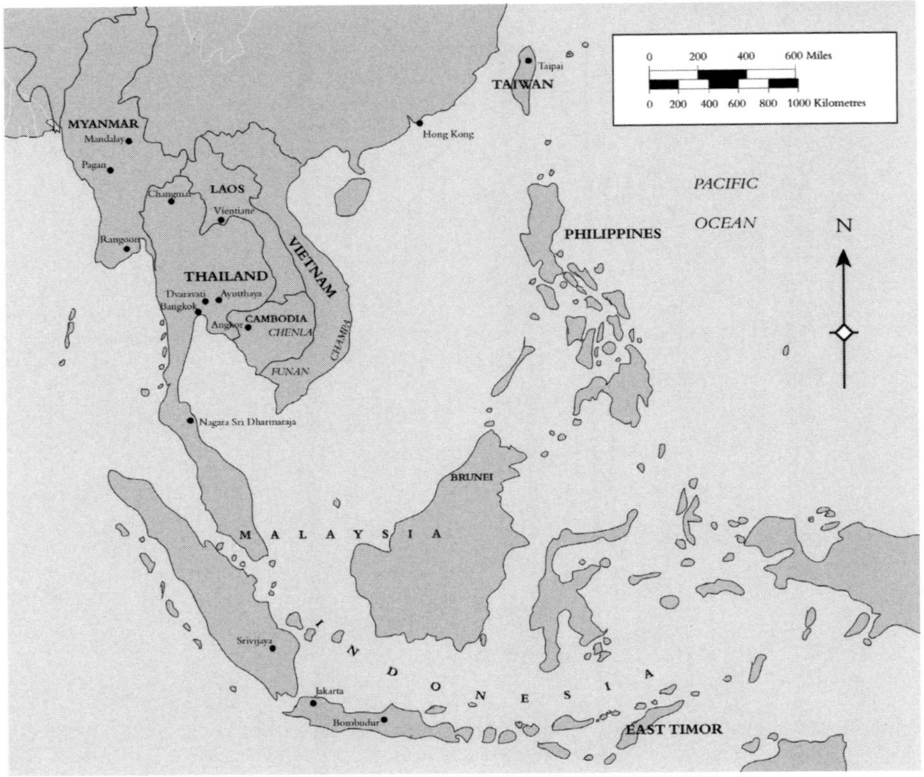

Map 4. Buddhist sites in Southeast Asia

Chapter I
A World Religion

> Wander forth, mendicants, for the good of the many, for the happiness of the many, out of compassion for the world, for the welfare and happiness of gods and men: may two of you not follow the same path.
>
> *Vinayapiṭka, Mahāvagga*

Buddhist Universalism

For a period of six years in the mid-fifth century BC, before he became the 'awakened one', Gotama, the historical Buddha, wandered around northern India as a homeless religious seeker. His quest finally came to an end near the village of Uruvelā, in the kingdom of Magadha: during a prolonged period of meditation, at a pleasant spot near a river in the woods, Gotama attained Nirvana. Whatever really happened under the tree of awakening, this was a decisive moment in the history of civilization. For soon afterwards the Buddha travelled to Sarnath to preach his first sermon, and then spent the remainder of his life establishing something unprecedented: a missionary religion, the first of its kind in the world, with a purpose to spread his teachings 'for the welfare and happiness of gods and men'.

In the hands of the Buddha and his followers the scope and purpose of religion was radically reconfigured. Henceforth the world would be dominated by a new kind of religious culture, one whose universal aims were initially spread across Asia by Buddhist missionaries. After some considerable time, similar missionary movements arose in the form of Christianity and Islam. But the adherents of both followed the Buddhist precedent by believing in something more than their universal teachings on ethics, salvation and so forth. The followers of all three religions, beginning with the Buddhists, were motivated by something quite unusual: the belief in the predestined or divinely chosen mission of their founders.

This peculiar teleological vision has inspired the devotees of all three religions to believe that their dispensations have a fundamentally important purpose in human affairs. Such a claim is not found in the other religions of the world, which have not been imagined as the medium by which all might participate in a divine order. Religious teleology was thus the essential aspect in turning missionary universalism into social reality, unlike other religions of the world, which have generally lacked the same missionary impulse even if occasionally expressing a comparable cosmic vision, or aspiring to a similar purpose. It follows that only Buddhism, Christianity and Islam can be called 'world religions', for only they have a truly universal vision and imperative.

The distinction between world religions and religions of the world helps explain why these three religions have played a disproportionately important role in the history of civilization. The belief in a predestined purpose fashioned cultural trajectories of immense significance, which affected the course of civilization in a most profound way. So great has been their influence that it is almost impossible to envision a world without them – almost as impossible, in fact, as it is to imagine a world without science. Religion and more recently science have played the greatest cultural role in human affairs since the emergence of sedentary life around 10,000 years ago, and the subsequent development of civilization proper.

The Historical Significance of the Buddha

If the religious universalism of the early Buddhists was something new, it would seem that the Buddha's life marks a watershed in the history of civilization. This is not widely recognized, perhaps because of the general tendency to regard all religions as essentially the same. According to the general understanding, a religion is any cultural phenomenon made up of various holy features, such as divine myths, revealed texts, contemplation, pilgrimage, sacred rituals, ceremonies of death, prayer and so on. The various religions of the world are thus assumed to be variations on essential themes, expressions of the sacred which differ according to cultural conditions determined by the time and place of their origin.

The general theory implies that the differences between local and international religions resulted from historical circumstance:

Fig. 1. Relief from the great stūpa *at Sanchi depicting worship at the Bodhi tree; the throne beneath it marks the spot where the Buddha attained his awakening*

sooner or later, so this thesis goes, some religion or other gained the support to turn it into a major movement, as happened in the case of Buddhism, Christianity and Islam. But the historical facts do not support this evolutionary view of religious history. Buddhism emerged in a society much less advanced than the contemporaneous civilization of ancient Greece, and the same is true of Christianity, the rural Palestinian origins of which were a world away from the sophistication of Rome. Even when a major religion such as Hinduism received extensive patronage from the Gupta empire (between the fourth and sixth centuries AD), this did not turn it into a universal movement.

These facts suggest that the development of religion on an international scale was not merely a consequence of major advances in civilization. It is true, of course, that the rise of Buddhism was aided by the patronage of Aśoka and the Mauryan empire, during the third century BC, just as the success of Christianity ultimately depended on support from Rome. But both movements had been widely disseminated before this political backing: imperial support mattered, but only in terms of furthering a religious purpose which had already been formulated in universal terms.

The course of history can only be explained on the assumption that both Buddhism and Christianity were missionary religions from the outset. That is to say, the zeal of their early devotees was the key factor in spreading the new creeds, and establishing a new cultural order. It is therefore a matter of great importance to determine how the universal imperative came about. Why did some men and women imagine that they belonged to movements of global and historical significance? Answers to these questions may possibly be found in the early Buddhist texts. For major sections of this extensive canon are only partially obscured by hagiography and myth, and so reveal much about the Buddha's impact. A careful reading of this literature may show how a new religious understanding was created.

Understanding Buddhism from the Beginning

This book introduces Buddhism by trying to understand how the Buddha inspired a world religion. By exploring the imaginative world of the early movement in its social and intellectual context, it attempts to identify basic themes which explain its appeal and success. This analysis is then elaborated to the spread of the movement throughout Asia, and its more recent transmission to the West. By starting with the Buddha's spiritual 'awakening', this study takes seriously the power of ideas to affect individuals and change societies.

While this might seem an excessively theoretical approach for an introductory book on religion, there seems little point in restating facts that are widely available in printed and electronic media. The 'bare facts' approach, although fundamentally important, is also easily misunderstood, as if presenting a picture of Buddhism as just another religion of the world. Pondering the deeper significance of Buddhist origins thus allows for a more inquisitive approach, one that attempts to deal with questions of 'why?' rather than 'what?' Rather than simply describing what Buddhism is, or has been, this book attempts to explain its diverse forms by exploring underlying speculative and institutional structures.

Investigating Buddhism in this manner is also a useful way of clarifying apparent contradictions in the tradition. One such problem is that of action (karma) and the liberation from it: although it is normally maintained that salvation (Nirvana) is an escape from the world of deeds, morality forms an essential part of the Buddhist path. This doctrinal problem is mirrored by the social fact that Buddhist monks and nuns do not simply leave the world to seek Nirvana, but also become deeply involved in local communities, as educators, doctors, landlords and even moneylenders. Since social engagement and seclusion have been important aspects of all Buddhist societies, it makes sense to begin a general study with the ideological features that inspired the mission in the first place.

A further point which suggests this approach is that Buddhism was profoundly complex from the very beginning. Early Buddhist thinkers did not merely contemplate the ordinary facts of existence and then present a solution to them: they also attempted to change the range of the given by experimenting in altered states of consciousness. This book will claim that the Buddha was the first person in history to reject, let alone entertain, the notion that the external world apprehended through the senses is a mind-independent reality. By approaching the study of Buddhism through an investigation of its founder, an attempt will be made to resolve the mystery at the heart of the movement: the fact that the first world religion was constructed around the idea that the 'world' is not objectively real.

Even if it might not be possible to access the content of the Buddha's awakening, to give the religion its due treatment we must explore these intriguingly subtle beginnings. The revision of Buddhist origins that this requires will in turn affect the general understanding of the various traditions that arose in India and beyond. This attempt to trace the genesis of ideas and institutions need not diminish the achievements of later Buddhist cultures. Locating the origins of Nāgārjuna's Madhyamaka philosophy in the Buddha's teachings, for example, does not imply that this philosophy was merely derivative.

Such an approach can rather highlight the creative genius of later Buddhists, for example by showing more exactly how Nāgārjuna added philosophical depth and rigour to intuitions which had not been systematically articulated.

In its focus on the historical Buddha this investigation differs from almost all modern scholarship on Buddhism. Some will object that this 'Orientalist' approach mistakenly reduces Buddhism to its texts; others will claim that early Buddhist literature is not sufficiently old to allow this sort of revision. But such concerns have surely been exaggerated in recent years. Even if it turns out that the canonical Buddhist literature cannot be taken back to the Buddha, a positivist approach is preferable to the assumption that the early literature has little historical worth, for this prejudice surely hinders scholarly curiosity and enquiry.

Cultural, Institutional and Speculative Structures

This book offers original perspectives on Buddhism in theory and practice: major themes are the significance of Buddhism as a material culture, the essential aspects of which go back to the Buddha's life (and death), as well as a new model of the relationship between Buddhism and the world, in the form of two fundamentally different ideals of ascetic engagement, which I have termed 'guild monasticism' and 'state Buddhism'. These structural models are based on a new account of the Buddha's emergence from the renunciant culture of ancient India, showing how he responded to the social, ritual and ideological trends of this fascinating period in human history.

The alternative intellectual history proposed here is perhaps more important than these cultural and institutional models. This is partly because it is based on a stratification of the canonical texts (a subject which at present is controversial), but also because it suggests that the entire history of Buddhist thought depends on one's understanding of the historical Buddha (a perspective which is at present unthinkable). According to my analysis a philosophy of 'constructed realism', implicit in the earliest stratum of the canonical teachings (which I believe goes back to the Buddha), sets a speculative trajectory quite different from the usual history of Buddhist thought.

The basic idea of this philosophy is relatively straightforward, for the Buddha's point that phenomena depend on the workings of the mind is surely well known: as the first verse of the *Dhammapada* ('Words of the Doctrine') states, 'all phenomena are preceded by mind, culminate in mind, consist of mind'. But the radical implications which follow from this have not yet been grasped. For if the perceived world is a sort of conceptual construction, it implies that space, time and individual existence are not objectively real, and that Nirvana is the ineffable truth of phenomena, rather than an absolute reality beyond it. This book's account of Buddhist thought in India revolves around these ideas, which are elaborated in some detail in the exploration of the early period, drawing out their implications in such subjects as the karma doctrine, cosmology and meditation.

On the basis of this conceptual analysis three major developments in the history of Buddhist thought in India are distinguished. The first two of these are divergences from the Buddha's constructed realism, which I have termed 'reductionistic realism' and 'meditative realism': both of these presume the perceived world to be objectively real, but that it is either lacking in 'self' (for the former) or grounded in an absolute reality, dissolution into which at death constitutes final liberation for a Buddhist saint (for the latter). While various Abhidharma thinkers developed reductionistic realism, I claim that meditative realism was a source for such schools as the Pudgalavādins ('Personalists'). The third development in this model consists of two related philosophical reformulations of the Buddha's constructed realism: first by Nāgārjuna and the Madhyamaka tradition (based on the *prajñā-pāramitā* texts), and then by Vasubandhu and other Vijñaptimātra thinkers.

If this estimation of intellectual history, from the Buddha to Vasubandhu, is roughly correct, it would seem to suggest that a chronological stratification of the canonical texts is unavoidable. Those who disagree with this approach, and prefer to interpret Indian Buddhist philosophy according to its later exegesis, should perhaps bear in mind that what ultimately matters is explanatory power; with regard to Indian Buddhism, this refers to the capacity of any theory to untangle the incredible network of connections which marks the Indian tradition as a whole. A superior theory, surely, is one which shows how the whole intellectual edifice hangs together, rather than simply proposing a new interpretation of any thread in isolation.

Even if the present analysis is deemed hopelessly misconceived by this yardstick, I believe it makes sense to introduce it to general readers with little background knowledge. For such an approach allows for the inclusion of aspects of Buddhism which are often ignored or dismissed, but which shed light into little-understood corners of the Buddhist tradition, and are highly interesting in their own right. At the least, it is to be hoped that this method of exploring Buddhism furthers contemporary understanding by highlighting problems, tensions and possible relations in the ancient sources.

These observations suggest there are compelling reasons for approaching Buddhism by trying to understand what happened in the beginning. This book thus begins with an investigation into origins, elucidating the inner workings of the early tradition, before attempting to make sense of the dense maze of Buddhist ideas and institutions which emerged from it. It is to be hoped that this leads to a more advanced understanding of the monumental impact of Buddhism on the world. And because Buddhism was the first religious movement of its kind, this analysis may perhaps further our understanding of the profound change in culture and civilization, still ongoing, set in motion by the Buddha's awakening.

Chapter II
Buddha

The noble disciple with a mind devoid of hatred and malevolence, whose thoughts are undefiled and pure, understands that if there really is karmic retribution, then after death he will be reborn in the heavenly world. But even if not, he knows that he fosters an untroubled and blissful state of being in the here and now.

Kālāma Sutta

Burning the Buddha

According to the early Buddhist texts, the ceremonies that marked the death of the Buddha were lengthy and elaborate. After he had passed away in a forest grove just outside the northern Indian town of Kusinārā, the locals erected a canopy of cotton around the body and decked it with wreaths of flowers. They then spent six days worshipping the corpse with garlands and incense, and with much singing, dancing and music. The townspeople of Kusinārā, some of whom are reported to have fallen to the ground in tears upon hearing of the Buddha's death, did not spare any expense.

On the seventh day, in accordance with the wish of the gods, the body was taken away by eight local chieftains. It was first carried in through the northern gate of the town and then out to the cremation site, a shrine to the east. On this journey the gods joined the locals in their worship, with flowers raining down from the heavens until the town was knee-deep in them, before the cremation was carried out according to royal rites. After being swathed in new cloth, and at some point immersed in an iron tank of oil, the body was placed on a scented funeral pyre, where it burst into flames spontaneously – but only after the senior disciple Kassapa had circumambulated it three times to pay his respects.

There is no reason to discount the essential elements of this account, despite its supernatural elements, for exactly the same rituals can be witnessed in India today. Perhaps the most celebrated funeral of a modern Indian holy man was that of the Maharishi Mahesh Yogi, who was cremated in an ashram next to the river Ganges soon after his death on 5 February 2008. The funerary customs were those normally administered to an Indian holy man: there was much incense, flowers, garlands, beating of drums and crashing of cymbals, before the dead sage was cremated on a funeral pyre of sandalwood. Perhaps the only concession to modernity, and a sign of the Maharishi's success promoting meditation in the West – he became famous in the 1960s as the guru of The Beatles – were the thousands of rose petals dropped from above by a helicopter (not the gods) on to the mourners gathered below.

The similarity between these two funerals shows that there has been a remarkable continuity in Indian religious custom: for nearly two and a half thousand years, since the death of the Buddha in around 400 BC, the ways of honouring dead seers have remained more or less the same. But it is curious that the textual evidence for this sort of veneration is not found in the Hindu scriptures until the *Bhagavadgītā*, a sacred text of around the first or second century AD. This book uses the Sanskrit term *pūjā* ('worship' or 'devotion') with regard to the reverence of sages and gods, and mentions the worship of Kṛṣṇa with flowers, leaves and water.

This means that for nearly 2,000 years Hinduism has been a religion of devotion, this being expressed in bright colours, sweet odours and divine, celebratory chaos. But the early Buddhist texts attest the same religious forms at a much earlier date; at a time, in fact, when no such mention of devotionalism can be found in the sacred texts of the Brahmins, the principal agents in the creation of what is now called Hinduism. The Brahminic texts of the early Buddhist period have nothing to say about the funeral rites described above or devotionalism (*pūjā*), which typifies modern Hinduism and whose forms are conspicuous in the ancient account of the Buddha's funeral.

The ancient texts thus indicate that funerary rites for holy men were originally associated with the Buddha and his movement, rather than the Brahminic priesthood. Since Buddhism was the first pan-Indian religion, it would seem that the culture of devotionalism was originally spread across India by the Buddha's followers. And not just India, but the whole of Asia too, for Buddhism was a world

Fig. 2. Statue of reclining Buddha at the time of his death (parinibbāna), *Wat Pho, Bangkok*

religion, the first of its kind. The early Buddhist movement harnessed the devotional aspect of Indian religiosity and turned it into something more than the celebration of the holy dead: Buddhism was a religion organized and institutionalized, indeed a missionary religion, the like of which had never been seen in the world before.

Was Buddhism an Historical Accident?

The Buddha's movement was initially just one among a number of similar groups which flourished on the Gangetic plains of northern India. While certain renunciant groups such as the Jains and Ājīvikas gained widespread support in India, only the Buddhists emerged from this shared heritage to achieve international success. Some of the early evidence suggests that this was an unlikely outcome. At least one text, the *Ariyapariyesana Sutta* ('Discourse on the Noble Search'), states that immediately after his awakening, the Buddha doubted whether anyone would understand his ideas, and suspected that the work of teaching would be a hassle. Although he eventually decided to teach, on the basis that just a few might understand him, the story suggests that the Buddha's mission was initially not meant for all, or even many.

This suggests the possibility that the Buddha's success was accidental, and that other holy men could have achieved the same degree of influence if historical circumstances had inclined in their favour. In support of this it could be argued that Buddhism is not particularly original, since much of its spiritual, ritual and doctrinal repertoire already existed in the religious culture of the Buddha's time. The devotionalism associated with the veneration of holy men, important ideas such as reincarnation and salvation from it, and the peculiar practice of cultivating altered states of consciousness: all these features of Indian religiosity, and many more, were the common heritage of most religious movements during the early Buddhist period.

To this it could be added that the central doctrine of Buddhism – the Four Noble Truths – seems to say nothing new. The First Noble Truth, that life in this world is unsatisfactory and painful (*dukkha*), was generally accepted by religious thinkers of the Buddha's time, and the notion that desire is the cause of suffering – the Second Truth – is already stated in the pre-Buddhist *Bṛhadāraṇyaka Upaniṣad*. The Third Truth of the cessation of suffering was also commonly accepted, and the Fourth Truth – of the way to the cessation of suffering, i.e. the Noble Eightfold Path – culminates in 'right absorption' (*sammā-samādhi*); that is to say, states of meditation similar to those taught by other teachers before and after the Buddha.

All this suggests that the Buddha merely reformulated the common religious ideas and practices of his time. And if so, perhaps the subsequent success of his movement was largely due to the third century BC patronage of Aśoka, a Buddhist convert who ruled the Mauryan empire, the largest pre-modern Indian polity (and one of the greatest empires of antiquity). A case can be made that without the aid of Aśoka, the Buddhists would have remained a minor sect of ancient Magadha, before disappearing like other ascetic groups such as the Ājīvikas. On the other hand, however, it can be argued that the Buddha's movement really did offer something different. For apart from old traditions such as the Buddha's reluctance to teach, the early teachings are charged with religious fervour, as if their authors were inspired to reveal a new message to the world.

Fig. 3. The Dhamek stūpa *marks the spot of the Buddha's first sermon in the deer park at Sarnath, near Benares*

This zeal can even be seen in the text that records the Buddha's initial reluctance to teach. Apart from his hesitancy, the *Ariyapariyesana Sutta* also indicates that the awakening was unprecedented, describing it as 'profound, difficult to perceive and understand, calm, supreme, beyond the scope of logic, subtle, to be known by the wise'. It goes on to add that the Buddha proceeded to Benares to 'beat the drum of the immortal in this blind world' and thus set in motion the 'wheel of Dhamma'. The composers of this text thus believed that they were part of an unprecedented mission to establish a new religious order (*dhamma*), which they presumed would continue due to its own mysterious momentum.

It is difficult to distinguish religious hyperbole from historical fact in this foundational story. That favourable circumstances aided the spread of Buddhism can hardly be doubted, but to establish if there was anything more than this requires a detailed consideration of two crucial issues: we must ascertain if the Buddha had sufficient charisma to have inspired men and women to follow him, rather than other teachers; and we must consider if, contrary to the initial evaluation of the Four Noble Truths, the Buddha's teachings (also termed *dhamma*) were original and possibly remarkable. In short, we must attempt to work out the role played by the Buddha in the success of the movement he founded.

Gotama, Sage of the Sakyas

Apart from his teachings, which are recorded in meticulous if disordered detail, we know little about the historical Buddha. Many items of personal curiosity have been transmitted in various Buddhist traditions, but since they are not found in the earliest sources they cannot be trusted. We do not know, for example, that the Buddha's personal name was 'Siddhattha' (S: Siddhārtha), for the early texts do not use this term, and its meaning – 'one who has achieved his purpose' – looks suspiciously like an honorific title. In the earliest sources the Buddha is instead addressed by his family name, Gotama, or referred to by the title 'sage of the Sakyas' (*sakya-muni*).

Other so-called facts about the Buddha are purely hagiographic. It is a myth that Gotama lived an exalted life as a prince in Kapilavatthu, being sheltered by his father from any knowledge of suffering and death, the eventual encounter with which prompted him to renounce the world. In the early texts this tale is associated with the former Buddha Vipassin, a mythological figure, rather than Gotama, whose life in Kapilavatthu during the fifth century BC must have been much more simple. There were no grand palaces, and no chance that a youth could have spent his childhood blissfully unaware of the basic facts of life. The Buddha's father is simply called 'the Sakyan' in the early texts; only in later literature is he termed a 'great king' (*mahā-rājā*). It is likely that he belonged to the class of chieftains that managed the tribal life of the Sakyas.

Apart from this, we can be reasonably sure that Gotama lived in the fifth century BC (probably from about 480 to 400), and that he was born to the Sakya tribe of Kapilavatthu, the remains of which lie within the Terai region of modern Nepal, or else somewhere nearby, close to the Nepalese border with India. It is also beyond reasonable doubt that at the age of 29 Gotama renounced the world and spent a number of years wandering the Ganges plains in search of religious truth, a period of striving that culminated in an experience he termed an 'awakening', at the age of 35, near the modern Indian town of Uruvelā (Bodhgaya). The Buddha then spent the remainder of his life teaching others and establishing a religious order, until he died, aged 80.

The early sources contain a little more biographical information than this: we know that Gotama's mother Māyā died giving birth to him, that he was then raised by his maternal aunt, Pajāpatī, and that he had a son called Rāhula, whose mother is called 'Rāhula's mother' in the old texts (and Yasodharā in later literature). There is also no reason to doubt the textual evidence which states that his stepmother and son eventually joined the Buddhist order. Although that is about as far as the historical record goes, it is fortunate that the Buddha's teachings have been preserved in the form of *ad hominem* responses to others: they are not stated in the abstract, but rather portray the Buddha in dialogue with various seekers, philosophers and holy men. In depicting the Buddha in different didactic situations, these teachings reveal much about his character.

Many texts suggest that the Buddha was polite and courteous, for example remaining outside a dwelling without interrupting his disciples' discussion, but then gently coughing to make his presence known at an appropriate point; the Buddha's welcoming manner to those visiting him is mentioned in numerous texts, which state that he would speak first to visitors. This is despite the fact that the Buddha is portrayed as a quietist who preferred to stay away from the crowd, as can be seen in the appeal of the wanderer Poṭṭhapāda for his fellow asctics to be quiet, so that the Buddha might join them:

> Be quiet, venerable sirs, do not make a sound. Here comes the ascetic Gotama, who delights in silence and praises quietude. Perhaps if he realizes that the assembly is silent he might decide to come over.

In the context of the rigorous ascetic standards of the time, the Buddha must also have been rather unconventional, occasionally lying down in the company of others, sometimes while teaching, and even taking an afternoon nap. Just as unusual was the Buddha's sense of humour. A number of early teachings have a hilarious, satirical undertone, suggesting that the Buddha was keenly aware of others' conceits, which he liked to dissect in humorous parodies, for example when spinning an elaborate tale to show that the ancestors of the haughty Brahmin Ambaṭṭha were once slaves of the Sakyas.

Other early texts reveal an absurdist streak to the Buddha's humour. This can best be seen in the texts which describe how a Brahmin wished to ascertain whether the Buddha was in possession of the 'thirty-two marks of a great man'. These include such things as the image of a thousand-spoked wheel on the soles of his feet, arms that reach down to his knees, a hairy mole between the eyebrows, a hidden (or sheathed) penis and an excessively long tongue. In their account of how the Buddha revealed the final two marks to enquiring Brahmins, the texts are quietly humorous: the Buddha is said to have revealed his sheathed penis through supernatural means before passing his large tongue all over his face, tapping both ears and nostrils before finally covering the whole of his face.

Whatever the truth-value of such texts, they at least show that their authors shared the Buddha's sense of humour, and even suggest that the Buddha did not take himself too seriously. This is in close agreement with many other texts where the Buddha stresses that his ideas are more important than himself. Such understatement can be seen in the Buddha's statement to his disciple Ānanda that after his death he should have no successor, with his followers instead remaining as a 'light unto themselves', with the teachings alone as their guide. What mattered most to the Buddha was the implementation of his ideas, rather than institutional offices or his own historical importance.

A similar refusal to take himself seriously can be seen in the Buddha's teaching to the Kālāmas, a tribe who were confused by the competing truth-claims of different holy men. The Buddha here directs his listeners to judge all teachers by a simple examination of ethical worth: if what any holy man says is morally good, it can be accepted, but if not it should be rejected. While the Buddha assumes that his ideas pass this simple moral test, he at least leaves this an open question – one that should be decided by each enquiring individual, on the assumption that the universal values of good and bad are more important than himself as a teacher.

All this suggests that the Buddha was an inspiring teacher: quietistic, humorous and self-effacing, with a commitment to imparting his ideas for the sake of others. Indeed, it is not difficult to imagine the Buddha encouraging his disciples in the following terms:

> What a compassionate teacher concerned with the welfare of his disciples would do, out of compassion, all that I have done for you, mendicants. Here, mendicants, are the roots of trees, here are empty houses: meditate, mendicants, do not dally, do not have any regrets later on. This is my instruction to you.

The early texts thus paint a compelling picture of the Buddha as a teacher more interested in the practical application of his ideas than their abstract truth value. This helps us better understand how his ideas had such an impact, and how they have managed to endure.

Skill in Means

Pragmatism is perhaps an unusual quality in a religious person: one might instead expect a missionary leader to be a person of belief, perhaps even a zealot with an ideology to impose on the world. By all accounts the Buddha was not like this. Instead it seems that helping people through his teachings, rather than inviting them to appreciate his ideas in the abstract, was most important to him. This is made vividly clear by the Buddha's famous statement that although his knowledge is as vast as the numbers of leaves in a forest grove, the teachings he has revealed are comparable to a single leaf. The reason for this parsimonious approach to teaching, the Buddha explains, is that he only imparts that which is most important: the Four Noble Truths of suffering, its cause, its cessation and the way thereto.

A famous simile that compares the Buddha's ideas to a raft also makes this pragmatism clear: just as a raft can help a person cross a river and thus reach safety, so too can the Dhamma help a person cross the dangers of transmigration (*saṃsāra*). The pragmatic point of this is emphasized when the Buddha points out that after reaching the far shore, there would be no point in carrying the raft around on one's head. In the same way the Dhamma merely serves a purpose – that of realizing Nirvana – and once this has been achieved it is to be left behind, just like a raft.

Other texts indicate that the Buddha went even further in limiting his ideas according to what would be useful. A good example is the *Sigālovāda Sutta* ('Discourse to Sigāla'): after coming across the householder Sigāla venerating the different regions of space (perhaps a way of worshipping the deities thought to inhabit them), the Buddha does not rubbish this practice, but instead tells Sigāla that he is not doing it properly: when worshipping thus he must recognize the cosmic regions as his parents (East), teachers (South), wife and children (West), friends and companions (North), servants and workers (nadir), and ascetics and Brahmins (zenith). An ethical dimension is added by this subtle change, one that the Buddha elaborates by advising certain moral norms, such as avoiding killing, stealing, lying and sexual misconduct.

Rather than impose his own ideas upon Sigāla, the Buddha here adapts meaningless ritual acts to his own ideas, thus drawing attention toward the universal values on which his teachings are founded. This is a vivid example of the ability to adapt his ideas to different levels, an intuitive talent traditionally referred to as the Buddha's 'skill in means' (S: *upāya-kauśalya*). What matters most, according to this didactic approach, is not so much the ideas themselves but the use made of them. This approach explains the Buddha's attitude towards the traditional Indian reverence of holy men. In the text that records his last days, the Buddha states that after dying his remains should be interred in a funerary mound (S: *stūpa*), so that the people who will worship there with garlands of flowers, scents and coloured powders – in the same devotional manner as at the Buddha's funeral – will thereby 'pacify' their minds.

In the same text the Buddha sets the stage for pilgrimage by describing four locations that are religiously inspiring: the places where he was born, achieved his awakening, began his ministry and will finally die. The reason for this is that the person who undertakes it might pacify his mind at these four sites. Just as in the discourse to Sigāla, the point of this teaching is that although the outer forms of worship are meaningless, they can be directed to a different end: that of inner peace, the cultivation of which furthers a person's moral and spiritual development.

The teachings to Sigāla, as well as those on relic worship and pilgrimage, are those of a skilled communicator and pragmatist, and with this we can begin to understand why the Buddhist movement was so successful. Because the Buddha taught that the real point of religious ceremony is the psychological states it promotes, his followers were able to utilize popular practices without taking them too seriously. The cultural forms in which Buddhism was transmitted were loosely defined and easily adaptable: they could be, and were, altered to accommodate local cults and traditions.

The Buddha cannot have guessed that this blend of the transcendental and the local would turn out to be so compelling. But in his intuitive response to individuals, and in his appropriation of local religious forms, his ideas were situated within a cultural vehicle of great utility and potency. The Buddha's teachings were thus crafted to create an ethical culture suitable for the northern Indian society of the fifth century BC.

The Social Background to Early Buddhism

It is not widely recognized that ethicization was a goal of the Buddha's teachings. For Gotama had originally been drawn into a culture of world-renunciation that gripped northeast India from about the sixth century BC onwards. As a wandering mendicant who left his family and possessions behind, most of the Buddha's teachings are unsurprisingly delivered to those who had also renounced the world. In common with other schools of religious strivers, followers of the Buddha were expected to dress in rags found in piles of rubbish, to be content to sleep at the foot of a tree, and to wander through the wilderness like a 'solitary rhinoceros'.

The early Buddhist texts paint a vivid picture of this vibrant renunciant culture. This was a world of social drop-outs meditating under trees, wizened ascetics subjecting themselves to painful austerities in the forest, and sophists and philosophers debating in the parks and towns. There has been nothing like it before it or since: the religious men and women of ancient India enjoyed 'the most perfect freedom, both of thought and expression . . . a freedom probably unequalled in the history of the world'.

Quite why this happened on such a massive scale is unknown. But the Buddha lived at the beginning of the second phase of urbanization in ancient India (the first being the defunct Indus civilization), a time when urban life rapidly overwhelmed earlier forms of social organization. The transformation from the secure world of the tribe and clan to the freer world of the town and city, would probably have been somewhat unsettling for those who lived through it, including the Buddha, whose life in the fifth century BC coincided with the rapid onset of social change.

These circumstances stimulated an atmosphere of enquiry, further contributory factors to which were epidemics of disease, for urbanization occurred primarily in the fertile wetlands around the Ganges. Indeed, a generally morbid atmosphere of intellectual enquiry is evident in the *Bṛhadāraṇyaka Upaniṣad*, a Brahminic text of roughly the fifth century BC. Situated in the northeastern kingdom of Videha, not far from the tribal home of the Sakyas, and in a society on the brink of urbanization, this text is preoccupied with unsettling pessimistic concerns, as can be seen in a question put to the sage Yājñavalkya in a riddling contest at the court of King Janaka:

> When this whole world is caught in the grip of death, when it is overwhelmed by death, how can the patron of a sacrifice free himself completely from its grip?

Such a question suggests that the emerging states were faced with an existential crisis, a loss of traditions and old ways made worse by illness and disease. The martial atmosphere which prevailed from the fifth century BC onwards, as the emergent states began to encroach on one anothers' territory, must also have contributed to the conflict and change which characterize the period. The centralization of power this entailed should not be overlooked: individual villages and more isolated tribal groups, such as the Sakyas, would have been increasingly subject to the will of the new polities. This mixture of creeping urbanization and the consequent loss of tribal freedom, as well as a new capacity to respond to events as individuals rather than clan members, can be seen in texts which describe the Buddha's renunciation. These describe Gotama's thoughts as follows:

> Life at home is restricted, a path of dust, whereas striving forth is the life of the open air. It is not easy for a person living at home to live the holy life that is completely pure and fulfilled, and as perfectly grooved as a conch shell. Why don't I shave off my hair and beard, don a discoloured robe and strive forth from home to homelessness?

The wish to leave one's dusty home for the 'open air' cannot easily be associated with a pastoral society. Such an idea must therefore be that of a recently urbanized individual, and shows that world-renunciation was a reaction, at least in part, to the emerging world of towns and cities. But whence the form of this reaction? Why did difficult times lead to the creation of a sub-culture of holy men? The more individualistic atmosphere of the towns would have stimulated an atmosphere in which accepted norms were questioned. But this does not explain why many left home to become religious drop-outs.

This development would probably not have happened unless the disaffected were able to draw upon existing ascetic traditions. The pre-Buddhist literature contains evidence for such figures, such as the 'quiet sage' (*muni*) of the Ṛg Veda who is said to wear dirty garments and fly through the air with the gods; 'strivers' (S: *śramaṇa*), ascetics (*tāpasa*) and wanderers (S: *pravrājin*) are also mentioned in those parts of the *Bṛhadāraṇyaka Upaniṣad* situated in the kingdom of Videha, perhaps the epicentre of the renunciant movement, located between the kingdoms of Kosala and Magadha. It is possible that these other-worldly figures from the religious fringe attracted a greater following during the period of urbanization; perhaps it was felt that they could provide old answers to new problems.

Whether or not this is correct, it is beyond doubt that most of the new renunciant groups, such as the Jains and Ājīvikas, reacted against the new world and consequently had little in the way of a positive doctrine for society. These movements proclaimed that the world is a bleak place of unrelenting suffering, with the normal woes of human existence compounded by the prospect of this misery being repeated over and over again, through the operation of the laws of karma and rebirth. The best that a person could hope for, these groups claimed, was simply to stop existing. In the case of Jainism this meant that some of its holy men went to the extreme of starving themselves to death.

Thus was the world of Gotama in the fifth century BC, with its rapid socio-political change, and opposed counter-culture of renunciation and asceticism. But as the Buddhist movement was to show, the opposition between urbane townsman and forest ascetic was neither inevitable nor inviolable. Urbanization was such a new development that it would have been possible to encounter the wilderness almost immediately outside the city walls. Since it would have been possible to act out the Buddhist ideal of living as a 'solitary rhinoceros' without moving far from the emerging urban civilization, a movement which encompassed forest and city-dweller was feasible.

Karma and Rebirth

The early Buddhist centres were usually situated just outside the new urban settlements, on the boundary between the town and country, in parks that were little more than domesticated versions of the wilderness. So although a favourite place of meditation for the Buddha was the 'great forest', a dense jungle which stretched from the foothills of the Himalayas to the edge of the urban centres, he was able to enter it from a park situated just outside the city of Vesālī. This close proximity to the urban world of northern India was further entrenched by the Buddhist practice of receiving alms daily from lay supporters. One gets the impression that the Buddhist movement was designed to bridge two worlds: that of ascetics and renouncers beyond society, and that of the new urban classes within the city walls.

Exactly this is suggested by the Buddha's reformulation of the karma doctrine, which overturned the pessimistic world-view of the renouncers. The subject of karma and rebirth dominated intellectual discourse during the Buddha's life and for a long time afterwards. The general idea is that all living beings are reincarnated after death according to the moral quality of their deeds (S: *karma*). Every action thus has a consequence: good deeds lead to good results in the future, and favourable rebirths after death (perhaps as a wealthy human being or a god), whereas bad deeds lead to bad results in the future, such as a bad rebirth (perhaps as a poor human being, an animal or a denizen of hell). This state of affairs was deemed miserable, because the sufferings experienced in this round of transmigration were believed to continue *ad infinitum* unless a person could find liberation from them.

The first explicit statements of these ideas are found in the pre-Buddhist Upaniṣads. Although these texts give the impression of ideas being worked out, they make it clear that since good and bad deeds bind a person to continued existence, an escape from both must therefore be found. The Upaniṣadic response to this problem was to propose a retreat from the world into a sphere of quietude and inaction. Only then could a person develop the altered states of consciousness in which a radical detachment from the world could be attained: in such a state of meditation, Upaniṣadic thinkers believed that a person's true identity could be realized. According to the mystic vision of the Upaniṣadic sages, this ultimately real 'self'

(S: *ātman*) is distinct from the body and identical to the immortal, cosmic essence (*brahman*).

More or less the same understanding of transmigration is found within early Jainism, although the liberated goal and method of escape were envisioned somewhat differently. The Jains believed that all action, both the good and the bad, must be avoided, and that a person's store of past karma must be eradicated through painful physical acts. The Jains were therefore antinomian outsiders, remaining beyond society as much as possible, avoiding action at all costs, and inflicting pain upon themselves in order to 'burn away' their karmic burden and liberate the soul from the cosmos.

These formulations of the karma doctrine imply that salvation cannot be gained from doing either good or bad deeds, which lead only to rebirth rather than liberation. According to early Jainism and speculative Brahminism, there is no role for morality in the spiritual life, for good deeds lead not to an ultimate religious good but rather perpetuate unsatisfactory existence within *saṃsāra*. While the positive results of good deeds provide a reason to act morally, this is undermined by the fact that even the good are doomed, for the sphere of religious truth transcends virtue. According to the karma theories of the Upaniṣads and Jains, to be good is not to be truly religious, for to be truly religious is to be amoral.

Early Buddhist Ethics

The general idea of karma and rebirth was accepted by the Buddha, albeit with some major changes. This is indicated by the Buddha's definition of the term *karma*, literally 'action', as *cetanā*, a word which generally means 'intention', but also covers cognitive states such as wishing, desiring, hoping and resolving. In simple terms the Buddha's point is that a person's states of mind, rather than actual deeds, condition all future states of being. This is why in a humorous episode the Buddha pointed out that canine and bovine ascetics – renouncers devoted to behaving like dogs and cows – can expect to be reborn as dogs and cows after death.

By psychologizing the doctrine of karma, the Buddha undermined the basic sociology of renunciant religion. For if karma is a matter of volitional states of consciousness, it follows that a person cannot escape the world by doing nothing: the renouncer gains nothing from physical inaction, whereas the layman does not necessarily add to his karmic balance through action (which might be involuntary, and so karmically neutral). This reimagining of the karma doctrine overturned the old dichotomy between action in the world and inaction beyond it: according to the new understanding of the Buddha, both layman and renouncer are equally caught by the activity of the mind.

The Buddha's subversion of karmic ideology did not stop there. A more radical innovation was the teaching that the religious path is one of virtue, so that morally good states of mind advance a person towards salvation. If the path is one of moral cultivation, the Buddhist saint must eventually realize a state of irreversible good, the goal of Nirvana being the ultimate fulfilment of virtue rather than its amoral transcendence. The Buddhist path is thus a process of karmic improvement rather than avoidance, in which moral and spiritual growth are identical and do not lead to an ultimate escape from good.

The Buddha's equation of spiritual and karmic progress is suggested by his use of the term *kusala*, which means both 'good' and 'skilful'. The term is used most simply in the sense of morally good states of mind, so that a person's 'foundation of good' (*kusala-mūla*) is defined as the absence of greed, hatred and delusion (states which are said to 'corrupt' a person). The most basic mental states of this kind are found in various lists of virtue (*sīla*), the most important of which advise a person to refrain from killing, stealing, sexual misconduct, false speech and intoxicating drinks. But since moral and spiritual virtues coincide in the Buddha's thought, the term *kusala* also denotes karmically beneficial states of mind generated along the path, such as concentration, mindfulness, joy, equanimity and so on: a person's cultivation of such states builds on simpler virtues and skilfully promotes spiritual good.

These ethical and psychological alterations to the karma doctrine transformed the religious dynamic of the age. It meant that world-renunciation was no longer a matter of necessity, but was rather a choice determined by inclination. A person could either follow a long spiritual path to salvation by performing good deeds, or else could become a mendicant and so achieve a more fundamental transformation in the here and now. Thus two fundamentally different kinds of religious lifestyle (householder vs. renouncer), based on separate modes of practice (merit-making vs. asceticism/contemplation) and distinct goals (a good rebirth vs. liberation), were brought together into a single path to be followed by all, leading to the same goal, the level of realization depending solely upon personal commitment.

All this is strikingly different from the amoral transcendence of early Jainism and the Upaniṣads. In contrast to these systems, the Buddha taught that the karma created by good deeds is spiritually efficacious, a vehicle for progression along the path to Nirvana. A person is not cast adrift in the infinite sea of reincarnation, therefore, but can take command of his destiny by doing good.

The importance of this idea in Buddhist India can be seen in the many hundreds of inscriptions which record religious gifts to the Sangha. These are often accompanied by a statement of purpose which articulates the belief that morality leads to Nirvana. A good example is a recently discovered fourth century AD inscription from Andhra Pradesh:

> The wheel which accompanies [the pillar] is the donation of the great general Ramanandinoka, set up for the sake of his own pre-requisites for Nirvana . . .

Kindness, Compassion and Nirvana

The Buddha's reinterpretation of the karma doctrine, and combination of moral and spiritual virtues, are stated most clearly in the teachings on the so-called 'divine abidings', four meditative states which illustrate how virtuous thoughts can advance a person towards liberation. The primary source for this teaching is the *Tevijja Sutta* ('Discourse on Three Knowledges'), which records the Buddha's dialogue with Vāseṭṭha and Bhāradvāja, two Brahmins who had come seeking advice on attaining union with the god Brahma (or godhead: the term *brahman* stands for both). The Buddha here uses the terminology of his Brahminic interlocutors to elucidate his understanding that good karma, in the form of meditative states of infinite moral potential, is a path to liberation:

> O Vāseṭṭha, the mendicant pervades all four directions with a mind steeped in kindness . . . compassion . . . joy . . . and equanimity. Thus above, below, across, everywhere, the entire world he continually pervades with a mind steeped in kindness . . . compassion . . . joy . . . and equanimity, a mind that is abounding, lofty, immeasurable, devoid of hatred and malevolence.

> Just as a strong conch-blower would make himself heard throughout the four directions with little difficulty, so too, Vāseṭṭha, does finite karma not remain once the mental liberations of kindness . . . compassion . . . joy . . . and equanimity have been cultivated: it does not persist in that state. This, Vāseṭṭha, is the path to union with Brahma.

The Buddha here states that immeasurable states of mind eradicate a person's 'finite' karma. In other words an immeasurable expansion of a person's spiritual state, achieved through the cultivation of virtuous thoughts (non-finite karma), wipes away the hindrances to spiritual progress (finite karma). The very idea of finite versus non-finite karma goes against the general karma theory, according to which all karma is finite, binding and deleterious. But it makes sense in the context of the Buddha's equation of karma with mental states, and his redefinition of the spiritual path as a progression in virtue: in this context, non-finite karma is a way of indicating immeasurably virtuous states of mind leading to Nirvana.

Similar ideas are found in numerous other teachings on the Buddhist path, which speak of liberation being achieved from the fourth stage of meditation (*jhāna*), an immeasurable state of mind in which all bad (*akusala*) thoughts have been eradicated. Since only bad karma is here abandoned, the fourth *jhāna* can be identified with the conclusion of the teaching to Bhāradvāja and Vāseṭṭha, and if so, this teaching on the divine abidings must be understood as another example of the Buddha's skill in means: to the two Brahmins who came enquiring about the path to union with Brahma, the Buddha instead taught an adapted version of his teaching that virtue leads to salvation.

The teaching to Bhāradvāja and Vāseṭṭha is a vivid example of the Buddha's ability to enter another person's mental world in order to communicate his ideas. The general discourse of karma and rebirth fits the Buddha's ideas very badly, since it permits no salvific role for morality and has little to say about psychology. But the Buddha was able to use its terminology to communicate a new idea: that spiritual progress is achieved through virtue. This skill in adapting these ideas to the general karma theory is taken one step further in the discussion with Bhāradvāja and Vāseṭṭha, for the Buddha here expresses his unique ideas on karma, virtue and liberation in the Brahminic idiom: the notion of 'union with Brahma' is retained, albeit as a metaphor for the attainment of Nirvana.

Divine Abodes

The Buddha taught that other states of mind designated *kusala* have a spiritual potency similar to the four divine abidings, a good example being faith (*saddhā, pasāda*). In early Buddhist thought faith is either a rational response to understanding the Dhamma, or an emotional response to witnessing the Buddha himself. Faith inspired in this way is both reassuring and therapeutic, for the term *pasāda* also means 'tranquillity', and in this sense is often used to denote advanced states of meditation. This implies that in the simple act of piety or devotion towards the Buddha and his Dhamma, a faithful Buddhist experiences a weak form of meditation. It was from this perspective that the Buddha advised the construction of reliquary mounds after his death: since devotional acts at these sites promote mental calm, faith can thus be said to have a meditative effect, and hence is the good karma that advances a person toward the ultimate spiritual good.

Early Buddhist teachings lack precise details on the pious person's path to liberation. But they clearly state that the spiritual path can be continued after death, in a divine abode or otherwise. The position of heavenly realms within a simple path structure can be seen in the Buddha's oft-repeated 'gradual discourse', a teaching which initially focuses on generosity, moral purity, heaven, the danger of sensual desires and the benefit of desirelessness. But once the Buddha realizes his interlocutor is ready to understand more profound ideas, he reveals the Four Noble Truths, so that the person realizes 'whatever has the nature of arising also has the nature of cessation'.

This teaching thus begins with the simple moral virtues always found at the beginning of the path (giving, moral purity, avoiding sensuality, etc.), continues with more advanced virtues (such as desirelessness), and finally concludes with the higher teaching on the Four Noble Truths. These virtues are thus stated in the order they should be developed on the Buddhist path, and so the attainment of a heavenly destiny after death occurs within the context of a broad teaching on the path to liberation. The implication of this is that heaven is a finite abode on the way to full spiritual realization, a relatively low level of attainment associated with simple religious virtues, but which precedes the eventual attainment of Nirvana.

Further evidence for the idea that heavenly abodes are part of the path is the Buddha's statement that the Dhamma is for 'the welfare and happiness of gods and men'. Some teachings thus suggest that gods are moral agents, whereas others describe how a person can attain liberation in the heaven of Brahma after death (after previously cultivating the divine abidings), or from some other high stratum of the cosmos (having previously cultivated the Buddhist path to a high degree of meditative realization). The same idea is contained in the scheme of four levels of spiritual attainment: the 'stream enterer' (who will not fall below the human realm before realizing liberation), the 'once-returner' (who returns to the human station only once before attaining liberation), the 'non-returner' (who attains liberation from a higher stratum of the cosmos after death) and finally the Arahat, the Buddhist saint liberated in life.

The concept of a 'stream-attainer' is most significant in the context of the religious aspirations of the laity, for it vividly evokes the idea that even a little progress along the path can carry a person along the 'stream' towards Nirvana. That a person's good karma has a lasting spiritual effect is certainly the message of the Jātaka tales. These popular fables narrate various past lives of the Buddha-to-be as he progressed along the path to awakening, and show how, in a variety of prior incarnations as human beings and various animals (monkeys, deer, etc.), he struggled towards liberation through simple and occasionally heroic acts of morality. Later Buddhist traditions understood these past lives in terms of the attainment of a series of virtues that culminated in the awakening of the Buddha-to-be, for example the tenfold Theravādin system: giving, virtue, desirelessness, understanding, endeavour, patience, truth, resolve, kindness and equanimity.

The first three virtues of this scheme correspond closely to the beginning of the Buddha's gradual discourse, whereas the final two virtues correspond to the divine abidings. A single, inclusive understanding can therefore be detected in all of these maps of spiritual progress: all are variants on a broad, multilevelled conception of the Buddhist path. The idea of spiritual progress over numerous lifetimes is not merely a feature of 'popular' lay Buddhism, but is firmly rooted in the Buddha's reworking of the karma doctrine. In the form of the Jātaka tales, the idea of a karmic progression towards Nirvana became a major ideological feature of Buddhist civilization.

Reality and Cognition

A positive understanding of the spiritual path as an ongoing progression in virtue helps explain the broad appeal of the early Buddhist movement. But other, more philosophical, aspects of the Dhamma help explain its appeal to the spiritual and intellectual elite. Subtler dimensions are suggested by the general failure of the early Buddhist teachings to provide a detailed account of the workings of karma: how mental states generate specific results in the future, in accordance with their moral worth, is not explained. Thus the gradual teaching does not state how virtue and giving enable progress along the spiritual path, in both the present and hereafter.

A lack of precision can also be seen in the early accounts of the different worlds in which an individual can be reborn. The general scheme is that the cosmos is made up of five cosmic realms: hell, hungry ghosts, animals, humans and gods. But other supernatural beings appear through the texts – *asuras, yakkhas, nāgas, gandhabbas* – and the heavenly realm is occasionally expanded to include various sorts of gods, and even purely mental realms corresponding to advanced states of meditation. Such cosmographic variation suggests that the Buddha did not have any clear teaching on this subject: even if supernatural beings feature throughout the teachings, he offered no picture of the world. The early Buddhist teachings also lack any serious cosmogony, the closest thing being the Buddha's joke about the god Brahma feeling lonely coinciding with the appearance of other beings through the natural workings of their karma (leading Brahma to believe he is the supreme being and creator of all).

While these omissions could be explained as a consequence of the Buddha's pragmatism, basic principles of Buddhist thought suggest a more profound reason. A fundamental aspect of the Dhamma is the redefinition of karma as states of mind, which shifts the focus towards individual experience and away from the existential structure within which it occurs. Other teachings define karma as 'mental constructions' (*saṅkhārā*), a term which directs attention towards the fact that an individual's experiential reality is fashioned by the workings of the mind. The Buddha's psychologism thus steers his Dhamma away from cosmographic descriptions of the different worldly realms, including how they are created and how a person is reborn in them.

The deeper reason for this avoidance of ontology, and focus on psychology, is that a person's entire world of experience is constructed in the mind. This is suggested by a famous teaching in which the Buddha claims that although the end of the world cannot be reached by any kind of travel, its end can be known within this 'fathom-long' body. It follows from this that the world's existence somehow depends upon a human being, and not the other way around. Other teachings imply that a person's very world of experience, and not just the particular experiences in that world, depend on the workings of the mind. A prominent example is the *Kevaṭṭa Sutta*, which tells the story of a Buddhist mendicant who, by meditative means, ascends the various heavenly realms in order to find an answer to the question of where the material constituents of the world (earth, water, fire and wind) 'cease without remainder'. When this mendicant is eventually told by the god Brahma that only the Buddha can answer this question, he returns to earth and is addressed by the Buddha as follows:

> Consciousness, which is intransitive, infinite and luminous all round,
> Here water, earth, fire and wind do not stand firm.
> Here the great and small, the minute and gross, the attractive and unattractive,
> Here name and form cease without remainder.
> With the cessation of consciousness, this [i.e. name and form] ceases.

In stating that the 'end of the world' is to be found in consciousness, the Buddha suggests that the world is not objectively real. This idea, that the world is dependent on states of transitive or objective consciousness, and ceases when such states of consciousness do not pertain, points towards a more profound philosophical reason for the Buddha's avoidance of cosmology and cosmogony. For both are based on the idea that the world is a transcendentally real domain beyond a person's perceptions and ideas. The Buddha's reworking of the karma doctrine, replacing action with states of mind without exactly specifying the real domains to which they lead, would thus seem to lead to a rejection of philosophical realism.

Constructed Realism

If the Buddha did not subscribe to philosophical realism, what other metaphysic might his teachings on morality and the spiritual path presume? An answer to this is provided in the *Brahmajāla Sutta* ('Discourse on the net of Brahma'), a text which provides a more subtle explanation for an individual's continuity in *saṃsāra*. The Buddha here claims that he understands things which are 'profound, difficult to perceive and understand, calm, supreme, beyond the scope of logic, subtle, to be known by the wise'. Exactly the same thought is said to have occurred to the Buddha immediately after his awakening, when he considered avoiding the responsibility of teaching. This statement thus suggests that the *Brahmajāla Sutta* is an attempt to articulate the Buddha's awakened gnosis: we should expect this teaching to outline the profound ideas that the Buddha initially considered too difficult for most people to understand.

Like virtually all early Buddhist teachings, the *Brahmajāla Sutta* does not present a systematic philosophy. But in explaining how a person continues in the round of suffering, it touches on abstract issues by offering a critique of 62 theses, attributed to unnamed thinkers of the Buddha's time. These include such things as the notion that the world has a beginning in time or does not, or is with or without spatial limits; or that the self comes into existence spontaneously and so has a beginning, or that it consists of a consciousness separate from the material body; or that the different constituents of individuality cease at death. In criticizing these views as a group, all of which deal with a human being's spatio-temporal existence in the world, the text suggests that there is something wrong with ontology *per se*. Exactly this is brought out in the Buddha's statement that the 62 views depend on the cognitive state of those who hold them:

> Whatever ascetics or Brahmins form ideas about the past, future or both . . . making all sorts of claims by means of these 62 statements with reference to the past and future, this comes about because what these venerable ascetics and Brahmins sense . . . is subjected to trembling and quivering.

The terms 'trembling' and 'quivering' here indicate that a person's primary sensations – sights, sounds, tastes, smells, touches and, according to the Buddha, mental objects – are distorted through a process of cognitive conditioning which makes them knowable. This means that the 'world' a person experiences is not the world as it really is, but is a conceptual construction of that reality. The same point is stated more clearly in the *Madhupiṇḍika Sutta* ('Honey-ball Discourse'):

> Dependent on the eye and forms arises visual consciousness. The coming together of all three is sense-contact, from which arises sensation. A person recognizes what he senses, thinks over what he recognizes, and makes conceptually diffuse that which he thinks over. It is because of this cognitive elaboration of thought that conceptualization, recognition and apperception assail a person with regard to past, future and present forms to be cognized by the eye.

This succinct teaching makes clear the fact that a person does not experience reality as it actually is, but rather reality as it is constructed by the cognitive process. It follows that the external world of space-time is a sort of mental fabrication, and not the objectively true reality it is assumed to be. Any philosophical attempt to grasp the true nature of the world of space-time is a categorical mistake, therefore, for it is based on the incorrect assumption that the constructed reality encountered in mundane experience is transcendentally real.

If all ideas about the human being and the external world depend on cognitive conditioning, it follows that a person's grasp of reality will change if the underlying cognitive structure is changed. This is exactly what the Buddha implies has happened to himself: he claims that his cognitive state and subsequent grasp of reality have been so utterly transformed that it is impossible to capture in terms of ideas about existence in time and space. But for those who naturally accept the cognitive construction of primary experience, and who are trapped in it, the forces of craving and attachment lead to a process of becoming that continues after death:

> All of their experience is fashioned by repeated sense-contact incurred through the six sense faculties. Dependent on sensation there is thirst, dependent on thirst there is attachment, dependent on attachment there is becoming, dependent on becoming there is birth, dependent on which arises this entire mass of decrepitude, death, sorrow, lamentation, suffering, depression and tribulation.

This is the Buddhist teaching of Dependent Origination, which outlines the causal processes which maintain the round of individual suffering: texts such as the *Brahmajāla* and *Madhupiṇḍaka Sutta*s show that the teaching is based on the idea that sentient beings are bound by the cognitive construction of experiential worlds, all of which are not objectively real but are dependent on sense contact. This is perhaps why the language of reincarnation is mostly avoided in the Buddha's teachings: there is a general preference for terms derived from the Sanskrit term *punar-bhava*, 're-becoming' (e.g. *punabbhava*, *ponobbhavika*), rather than the word 'rebirth' (S: *punar-jāti*). This nomenclature presupposes a dynamic process of experiential conditioning, rather than the idea of actual rebirth into an objectively real world.

Further support for this is suggested by the fact that realms of experience (especially the human realm) are often said to be a state of 'hereness' (*itthatta*). This peculiar term suggests that beings do not exist in ontologically distinct worlds, situated somewhere in an objectively real cosmos, but are instead bound to particular states of experience, in which there are particular types of cognition characterized by their own, distinct, qualities. The general metaphysic could be termed 'constructed realism': 'constructed' in the sense that the world of experience is a mental construction; and 'realism' in the sense that cognitive processes and the underlying reality that they fashion are both objectively real. This means that the various realms of the cosmos, such as those of gods, humans and hell-beings, do not actually exist as real places in a mind-independent reality, but are states of experience which depend on qualitatively different constructions of reality.

This philosophical understanding explains why, when asked whether the gods exist, the Buddha replied that it 'depends upon the context' – an answer which implies that gods are effectively real in one state of consciousness but not necessarily in another. In other words, all possible modes of individuality could be said to 'exist' for those who experience them, but in a different context – such as the experiential reality of a Buddha, which is in direct contact with the non-constructed way things really are – the very notion of existence (or non-existence) does not pertain. The Buddha's equivocal response to this question about the gods' existence is reminiscent of his silence when asked the following ontological questions:

> Is the world eternal? Or is the world not eternal?
> Is the world finite? Or is the world not finite?
> Is the soul the same thing as the body? Or is it different from the body?

> Does the Tathāgata exist after death? Or does the Tathāgata not exist after death?
> Does the Tathāgata both exist and not exist after death? Or does the Tathāgata neither exist nor not exist after death?

When pushed to explain his refusal to answer these questions, the Buddha sometimes stated that any answer to them would serve no salvific purpose. But other texts indicate a fundamental problem with the realistic presuppositions of the questions: since the questions assume the mind-independent reality of the world, the Buddha can neither affirm nor deny them, for to do so would be to assent to philosophical realism. To indicate the categorical mistake that such questions commit, the Buddha thus remained silent, or instead advocated that a person should not have any 'view' (*diṭṭhi*); that is to say, no ontological opinion of the kind listed in the *Brahmajāla Sutta*.

The Buddha on the Reality of the Soul

A consequence of this philosophy of constructed realism is that a human being's most basic existential presupposition is fundamentally mistaken: the notion of being an individual who exists in an objectively real world 'out there' is incorrect. This cognitive error lies at the root of the forces that confine a person to continued becoming in *saṃsāra*: ignorance, in particular the belief that the 'I' is an entity that remains stable over time and endures into the future; and grasping, otherwise referred to as craving, greed, thirst and volitional forces, which are the expression of the 'I', the inevitable state of wanting that results from the conceptual construction of reality into self and world.

This philosophy explains why the Buddha criticized the tendency to hypostasize the subject of experience into an ultimately real existent: numerous early Buddhist teachings focus on the delusion of conceiving the 'I' in terms of an ultimately real 'self' or 'soul' which is permanent and unchangeable. The form of such teachings was determined by the version of this idea taught in the early Upaniṣads, according to which the true subject of experience – the 'I' that is the thinker of thoughts and perceiver of objects – is said to consist of a pure, subjective consciousness. Upaniṣadic thinkers believed that by realizing this true identity (S: *ātman*: 'Self'), a person would be released from the suffering of *saṃsāra*.

According to the Buddha's teaching of Dependent Origination, this idea is fundamentally and dangerously misconceived. For this teaching points out that the sense of individual identity pertains only under particular cognitive conditions, those through which a constructed reality is manufactured out of primary experience. As the Buddha pointed out to his disciple Ānanda, it would not be possible to imagine such a self in the absence of these cognitive conditions:

> Ānanda, to the person who claims 'My self is beyond sensation and experience', one should say: 'Is it possible to have the notion "I am" when there is no sensation whatsoever?'
>
> 'It is not so, master.'
>
> Therefore, Ānanda, it is because of this that it is not suitable to think that one has a self beyond sensation and experience.

In this critique of a true personal identity beyond all phenomena – a transcendent self, in other words – the Buddha points out that any notion of identity is a manifestation of self-consciousness, the state of awareness in which a person is able to think 'I am'. But when a person passes beyond sensations, perhaps in an advanced stage of meditation or in deep sleep, the cognitive conditions upon which self-consciousness depends disappear, and no sense of self pertains. The notion of a 'transcendent self' is therefore a contradiction in terms, for the self is cognitively contingent rather than a transcendent essence beyond conditions.

Thus the Buddha directed his followers to see the mistake of imagining the subjective aspect of experience as an ultimately real entity, one that might even be eternal. Another way of making this point was through the 'not-self' (*anattā*) teaching, which shows that no aspect of a person's individual being, including consciousness, is either permanent or transcendentally real. This point is made by analyzing experience into five different aspects – form, sensation, apperception, mental constructions and consciousness – before pointing out that since each is impermanent, it would be mistaken to think about them in terms of a transcendent self:

> What do you think, mendicants, is form permanent or impermanent?
>
> 'Impermanent, master.'

> Is that which is impermanent unsatisfactory or satisfactory?
>
> 'Unsatisfactory, master.'
>
> And is it suitable to regard that which is impermanent, unsatisfactory and subject to change as 'This is mine, I am this, this is my self?'
>
> 'No, master.'

With this simple series of questions the Buddha undermines the grounds for believing in an ultimately real personal identity, some aspect of the 'I' that might endure beyond this life. This is achieved indirectly: the point that there is no permanent identity in conditioned experience is teased out in stages, as the Buddha leads his disciples through a thought experiment. But the process of reflection does not culminate in any positive statement of truth, for the disciples are instead led into a sort of cognitive vacuum, in which misconceived ideas have been negated. The Buddha goes on to explain that this state prepares the way for a more profound detachment, and eventually liberation:

> When the learned, noble disciple sees things in this way, mendicants, he becomes disillusioned with form, sensation, apperception, mental constructions and consciousness. Being disillusioned he becomes dispassionate, and through dispassion he is released. When released there is the knowledge 'I am released', and he understands: 'Birth is destroyed, the holy life has been lived, done is what had to be done, there is no more of "hereness" (*itthatta*).'

The denial of a true identity in conditioned experience is thus framed in such a way as to deconstruct a person's mundane grasp of things, and so begin the process of inner transformation. That process is here outlined in brief; other teachings describe the way to Nirvana in much greater detail. But we can here note the attempt to incite understanding of the problem of suffering, rather than trying to find any special kind of experience within it. This brings into focus the Buddha's intellectual and empathetic genius, and allows us to draw some tentative conclusions about the appeal of the Buddha's ideas, and their possible impact in ancient India.

An Estimation of the Buddha's Impact

At the heart of the Buddha's teachings is the idea that experiential worlds are created by mental states, their quality depending on the moral worth of a person's thoughts. As a spiritual pragmatist the Buddha focused his teachings on the moral aspects of this philosophy, in particular the simple point that pure mental states result in desirable worlds of experience (which lie closer to Nirvana), whereas morally corrupt states of mind lead to experiences in painful realms (which are far from Nirvana). These ideas were presented through a fundamental reworking of the karma doctrine, according to which the idea of escaping the whirligig of *saṃsāra* was transformed into the idea of cultivating a potentially irreversible 'stream' of good leading to Nirvana, the end of suffering, a state of virtue in which all mental construction ceases. The appeal of the early Buddhist movement is thus to be explained through the combination of the following factors: profound ideas, their formulation in positive religious terms, and their embodiment in the charismatic figure of the Buddha, who was able to vary his teachings according to time and place so as to maximize their impact.

In the early texts these factors are often combined within single teachings, for example the gradual discourse, which begins with simple ideals but then goes further when the Buddha judges the revelation of more profound truths suitable for the occasion. It is not difficult to see in this approach an attempt to build a broad church, one with room for mystical quietists alongside city-dwellers, both of whom adhere to the same conception of the spiritual path, in which the boundary between renunciation and lay life is replaced by a single continuum of religious ideals, practices and goals. Early Buddhist ethics are therefore the connecting point between meditators beyond the world and those pursuing mundane ends within it: the purpose of the former is the realization of the highest good, whereas the latter focus more simply on the virtuous deeds which place them on the path towards this end.

Within this conceptual structure two aspects are particularly important: ethical universalism and intellectual innovation. The early Buddhists were certainly aware of this, for within a century of the Buddha's death they placed him at the centre of a mythology focused on these features of the Dhamma. They came to believe that Gotama's strivings were the final act in a dramatic religious career, one in which he had previously been a Bodhisatta ('devoted to awakening'), pursuing moral and spiritual perfection, in a variety of incarnations for a vast stretch of cosmic time. After being born as a human being for the last time, the myth states that the mass of good karma acquired by the Bodhisatta enabled him to finally awaken to his Dhamma as a Buddha, the seventh such figure in recent world ages. The early Buddhists thus essentialized their founder's significance into his ethical universalism (the idea of a lengthy path of virtue which finally resulted in liberation), and his awakening to eternal truths (Dependent Origination, the Four Noble Truths, etc.). Based on these beliefs the early Buddhists imagined a unique purpose for their mission, one that was believed to be an expression of the religious essence of the cosmos.

The zeal which motivated this mythological formulation suggests that the Buddha had a profound impact on his followers. But impressive teachings and a new understanding of religious purpose do not necessarily translate into missionary success. Patronage is required, and in this respect it is notable that the early Buddhists seem not to have attracted significant royal support, despite the Buddha being on friendly terms with the royalty of the fifth century BC: King Bimbisāra of Magadha, his successor Ajātasattu, and King Pasenadi of Kosala. Some Buddhist records even state that Pasenadi's son Viḍūḍabha massacred the Sakyas around the time of the Buddha's death, whereas the later royal dynasties of Magadha did not favour the Buddhists: reliable tradition states that both the Nandas and the first two Mauryan kings were supporters of the Jains and Ājīvikas.

If not from the royalty of the fourth century BC, support for the early Buddhists must therefore have come from the emerging urban centres of the Gangetic plains. The appeal of the Buddha's Dhamma to these communities is not difficult to explain. Apart from its ostensible religious purpose, the ethos of moral responsibility, rather than pessimistic escape, was well suited to an increasingly open and individualistic world. While the gruesome practices of some ascetics might have drawn attention and support through their shock value, the Buddha's ideas instead appealed through presenting a positive and life-affirming ethos.

By promoting such values as diligence, thrift, patience, empathy, and a long-term perspective, the Buddha thus turned the karmic individualism of the renouncers into a force for social good within an emerging civilization. As well as teaching an ethical way of life as the means of achieving the spiritual goal, the Buddha thus provided individuals with the means of making sense of a new world of towns, culture and money.

Chapter III
Meditation

> He forms not even the slightest conception with regard to worldly phenomena: that which is seen, heard or thought. That Brahmin does not grasp at views, so how could anyone here, in this world, conceptualise him? They form no views, they have no preferences, they do not depend on phenomena. The Brahmin cannot even be inferred through virtue or vows: such a being has gone to the far shore and depends on nothing.
>
> *Paramaṭṭhaka Sutta* (Sutta Nipāta 802–803)

The teachings which emerged over the course of the Buddha's mission came to comprise a broad spiritual system. But it must not be forgotten that the Buddha's primary concern was to share his awakened understanding with the few that might grasp it: establishing a spiritual elite was a necessary step in creating a movement of vitality and purpose. To this end the Buddha worked the basic principles of his anti-realist philosophy into a range of spiritual practices. By providing his followers with the meditative means of touching the unknowable reality of Nirvana, the Buddha endowed his movement with an intangible, mystical, dynamic – one that ensured the transmission of his spiritual charisma beyond his immediate circle of disciples.

The term 'meditation' can be used to describe the spiritual practices of early Indian Buddhism in two overlapping senses. First is the general sense in which it denotes a plurality of spiritual exercises and disciplines, including such things as inner absorption, philosophical contemplation and various thought experiments in which the Buddhist adept attempts to master some essential idea or aspect of the path. More specifically, the term refers to a particular type of spiritual practice in which a person cultivates altered states of consciousness by minimizing thought.

These two senses of the term 'meditation' are reflected in the early Buddhist use of forms of the verb *jhāyati*. In its basic meaning of 'thinking', 'imagining' and 'contemplating', this word denotes the various mental disciplines included in the Buddhist path of spiritual cultivation (*bhāvanā*). But the nominal form of the term (*jhāna*) also refers to four stages of a particularly Buddhist sort of spiritual development, one based on the cultivation of states of inner absorption, a practice unknown among religious traditions with no historical connection to India.

A key term applied to all such practices is *samādhi*, the root meaning of which is to 'put together' or 'unite'. This word thus denotes the attempt to focus the mind within and empty it of all content. Meditation in this sense is an entirely impersonal affair, without any concept of a divinity or deity: the person who pursues the path of absorption does not supplicate to a supernatural being or focus on it, but instead attempts to calm the mind before abstracting it into states of consciousness beyond the phenomenal world.

In his struggle to realize Nirvana, the canonical texts state that Gotama tried out various types of meditation, sometimes under the instruction of different teachers, before rejecting the idea that altered states of consciousness alone are liberating. But the meditative methods recommended in the early Buddhist texts include those that the Buddha experimented with. As such, these practices mark the historical starting point of Buddhist meditation. Even if the Buddha found the methods of his teachers insufficient, it seems he believed that they could play a useful role in a person's spiritual path.

Pre-Buddhist Meditation

The obscure origins of the meditative tradition in India can probably be located within the mysticism of the ancient Vedic poet-seers (*ṛṣi*). The *Nāsadīya-sūkta*, a late poem of the Ṛg Veda, perhaps composed some time between 1200 and 1000 BC, describes, elliptically, how the world was created from a state of divine perfection, a process founded on the initial arising of cosmic consciousness. This poem makes no mention of meditative practices, but in stating that the seers found the 'connection of the existent in the non-existent through inspired thinking', it suggests the existence of an old mystical tradition focused on grasping the mystery of cosmic creation.

Actual evidence for meditation does not appear until the *Bṛhadāraṇyaka Upaniṣad*, a Brahminic text that can be dated immediately prior to the Buddha. But the portions of this text which mention meditation indicate that its goal is identification with the divine source of the cosmos, and if so it can be logically connected to the *Nāsadīya-sūkta*, which is many hundreds of years older: both texts share the idea of realizing a primeval state of cosmic consciousness. The *Bṛhadāraṇyaka Upaniṣad*'s key passage on meditation occurs when the sage Yājñavalkya describes the realization of the 'world-self' as follows:

> A man who knows this teaching thus becomes calm, composed, cool, patient, and concentrated. He sees the self within, and all things as the self.

This brief statement indicates an attempt to identify with the cosmic source of all through inner concentration. It was almost certainly this tradition that Gotama encountered in the mid-fifth century BC, when he studied meditation under two teachers: Āḷāra Kālāma, who taught a system culminating in the state of 'nothingness', and Uddaka Rāmaputta, who taught a system which culminated in a state of 'neither perception nor non-perception'. Both goals were probably different ways of imagining the cosmic self, but Gotama found neither ultimately satisfying: the early texts state that in spite of realizing these goals, and then being proclaimed a master by his teachers, Gotama rejected the idea that he had achieved Nirvana. It was perhaps at this point that Gotama began to question the metaphysics of meditation, and so came to doubt that liberation can be achieved in any state of conditioned experience. The roots of the Buddha's understanding of how consciousness is constructed, and the beginnings of the enquiry that ultimately resulted in his awakening, can perhaps be traced to this spiritual failure.

Despite the disappointment of these meditative experiences, the Buddha allowed his teachers' methods, albeit stripped of their old metaphysical significance. The objects of meditation related to the two teachers, such as the material elements earth, water, fire and wind, were instead used as simple objects of concentration, and were not understood as subtle realities of the cosmos leading back to the cosmic self (as they are in early Brahminic texts). Some of these meditative states retained some cosmological significance, however, a good example being the four 'formless spheres' (space → consciousness → nothingness → neither perception nor non-perception). Certain Buddhist texts imagine these not as the subtle, inner realities of an objectively real world, but rather as rarefied cosmic strata found above the heavenly realms of the Buddhist cosmos.

An indication of how this sort of meditation was practised is given in early Buddhist texts such as the *Cūḷa-suññatā Sutta* ('Shorter Discourse on Emptiness'). This describes how the meditator first focuses his attention on the forest, and thus clears his mind of disturbances found in the village. After developing a more refined state of awareness, the meditator then focuses on 'earth' in order to clear his mind of the diverse features of a forest (such as rivers, tree-stumps, thorns and so on). The meditator's state of awareness thus becomes even more tranquil, and is said to be just like a 'smooth bull's hide stretched out with pegs'. Following this uniform and contentless state of mind is the development of the formless spheres: 'the sphere of the infinity of space', 'the sphere of the infinity of consciousness', the 'sphere of nothingness' and 'the sphere of neither perception nor non-perception'.

This 'descent into emptiness' is thus achieved by cultivating states of inner absorption, increasingly empty of content, which finally result in a state of mind termed the 'signless concentration of mind'. But this state was not viewed as an end in itself, as the text goes on to describe how the mendicant understands that this meditation is 'constructed and volitionally produced', and so impermanent – a point which once grasped effects liberation. A similar idea is expressed in the Buddha's dialogues with the renouncer Upasīva. To this enquiring Brahmin the Buddha states that the meditator, having reached the state of 'nothingness' – the meditative goal of Āḷāra Kālāma – should then become 'mindful' and observe 'the destruction of thirst night and day'. The Buddha thus taught that altered states of consciousness are useful only insofar as they prepare the way for a more profound understanding of conditioned experience.

The Art of Meditation

Apart from the meditative training under Āḷāra Kālāma and Uddaka Rāmaputta, the early texts state that Gotama tried out a number of ascetic practices. Some of these accounts describe Gotama's efforts in graphic detail:

> Because of eating so little my backside became like a camel's hoof . . . the joints in my spine were curved like a chain of beads . . . my ribs were just like the ramshackle rafters of an old barn . . . the sparkle in my eyes was sunk deep inside their sockets, just like the sparkle of water lying deep within a well . . . my scalp was cracked and withered, just like a bitter gourd cracked and withered by the wind and heat . . .
>
> The skin on my stomach clung to my backbone, so that when I stroked the skin on my stomach I felt my backbone, and when I stroked my backbone I felt my the skin on my stomach . . . when I defecated or urinated, I fell down head-first right there . . . when I soothed the body by rubbing my limbs with my hands, as I rubbed the hair, rotten at its roots, fell from my body.

Gotama's attempts to meditate without breathing are described in a similarly vivid manner:

> Just as a strong man might tie a tough leather strap around someone's head, so too did I feel excessive pain in my head when I stopped breathing in and out through my mouth, nose and ears. Although vigorous energy was aroused in me, and clear mindfulness established, my body was strained and disturbed by my overwhelming exertions.

The stories of Gotama's ascetic practices are meant to show that he achieved nothing by pushing the painful path to liberation to its farthest point. Whether or not any of this actually happened, the accounts at least suggest the correct way through a simple contrast: a mendicant should not do anything remotely like the acts of starvation and breath-suppression practised by other ascetics of the time. This point is emphatically made by the concluding episode in the stories of Gotama's asceticism, which state his remembrance of falling into a meditative state as a boy, when he sat under a rose-apple tree as his father worked the fields. Delving further into this memory Gotama realized that this natural state of meditation was not merely a kind of sensual pleasure, and so became convinced that it is the way to awakening.

Gotama's rejection of asceticism, and his meditative experience as a child, set up the Buddhist path as the 'middle way' between harsh asceticism and worldly pleasure, which directs the meditator towards a diligent rather than zealous cultivation of meditative states. This gentle approach can be seen in the Buddha's teaching to Soṇa, who practised walking meditation too strenuously, turning his feet into a bloody mess. When he wondered whether it would be better to return to lay life, the Buddha advised Soṇa to cultivate his practice like he would formerly have strung his lute: just as a lute does not play properly when the strings are too tight or slack, so too is it impossible to meditate properly when one is agitated (due to too much zeal) or indolent (due to sloth). A similar analogy which elucidates the diligent and unforced approach of Buddhist meditation is that of the turner:

> Just as a skilled turner or his apprentice, when making a long turn, understands 'I make a long turn', or, when making a short turn, understands 'I make a short turn', so too, in breathing in deeply, the mendicant understands 'I breathe in deeply' . . . or, when breathing in lightly, he understands 'I breathe in lightly'.

The Buddhist meditator is here advised to watch his breath carefully, not zealously, just like a meticulous artisan, in an almost effortless attempt to cultivate altered states of consciousness. Buddhist meditation is therefore a subtle art, in which attention is applied diligently, without pushing too much or slacking off. This gentle approach is in harmony with the philosophy of Dependent Origination. For if the problem of suffering is essentially a matter of mental construction, it follows that force will only perpetuate the forces of conditioning. A more suitable approach would be for the mind to be gently directed towards a state in which volitional activity subsides, so that the mentally created world of individual experience might naturally unravel. Such a philosophy of meditation is suggested by the following early teaching:

> Radiant is the mind, *bhikkhus*, but it is spoilt by defilements that enter it.

This statement suggests an approach to meditation in which harmful or unwholesome (*akusala*) states of mind must be dissolved, through a gentle but diligent application of attention, rather than by strenuous effort. Just as the mind of a craftsman or artisan is naturally focused and uncluttered, so too must the mind of a meditator be simply directed in such a way that conceptual proliferation is minimized, and defilements excluded, the end result being that they fall away without any effort.

The Middle Way

The early texts therefore explain the Buddhist path as a middle way (*majjhimā paṭipadā*) between sensual indulgence and ascetic penance. This middle way is the Noble Eightfold Path which brings about the complete cessation of suffering, as explained in the First Sermon of the Buddha, at Sarnath:

> There are two ends, mendicants, to which a renouncer ought not resort. Which two? Devotion to sensual pleasures, which is inferior, village-like, for normal people, ignoble and not connected with the purpose; and devotion to self-mortification, which is painful, ignoble, and not connected with the purpose. Avoiding both these ends, mendicants, the Tathāgata has completely awakened to the middle way, which brings vision and knowledge, and leads towards calming, understanding, full awakening and Nirvana. What, mendicants, is that middle way to which the Tathāgata has awakened? It is this very Noble Eightfold Path, namely: Right View, Right Resolve, Right Speech, Right Action, Right Livelihood, Right Endeavour, Right Mindfulness and Right Absorption.

If the Buddha's Dhamma does steer a course between the extremes open to the householder (indulgence) and renouncer (penance), the middle path should be open to those following both lifestyles, as long as the extremes associated with both are avoided. The logic of the 'middle way', and the teachings on which it is founded, thus suggests that the Buddhist path should be a broad and inclusive vehicle to Nirvana. Its eightfold structure shows that this is in fact the case, since the eight steps begin with simple moral observance and end in the higher levels of meditation; the path so imagined thus blends the ethical and spiritual virtues taught by the Buddha, and therefore excludes nobody from it.

The first two stages of the path, Right View and Right Resolve, are relatively straightforward but crucially important. For if a person does not grasp the Buddha's ideas and resolve in accordance with them, mental construction will maintain the conditioned world of *saṃsāra* rather than lead out of it. As the *Brahmajāla Sutta* points out, wrong ideas trap a person in the ongoing process of becoming, just like a fish in a net. It is for this reason that the path begins with knowing basic Buddhist ideas such as the Four Noble Truths (Right View) and the aspiration to act in accordance with Buddhist ideals of desirelessness, kindness and compassion, at the same time avoiding such things as desire, hatred and violence (Right Resolve).

The next three stages of the Path consist of actual moral observance: Right Speech, Right Action and Right Livelihood – stages of virtue elaborated in various codes of conduct, and which lead to stage six of the path, Right Endeavour. This consists of a moral introspection whereby a person attempts to eradicate bad states of mind and cultivate good ones, and so develop a more profound level of karmic virtue, one in which moral progress is interiorized in such a way that it leads to the higher stages of meditation:

> And what, mendicants, is Right Endeavour? Here, mendicants, the mendicant endeavours and exerts himself for the non-arising of non-arisen bad states of mind, for the abandoning of bad states of mind that have arisen, for the arising of unarisen good states of mind, and for the persistence of good states of mind that have already arisen. This, mendicants, is called Right Endeavour.

This stage of the path is therefore a bridge between two basic spiritual orientations: the good deeds which can be easily performed by a layperson, and the meditative endeavours that are more naturally the domain of the renouncer. But Right Endeavour is not merely a simple starting point for higher states of meditation. A number of early texts on Gotama's spiritual strivings explore this sort of discipline in great detail, and show that it is an essential preparation for the higher meditations that follow.

Dealing with Thoughts

Whatever the truth of Gotama's attempts to coerce his thoughts through breathless meditation, this story is in agreement with the Buddhist practice of watching the breath, without resorting to force and thus causing pain. The Buddhist way of diligently paying attention to an object, just as an artisan would focus on a craft, was obviously devised in opposition to the severe ascetic tendencies of the age. Exactly the same approach can be seen in a couple of early texts which describe different aspects of Gotama's strivings. These texts describe how Gotama applied his attention with care and diligence so as to observe and resolve unwholesome psychological states, rather than forcing his mind in an attempt to arrive at a pre-ordained result. These introspections thus exemplify the sixth stage of the Eightfold Path, Right Endeavour, in a highly idiosyncratic manner.

The two texts in question are the *Bhaya-bherava Sutta* ('Discourse on Fear and Dread') and the *Dvedhā-vitakka Sutta* ('Discourse on the Two Types of Thoughts'). The former describes how Gotama spent holy nights at religious shrines in order to invoke his inner fears. When a wild animal would approach, or a peacock would move a branch, or even when the wind rustled the trees, the discourse reports how fear came upon Gotama, in response to which he introspected 'Why do I live in constant expectation of fear and dread?' Gotama thus resolved not to alter his position or action at the very moment of fear, but to wait for it to abate, in the process arriving at a state of mindfulness, energy, bodily calm and focus. This state of mind then forms the basis for the development of higher states of meditation, which are achieved not through forcing the mind to concentrate on an object, but rather by working out thoughts diligently.

A similar approach is articulated in the *Dvedhā-vitakka Sutta*, which describes how Gotama investigated his thoughts by classifying them into two types: those of sensual desire, malevolence and violence, and those of desirelessness, benevolence and non-violence. When a thought of violence arose, Gotama thus reflected on the harm caused by such thoughts, which obstruct understanding and so lead away from Nirvana. The text states that by introspecting in this manner, Gotama's morally bad thoughts naturally subsided. When a thought of non-violence arose in Gotama, however, he is said to have realized that this causes no harm but instead increases understanding and leads towards Nirvana. But since continually contemplating his morally good states of mind would be tiring, Gotama thus concluded that he only had to be aware that these states were present, rather than actively contemplate them, in order to create a morally pure basis from which to achieve higher states of meditation.

Both texts state that moral introspection prepared the way for Gotama's spiritual progress: through observing his own mental states, Gotama resolved negative thoughts and came to understand how states of mental purity (*kusala*) aid meditative absorption. In these texts we therefore see how dealing with thoughts is a bridge between outer acts of morality and the cultivation of inner states of meditation. Exactly this approach to spiritual development is expressed in the Noble Eightfold Path as Right Endeavour: the same mental attitude, of diligent observance rather than struggle and suppression, leads to more advanced stages of the Buddhist path.

Cultivating Attention

In the Noble Path, the sixth stage of Right Endeavour precedes the seventh stage of Right Mindfulness and the eighth stage of Right Absorption. The introspection of the sixth stage of the path thus prepares the way for meditation proper: Right Mindfulness is a similar but more radical sort of introspection, one usually explained in terms of the Four Establishments of Mindfulness, a fourfold practice of cultivating a presence of mind with regard to the body, sensations, thoughts and mental states (especially those to be avoided or cultivated on the Buddhist path).

This scheme envisions the meditator developing his awareness of experiential states as they actually are (body, sensations, thoughts), before contemplating the degree to which they accord with the ethical and spiritual states to be cultivated on the path. The introspective habit of the sixth stage of the path is therefore extended into a more comprehensive observation of the human condition, a process which according to the *Satipaṭṭhāna Sutta* ('Discourse on Cultivating Mindfulness') begins with observing the breath:

> Sitting down in the forest, or at the foot of a tree, or in an empty hut, the mendicant should cross his legs, keep his body erect and establish mindfulness around his face. He breathes in mindfully, and breathes out mindfully. If he breathes in deeply, he knows he breathes in deeply. If he breathes out deeply, he knows he breathes out deeply. If he breathes in lightly, he knows he breathes in lightly. If he breathes out lightly, he knows he breathes out lightly. He disciplines himself thinking 'I breathe in experiencing the entire body', or 'I breathe out experiencing the entire body', or 'I breathe in tranquilizing the bodily impulses', or 'I breathe out tranquilizing the bodily impulses'.

A number of texts on the cultivation of mindfulness indicate that watching the breath leads to the attainment of absorbed states of meditation. According to the *Ānāpāna-sati Sutta* ('Discourse on Cultivating Mindfulness of Breathing In and Out'), this practice leads to the development of the 'Seven Limbs of Awakening' (mindfulness, investigation of mental states, energy, joy, tranquillity, absorption and equanimity), and also involves the direct cultivation of meditative qualities (through observing the breath):

> He disciplines himself thinking 'I will breathe in . . . and out . . . experiencing joy', 'I will breathe in . . . and out . . . experiencing bliss', 'I will breathe in . . . and out . . . experiencing the mental formations', 'I will breathe in . . . and out . . . pacifying the mental formations', 'I will breathe in . . . and out . . . experiencing the mind', 'I will breathe in . . . and out . . . gladdening the mind', 'I will breathe in . . . and out . . . absorbing the mind', and 'I will breathe in . . . and out . . . releasing the mind'.

This teaching could be read as a way to liberation in its own right, although if read in conjunction with the other discourses on mindfulness, observing the breath could instead be read as a means of attaining a heightened awareness of sensations and thoughts. These second and third establishments of mindfulness are described in very simple terms: the mendicant is said to become aware of his pleasant, unpleasant or neutral sensations (sights, sounds, tastes, smells, touch and simple mental objects), before considering whether thoughts of greed, hatred and delusion have arisen, and whether the mind has any meditative quality (whether it is focused or distracted, lofty or lowly, mundane or transcendent, or concentrated or 'released').

The fourth and final exercise in mindfulness consists of paying attention to the spiritual value of one's states of mind (*dhamma*). The meditator is here advised to consider whether his mental states are spiritually beneficial in the Buddhist sense (whether they correspond to the Seven Limbs of Awakening), or spiritually harmful (whether they correspond to the 'five hindrances' of longing, aversion, sloth, restlessness and doubt). In this final part of the practice, the mendicant therefore considers the overall quality of his experiential state, as a guide to his spiritual progress.

The Four Establishments of Mindfulness thus present a way by which the Buddhist mendicant can turn his entire life into a meditation: rather than simply achieve altered states of consciousness, the meditator instead uses such states as a means of observing the totality of his experience. In other words, meditation is not limited to secluded sessions of quiet sitting, but is to be abstracted into every aspect of life, in such practices as walking intensely along a prepared stretch of ground. The purpose of this approach to meditation is to develop an impartial and detached state of being, as one of the Buddha's teachings to his son Rāhula makes clear:

> Cultivate a meditation that is just like the earth, Rāhula, for pleasant and unpleasant sense-contacts will not invade and obsess your mind when you do so. Rāhula, when people throw something pure or impure onto the earth – such as excrement, urine, spit, pus or blood – the earth is not troubled, harassed or disgusted by that. In the same way, Rāhula, cultivate a meditation that is just like the earth.

The early Buddhist texts present breathing and walking in a disciplined manner as a means of simplifying experience, of reducing it to its bare essentials, so as to observe it as it is, at the same time keeping in mind states which incline towards Nirvana and states which do not.

Mindfulness and the Buddhist Path

The discourses on mindfulness present a homogeneous and apparently complete vision of the Buddhist path. But a different perspective is presented by the Eightfold Path, in which mindfulness is the penultimate rather than concluding aspect. Other texts which contain different accounts of the path are in general agreement with the Eightfold Path, such as the Seven Limbs of Awakening and the Five Faculties or Powers (faith, energy, mindfulness, absorption and insight). All these seem to be variations on the same theme, imagining the same general progression to Nirvana, in which virtue is followed by introspection and mindfulness, and finally the altered states of consciousness produced by inner meditation.

The discourses on establishing mindfulness stand apart from this general understanding although this might only be because of its style of presentation, rather than substance. Indeed, the texts on *satipaṭṭhāna* articulate an atemporal rather than progressive understanding of the path, a point made clear in the concluding statement that whoever should practise them for an extended period of time – for as little as one week or as much as seven years – can expect to be liberated or else achieve the state of non-return. This means that the four *satipaṭṭhāna*s constitute the practices which lead on, even if the discourses on them do not describe how the practice plays out over time. Furthermore, the Seven Limbs of Awakening, a temporal path scheme beginning with mindfulness and culminating in a refined state of equanimity, is mentioned in both the fourth establishment of mindfulness and in the *Ānāpāna-sati Sutta*. This implies that the texts on establishing mindfulness expand upon a key stage in the path, rather than offer a complete account of the path in its own right.

Besides the atemporal accounts focusing on the four *satipaṭṭhānas*, and the summary temporal lists such as the Eightfold Path and Seven Limbs of Awakening, a more detailed temporal account of the path is found throughout the early texts. This account describes the ideal spiritual biography of the Buddhist mendicant, one that corresponds closely to the Noble Eightfold Path and offers yet another perspective on the cultivation of mindfulness. Its description of how a person hears the teaching of a Buddha, decides to renounce the world and then observes various moral precepts corresponds to the first five aspects of the eightfold way: Right View, Resolve, Speech, Action and Livelihood. In the next stage of the path the mendicant is advised to guard his sense faculties, so that spiritually deleterious states of mind do not overwhelm him:

> When he sees a form with the eye, he does not grasp at the qualities or details because of which, if he were to pass his time without restraining the eye, unwholesome states such as greed or distress might assail him.

This close observation of mental states, and attempt to ward off those that are ethically corrupt, is a sort of applied version of Right Endeavour. A close approximation to the Eightfold Path continues in the next stage of the detailed description, which corresponds to Right Mindfulness, albeit in a greatly simplified form, as a short description of becoming fully aware of mundane experience:

> The mendicant pays full attention when going forward and backward, when looking ahead or around, when bending and

> stretching, when carrying his outer robe, bowl and inner robe, when eating, drinking, chewing and tasting, when defecating or urinating, when moving, standing still, sitting down, asleep, awake, speaking or being quiet. In this way the mendicant is endowed with mindfulness and full awareness.

The next stage of the detailed description is inner meditation: the mendicant is said to seek out an isolated place, sit down cross-legged and establish mindfulness 'around his face' (*pari-mukham*). This introduction to the account of inner meditation is identical to the opening of the accounts on establishing mindfulness by paying attention to the breath, a correspondence which suggests the four *satipaṭṭhānas* elaborate the means of attaining higher states of meditation as stated in the detailed description. Some connection is undeniable, although it is also possible the authors of the discourses on mindfulness used the detailed description as their starting point for a new and complete account of the path. Whatever the case, it would seem that the discourses on mindfulness and the detailed description present a similar understanding of the relationship between mindfulness and absorption. But whereas the detailed description imagines mindfulness as basic self-awareness of daily actions, which comes after much preparation and precedes meditative absorption, the *Satipaṭṭhāna Sutta*s envision mindfulness as a complete meditative discipline to be applied from the start, in which meditation apparently precedes the close application of attention to mundane experience.

What the Buddha actually taught is difficult to establish given these differences. Nevertheless, the texts are in close agreement over what really matters: the mental states considered spiritually valuable, and the manner and direction of their development. Maybe the variation between the different accounts is merely one of presentation, perhaps due to the Buddha's habit of varying his teaching according to the context. But it is also possible that the discourses on mindfulness were composed by an early *satipaṭṭhāna* school of thought, one located in the town of Kammāsadhamma in northwestern Kuru kingdom.

The Four Stages of Meditation in Context

The final stage of the Noble Eightfold Path is Right Absorption, usually explained as the four stages of meditation (*jhāna*). In the long temporal description of the path, these meditations also comprise its final stages, and are roughly equivalent to the states listed as the final four of the Seven Limbs of Awakening (joy, tranquillity, absorption and equanimity). According to the long temporal account, these four states are realized after the mendicant sits down, establishes mindfulness 'around the face' and then abandons the five hindrances:

> He abandons longing for the world and abides with a mind devoid of longing: he purifies his mind of longing. He abandons malevolence and enmity, and abides without malevolence and full of compassion for the welfare of all beings and creatures: he purifies his mind of malevolence and enmity. He abandons lethargy and drowsiness, and abides devoid of them, conscious of light, mindful and fully aware: he purifies his mind of lethargy and drowsiness. He abandons agitation and worry, and abides without disturbance, with a mind quiescent within: he purifies his mind of agitation and worry. He abandons perplexity and abides in a state beyond it, having no doubts with regard to good states of mind: he purifies his mind of perplexity.

At this point of spiritual development the mendicant is likened to a person recovered from a serious illness, or to someone released from jail, or slavery, or arrived home after being lost. In this state of freedom the mendicant progresses through the four stages of meditation as follows:

> Aloof from sensual pleasure and bad states of mind, he enters and sustains the first stage of meditation, a state of joy and bliss born from seclusion in which there is discoursive thought.
>
> With the calming of discoursive thought he enters and sustains the second stage of meditation, a state of internal tranquillity and unity of mind devoid of discoursive thought, in which there is the joy and bliss of concentration.
>
> With the fading away of joy, he abides in a state of equanimity in which he is mindful and fully aware, and experiencing bodily bliss: he enters and sustains the third stage of meditation, about which the noble ones say 'he abides in bliss, mindful and equanimous'.
>
> With the abandoning of pleasure and pain, and with the disappearance of all previous states of happiness and sadness, he enters and sustains the fourth stage of meditation, a complete purification of equanimity and mindfulness.

The series of four meditations implies that over time, the person is transformed by a subtle co-development of mindfulness and absorption. In the first two stages the mind becomes calm and still, so that the capacity to conceptualize experience disappears, with the mind becoming increasingly empty of content. The first meditation is likened to a moist ball of lathered soap powder which does not leak, indicating a basically unified state of mind, one that is fully developed in the second *jhāna*, which is described by a more elaborate simile: this experience is compared to a deep pool without any inlet or outlet, with its cool, pellucid waters being fed from within by an underground spring.

Whereas the mendicant develops inner absorption at the expense of awareness in the first two stages of meditation, this situation changes in the next two stages. To be 'mindful and fully aware' in the third stage indicates the resumption of sensory experience and objective consciousness, even if there is no indication that the ability to verbalize has returned. The meditator would instead seem to have entered a more vivid form of transitive consciousness, one devoid of the conceptualization which usually arises in the process of cognitive conditioning. In the fourth stage this state is taken much deeper, or completely 'purified', with all cognitive and affective responses to primary experience fading away, so that the mental construction of primary experience apparently all but ceases.

The similes used to describe the third and fourth stages reflect the change from inner absorption to purified objective awareness. Thus the third state is compared to a lotus immersed in water, and the fourth likened to a person sitting wrapped from head to toe in pure white cloth, with a body entirely pervaded by a 'perfectly purified and translucent mind'. These similes indicate a transformation of the adept's entire psycho-physical being: it is not simply the case that consciousness is focused within, and so cut off from bodily awareness and experience, but rather that the totality of the person's experiential state is transformed, in body and mind.

The four stages of meditation show that advanced stages of the path are reached through more than the mere cultivation of altered states of consciousness. Since the four meditations are stages in an idealized spiritual biography, they should be understood not just as altered states of consciousness, perhaps to be achieved in a single meditative session, but rather as stages of life, which develop naturally from a disciplined lifestyle of restraint, introspection and observation. The mendicant does not simply attain (*upasampajja*) altered states of consciousness, but rather passes his time in them (*viharati*), as his basic experiential state, so that at the higher reaches of the process he is at the point of realizing the radical deconstruction of conditioning that is Nirvana.

Nirvana

According to early Buddhist thought Nirvana is the cessation of Dependent Origination. This means it is a state in which the karmic perpetuation of individual experience in space-time ceases for good. But it is difficult to understand how this can be brought about: how can a person deconstruct the sense of individual existence in the world, if the 'I' who acts to achieve this end is part of the problem that must cease? The principles of early Buddhist thought suggest that a person cannot, in the final analysis, do anything to bring salvation about, for any such effort would merely perpetuate conditioned reality. These problems are reflected in the fact that the Noble Eightfold Path ceases at Right Absorption, just as the Seven Limbs of Awakening cease with equanimity: both imply that nothing can be done once the highest level of meditation has been reached.

Much the same point is implied by the use of fire imagery in the early teachings: whereas conditioned experience is likened to a burning fire, the term 'Nirvana' is derived from the verb *nir-vā*, meaning to 'blow out'. Nirvana is therefore an experience in which conditioned experience – of greed, hatred and delusion – ceases, just as a flame goes out when its fuel is exhausted. Fire imagery is also implied in the definition of the five aspects of conditioned experience (form, sensation, apperception, mental constructions and consciousness) as 'masses of fuel' (*upādāna-kkhandha*). Since the fuel of the five 'aggregates' includes a person's consciousness (*viññāṇa*) and volitions (*saṅkhāra*), and since this must be 'blown out' in order for Nirvana to be realized, it would seem that the person cannot finally do anything in order to escape *saṃsāra*.

But this does not imply complete helplessness in the matter of spiritual realization. The *Sekha Sutta* ('Discourse on Training') explains the situation through a simple analogy: just as a chick will emerge from its shell as long as the egg has been properly incubated, without the mother-hen wishing for this to happen, so too is the person 'incubated' by the four stages of meditation able to attain liberation even without wishing to do so. Another account of effortless liberation is contained in the *Mahā-taṇhāsaṅkhaya Sutta* ('Greater Discourse on the Destruction of Craving'). After the lengthy description of the temporal path, this teaching explains how the forces which fuel conditioned experience naturally cease after the fourth stage of meditation has been achieved:

> When he sees a form with his eye (or perceives any other sense object), he is neither attracted to a pleasant form nor repulsed by an unpleasant form. For he abides with mindfulness of the body firmly established, with an immeasurable mind, and understands as it really is (*yathā-bhūta*) that release of mind, a release through insight, in which all bad states cease without remainder. Having thus abandoned favouring and opposing, whatever sensation he experiences, be it pleasant, unpleasant or neither, he finds no satisfaction in it and does not welcome it. Since he abides without delighting in or welcoming sensation, all delight in it ceases for him. Due to the cessation of delight, attachment ceases; with the cessation of attachment, becoming ceases; with the cessation of becoming, birth ceases, with the cessation of birth, decrepitude and death cease; with the cessation of decrepitude and death, sorrow, lamentation, pain, depression and tribulation cease: thus ceases this entire mass of suffering.

The key aspect of this transformation is the realization of a meditative state described as a 'release of mind, a release through insight'. Numerous texts conclude the Buddhist path with this state, which thus marks the point from which the attainment of Nirvana becomes inevitable: at this point, the person has apparently attained a transformed state of gnosis, of seeing things 'as they really are'. The description of seeing things as they really are (*yathā-bhūta*) in the *Brahmajāla Sutta* mirrors this account, as it similarly describes an insight into the structure of experience (the 'rise, fall, pleasure, danger and release from the six spheres of sense-contact'). In his discussion with the Brahmin Posāla, the Buddha similarly explains that the meditator must understand the underlying cause of experience while in the meditative state 'nothingness':

> Once one knows that the origin of nothingness is the fetter 'delight', one must understand it thus and have insight into it. This is the true knowledge of the liberated Brahmin.

In explaining that a person must comprehend the root cause of the state of nothingness, the Buddha implies that understanding the underlying structure of experience comes about in a trans-conceptual meditative state. The underlying principle is that a combination of mindfulness and meditative absorption enables a person to see into the true nature of experience. Of course, to understand that delight is the root cause of conditioned experience is another way of stating the Second Noble Truth, that suffering is caused by thirst. If so, it seems likely that this account influenced the conclusion of the detailed description of the path, which states that liberation is finally effected by understanding the Four Noble Truths. But describing liberating insight in this way goes beyond comprehending the structure of experience in a highly refined state of mindfulness, since comprehending all four Truths includes the Fourth Truth (the Eightfold Path), the understanding of which requires conceptualization.

The same applies to early texts which state that insight arises from contemplating the teaching of Dependent Origination. For such a contemplation implies that a person has not abandoned ideas and abstract thought – a notion that goes against the philosophy of constructed realism, and the basic sense of the path structure described throughout the early texts. In the earliest Buddhist period, of the Buddha and his disciples, Nirvana was not regarded as a knowable experience as such, but was rather thought to be a sort of meta-experience, in which the structure of conditioned experience ceases.

Meta-experience

The fact that Nirvana was originally considered a kind of meta-experience, rather than an elevated sort of objective consciousness, is made clear by the fire imagery used to describe conditioned experience and its cessation. The image of an extinguished flame indicates that the cessation of Nirvana is completely unknowable, as illustrated by the Buddha's teaching to Upasīva:

> Just as a flame blown with the force of the wind goes out and cannot be reckoned, so the sage released from the category 'name' goes out, and cannot be reckoned.

The cessation of 'name' here indicates the cessation of conceptualization, the key aspect in the process of cognitive conditioning which causes suffering. A different and fuller application of the same simile is found in one of the Buddha's teachings to the wanderer Vacchagotta, in response to a question about what happens to a liberated person after death:

> If, Vaccha, you were to be asked: 'When this fire in front of you is blown out, in which direction does it go from here – to the East, West, North or South?' Being questioned thus, how would you explain it?
>
> 'The issue does not arise, Gotama. For the fire burnt dependent upon its fuel of grass or firewood, and when the fuel has been consumed, and no more is provided, being without fuel it is reckoned as "blown out".'
>
> In just the same way, Vaccha, the form, sensation, apperception, mental constructions and consciousness by means of which someone might designate the Tathāgata, has been abandoned, uprooted, extirpated, annihilated, and is not liable to arise in the future for the Tathāgata.
>
> The Tathāgata, Vaccha, is released from that which is reckoned as 'form' (and sensation, apperception, mental constructions and consciousness): he is deep, immeasurable and unfathomable, just like a great ocean. The propositions 'he is reborn', 'he is not reborn', 'he is both reborn and not reborn' and 'he is neither reborn nor not reborn' – these do not apply.

In this teaching the image of an extinguished flame is applied by the Buddha to himself, and so focuses on the complete transformation of a liberated person's experiential state: the different aspects of conditioned experience disappear, leaving him in a state beyond reckoning. Just as an extinguished flame no longer exists in space-time, so that one cannot ask in which direction it has gone, so too does the person liberated in life realize a state outside the conceptually constructed world of time and space, and hence ontologically inexplicable. The early teachings do not fail to draw this radical conclusion, for example the *Kalahavivāda Sutta* (of the *Aṭṭhakavagga*, book four of the Sutta Nipāta), where the Buddha suggests that the awareness of being an embodied individual ceases in liberation:

> Not cognizant of conceptualization, not cognizant of misconceptualization, not uncognizant but not cognizant of what is untrue: form disappears for the one who has reached this state, for the discernment of manifoldness originates in conceptualization.

This statement is complex but essentially equivalent to the teaching given to Vaccha: both note the disappearance of physical form in the liberated state. But the Buddha here adds that this occurs when spatio-temporal awareness – 'the discernment of manifoldness' – ceases. Other teachings from the *Aṭṭhakavagga* describe the cessation of this mentally constructed world of time and space, for example the *Tuvaṭaka Sutta*:

> 'I ask you, kinsman of the sun, great sage, about detachment and the state of peace: with what sort of vision is a mendicant quenched, so that he grasps at nothing in the world?'
>
> The Blessed One said:
>
> The contemplative should put a stop to the notion 'I am', which is the root cause of discerning manifoldness. He should ward off whatever inner thirst he has, training himself to be ever mindful.

The Buddha here states that in liberation a person's sense of existing as an individual in the manifold world stops. In the *Purābheda Sutta* the Buddha further points out that the liberated person transcends time:

> Devoid of thirst even before death, not dependent upon the past, immeasurable in the middle, for him nothing is fashioned with regard to the future.

The statement that the liberated sage is 'immeasurable' in the 'middle' – i.e. the present – is a poetic way of describing the transcendence of time. The liberation of Nirvana is therefore indescribable, a state in which the construction of primary experience into the world of time and space ceases, a point explicitly made in the *Mahā-nidāna Sutta* as follows:

> The extent of articulation and its range, of utterance and its range, of designation and its range, of understanding and its scope, and of existence in *saṃsāra* and its 'movement' (i.e. time): the mendicant is released from all this through higher understanding.

This teaching implies a nominal theory of reality, according to which existence and time are equivalent to words and thoughts ('articulation', 'utterance', 'designation' and 'understanding'). But the Buddha is beyond this conceptually constructed world of space-time, and in touch with reality as it actually is.

Ineffability

The early Buddhist teachings imply that the ineffability of Nirvana is more than just a qualitatively indescribable experience, such as a flavour or smell experienced for the first time. It is rather suggested that Nirvana is ineffable in the more radical sense of being the dissolution of individual experience *per se*, private or otherwise, a meta-experience in which the cognitive basis of all individual conditioning ceases. In his teaching to Udaya, the Buddha states that this is equivalent to the cessation of consciousness, which occurs while the person is awake and aware:

> Not delighting in internal or external sensations, consciousness ceases for the person who passes his time mindful in this way.

In early Buddhist thought the term 'consciousness' denotes transitive awareness – the perception of objects – but here it is said to cease while a person attends to the sights, sounds, smells and so on that are the objects of experience. This statement draws attention to two apparently contradictory aspects of the liberated experience, and thus encapsulates the conceptual difficulty posed by the early Buddhist teachings on Nirvana. These two aspects are the notion that transitive awareness must be dissolved, and the notion that the liberated person nevertheless remains mindful. In the *Alagaddūpama Sutta* the Buddha elaborates on this baffling state as follows:

> Therefore, mendicants, I say that when Indra, Brahma, Pajāpati and the gods search for a mendicant thus released in mind, they cannot establish the location of the Tathāgata's consciousness. Why is that? O mendicants, I say that the Tathāgata is untraceable even in the present.

The reason a liberated person's transitive consciousness (*viññāṇa*) cannot be found is that it does not pertain in liberation: it is an aspect of conditioned experience that the Buddha, in his teaching to Vacchagotta, claims to have 'annihilated'. Since this vital aspect in cognitive conditioning – and thus the mental construction of space-time – is not part of the awakened experience, it follows that a liberated being cannot be spatially located, even if he somehow remains mindful and fully aware. The lack of a spatio-temporal location for the liberated person is also reflected in the term 'Tathāgata'. This word is a compound made up of the terms *tathā* – 'thus' – and *gata* – 'gone', and is usually rendered 'Thus-gone'. But there are reasons for believing that in the language spoken by the Buddha, words ending in *-gata* were used to describe conditions or states of being rather than motions or acts. If so, the term indicates a condition (*-gata*) that is indescribable (*tathā*): the liberated person is 'the one whose state (*-gata*) is thus (*tathā*)'.

By using a term of motion (*-gata*) in a sense in which it lacks any sense of movement, the Buddha thus implies that he had gone beyond the possibility of going or being anywhere. In the Buddha's Dhamma, liberation is not simply a matter of having a private and indescribable religious experience, then, but is ineffability of an entirely different order, an irrevocable deconstruction of conditioning that liberates a person from the knowable reality of spatio-temporal being.

Miracles

This understanding of Nirvana helps explain a peculiar but generally misunderstood aspect of early Buddhism: the belief that the Buddha and other liberated saints were able to act contrary to the laws of nature. Such a belief is the logical consequence of the philosophy of constructed realism, which states that a Tathāgata is beyond the constraints of time and space, and thus implies that he can perform miraculous acts. This is indeed what the early texts claim: miracles are attributed to the Buddha and some of his disciples, and many of the detailed accounts of the path state that powers such as flying, becoming invisible or walking on water become possible after the fourth stage of meditation.

It is easy to explain the belief in miraculous powers away, a fancy of the more imaginative members of the early Buddhist community. But a consequence of the doctrine of Dependent Origination is that a Tathāgata should indeed be able to fly through the sky 'like a bird with wings', for such a person has deconstructed laws of nature that are merely contingent. Even if this seems absurd, it is not without a rational basis. For it can hardly be denied that a sensation triggers a complex series of psycho-physical events which enable a person to perceive an object, and which therefore represent an object as it is constructed rather than as it actually is: process implies change, and if so the basic idea of constructed realism is sensible, even if the Buddha takes it to extreme lengths in rejecting philosophical realism.

Although early Buddhist teachings offer no conceptual analysis of miracles, they occasionally imply that such things are philosophically grounded. This can be seen in the *Kevaṭṭa Sutta*, which begins with the lay-disciple Kevaṭṭa imploring the Buddha to let a Buddhist mendicant perform a miracle (in order to inspire faith among the townspeople of Nāḷandā). But the Buddha refuses this request, pointing out that even if he did this a sceptic would simply explain it away as a magical trick, in which case no faith would be inspired. The Buddha then narrates the peculiar story of a Buddhist mendicant who, by supernatural means, travels through the higher heavens as far as the god Brahma, in order to find out where the material elements 'cease without remainder'. Eventually the mendicant returns to the Buddha and is told that they cease in 'Consciousness, which is intransitive, infinite and luminous all round' (the full statement is on p. 30). This juxtaposition of themes is peculiar: in a discussion about miracles, the Buddha narrates a story which apparently suggests why miracles are possible, i.e. because the material elements that make up the world are contingent on transitive consciousness. As a whole, the discourse suggests a philosophical reason for miracles, even if ordinary people are likely to explain them away as a magical illusion.

Another suggestive text is a discourse which reports the Buddha's encounter with the brigand Aṅgulimāla. Advised not to follow a forest path in the vicinity of this fierce murderer, famous for threading the fingers of his victims into a garland which hung around his neck, the Buddha nevertheless set off and was pursued by him. But Aṅgulimāla was unable to reach the Buddha no matter how fast he ran, and had the sense of going nowhere while the Buddha walked on at his own pace. When Aṅgulimāla eventually gave up and called out for the Buddha to stop, the Buddha gave the following enigmatic response: 'I am standing still, Aṅgulimāla, whereas you are not.' The Buddha then offered the following explanation to his puzzled interlocutor:

> I stand still, Aṅgulimāla, since I have utterly laid down the stick with regards to all creatures, towards whom you lack restraint. Therefore I am still, whereas you are not.

The Buddha here explains that he is 'still' in a more essential sense than Aṅgulimāla, in that he occupies a state of complete non-violence towards all living beings. Since this state of non-violence is transgressed by Aṅgulimāla, it is he who remains in motion in a more essential, mental sense, despite his physical inaction. The Buddha's stillness is defined as a state of ethical purity, which means that it is devoid of bad karma. But such a state is exactly the aim of absorption, and is reached at the fourth stage of meditation. It therefore follows that the nature miracle of the *Aṅgulimāla Sutta* occurs in a state in which mental construction has ceased.

Miracles are therefore a consequence of the radical deconstruction achieved by a Tathāgata, the being who is beyond time and space. The Buddha's encounter with Aṅgulimāla can thus be taken as a narrative exploration of a Tathāgata's state: the person who, being beyond the conceptual construction of individual existence in space-time, who does not and cannot go anywhere, is still even when physically active, unlike Aṅgulimāla who is physically still but trapped in the mental construction of his karma. Whether or not the Buddha was able to perform nature miracles, such things are a logical consequence of his teachings on Dependent Origination, which imply that the liberated person's spiritual release places him within the ineffable, but inherently virtuous, way things really are.

Apotropaic, Karmic and Gnostic Buddhism

The individual quest for salvation, to be achieved especially through the cultivation of altered states of consciousness, lies at the heart of the early Buddhist movement: it is not possible to understand Buddhism without understanding meditation, the primary pursuit around which all other religious concerns revolve. But this does not mean that Buddhism is only about private states of religious experience. For the Buddha devised a broad spiritual path, the lower levels of which consist of non-meditative activities such as making merit through pious offerings to the Sangha, living in accordance with Buddhist moral values, pilgrimage, *stūpa* devotionalism and so on.

These two different levels of religious activity could be categorized by the terms 'karmic' and 'gnostic': the purpose of the former is to generate good karma for a person's spiritual progress in the future (in this life or the next), whereas the concern of the latter is to fully understand the Buddha's teachings. Gnostic Buddhism therefore lies within the domain of the Buddhist intelligentsia and virtuoso meditators, the thinkers bent on penetrating the truth of the teachings, and those for whom salvation is a primary concern to be approached through meditation and contemplation.

This distinction between two levels of religious observation is a theoretical construct, for there is no separation between the two in any Buddhist culture or even in the canonical teachings. These two orientations are bound together by the karma doctrine, which asserts that moral observances are a preparatory spiritual purification, and that the good karma created by simple acts of piety is akin to weak states of meditation. The doctrinal unity of karmic and gnostic Buddhism is also supported at the cultural level by the aesthetics of Buddhist devotionalism: the ceremonial forms described in the accounts of the Buddha's funeral, and in his directions to perform simple rituals at *stūpa*s, established a common religious culture within which devotionalism and meditation have always been practised.

Another dimension of Buddhist practice was appended to this broad synthesis of karmic and gnostic ideology, almost certainly in the first century of the Buddhist era, but perhaps not during the Buddha's life. This could be termed 'apotropaic' Buddhism, for it consists of ritualistic and magical practices intended to bring about protection and success in the present life. The idea of achieving well-being through a ritual act would seem to violate the very foundations of the Buddha's teachings, but is articulated in canonical texts such as the *Maṅgala*, *Ratana* and *Āṭānātiya Sutta*s. Any discord is minimized, however, by the fact that the protective formulae of these texts express simple ethical ideals, so that the act of chanting invokes Buddhist values in the practitioner's mind. Such ritual chanting could thus be described as a way of contemplating Buddhist ethics (at a basic level); since good mental states are thereby generated, apotropaic Buddhism could be viewed as an extension of karmic Buddhism to a more basic level of religious activity.

The integration of apotropaic practices into the Dhamma was aided by the fact that the achievement of worldly well-being was an aspect of Buddhism from the very beginning. This is most obvious in the Buddha's dialogue with King Ajātasattu of Magadha in the *Sāmaññaphala Sutta*: in a discussion about whether or not any worldly rewards are gained through being a renouncer, the king informs the Buddha that all other contemporary teachers avoided this issue, preferring to focus on the theoretical aspects of their doctrines, 'as if explaining a bread-fruit when asked about a mango'. In contrast to this, the Buddha presents the spiritual path as a means of achieving tangible rewards in the here and now, which lead gradually to the ultimate religious good. The inclusion of apotropaic elements in the Dhamma could be seen as an extension of this aspect of the Buddhist path, albeit at a lower level.

Very early in the history of Indian Buddhism, the pious acts believed to generate good karma were extended to include protective rituals. And as Buddhism expanded across and beyond northern India, the apotropaic dimension of the Dhamma was gradually expanded to include purely magical rituals with hardly any moral content. Apotropaic and karmic Buddhism have been more or less indistinguishable ever since: in all Buddhist cultures, devotional acts and protective rituals are at once an attempt to achieve well-being in the present as well as a good destiny beyond the grave. Both levels of observance thus lead towards the higher aims of the Dhamma, with practitioners at all three levels expressing their commitment within a single religious culture framed by the devotional aesthetics of old Magadha.

Chapter IV

Embellishing the Dhamma-Vinaya

> Therefore, Ānanda, live as a light unto yourselves, taking refuge in yourselves and nobody else, with the Dhamma as your light, with the Dhamma as your refuge, taking refuge in nothing else.
>
> *Mahā-parinibbāna Sutta*

These words of the Buddha, uttered shortly before his death, must be reckoned as one of the most important statements in the history of civilization. For the advice not to appoint a successor directed the Buddha's followers towards institutional independence and individual freedom of thought, factors which promoted missionary zeal and speculative creativity. The focus on personal responsibility, without parallel in all other world religions (or religions of the world) was thus a key factor in the creation of dynamic Buddhist cultures throughout Asia. Such advice could have been disastrous, causing the Sangha to quarrel about the true meaning of the Dhamma, perhaps leading to schism, as occurred with the Jains after the death of their founder, Mahāvīra. Since this did not happen even when different interpretations of the Dhamma arose, it would appear that the Buddha's followers remained in agreement about the essentials of his teachings.

At the very least, the general theoretical framework of the teachings, especially the reworking of the karma doctrine and the notion of an inclusive path, must have been generally agreed, as must the lifestyle and practices of the community. Perhaps most important of all, the memory of the Buddha as a non-disputatious teacher remained strong among his followers. The Buddha's courteous example would thus have endowed the early community with a pragmatic and flexible approach to furthering the mission. Even though disagreements are suggested as early as the texts which record the Buddha's death, these did not affect the general course of institutional development.

This can be seen in the account of the First Council at Rājagaha, the old capital of Magadha, convened just after the Buddha's death in order to gather and preserve the teachings.

The First Council

The Pali account of this council includes the curious story of the mendicant Purāṇa, who formally assented to the proceedings, but stated his preference for the Buddha's teaching as he remembered it. Such an episode suggests the possibility that inauthentic teachings were included in the primitive Buddhist canon from the very beginning. But even if so, it does not follow that all information about the Buddha is flawed. Indeed, the very preservation of this story reflects well on the proceedings of the council, for it suggests there was no attempt to silence critics. Even if Purāṇa's scepticism raises the possibility that not everything attributed to the Buddha can be so regarded, the story gives the impression of an open and honest attempt to preserve the Buddha's teachings – reason enough to suppose that genuine teachings of the Buddha were preserved.

That any memory of the Buddha's teachings was preserved is remarkable, for the First Council took place before writing existed in ancient India. But since the Vedic literature of the Brahmins had already been transmitted verbatim without writing for up to 1,000 years, the Buddhist community knew that a massive feat of memorization was a feasible, if daunting, task. As an aid to transmission, stories of the Buddha's teachings were put into a highly repetitive form suitable for group recitation, all based on a limited number of formulaic templates. Such a style of composition could have emerged from the First Council itself, for this event is remembered as a 'group recitation' (*saṅgīti*) rather than a 'council'. The practice of group recitation, along with repetition and other mnemonic techniques, reduced the effort required to remember the teachings and so minimized the possibility of individual errors in transmission. As the body of oral literature grew, different groups of recitors (*bhāṇakas*) began to specialize in different categories of text.

The only complete Buddhist canon which survives in an ancient Indian language is that of the Pali tradition, transmitted from northern India to Sri Lanka in the mid-third century BC, and from there to

South India and Southeast Asia. Like all canonical Buddhist literature, this canon is divided into three 'baskets' (*piṭaka*): the Sutta-piṭaka (the Buddha's discourses plus a few other early texts in a similar form), the Vinaya-piṭaka (disciplinary rules to be followed by individual mendicants and the community as a whole), and the Abhidhamma-piṭaka (seven books that explore the Buddha's teaching in a more abstract and analytical manner). But these three baskets were not known at the beginning of the attempt to preserve the Buddha's teachings: the Pali account of the First Council instead describes the works preserved as Sutta and Vinaya, indicating that the scholastic compositions of the Abhidhamma did not exist at that time, and so cannot go back to the Buddha.

A period of literary development must also be assumed for the Sutta and Vinaya portions of the canon. The Vinaya evolved over time, as the community expanded and began to adopt a more settled monastic life, whereas the Sutta-piṭaka contains a variety of teachings that cannot go back to a single person. Some individual discourses (Suttas) even depict an advanced state of debate, and can only have been composed after a considerable period of doctrinal development. The Sutta-piṭaka therefore contains not only the Buddha's teachings, but also the contribution of early Buddhist teachers and thinkers to their master's Dhamma. While the creation of new 'words of the Buddha' (*buddha-vacana*) might appear fraudulent, the early thinkers and teachers probably believed they were faithfully drawing out the meaning of the teachings; passing off their ideas as teachings of the Buddha was initially the only way of preserving their creative endeavours.

Because oral tradition was accumulated gradually, with no attempt to preserve chronological distinction, the teachings of the Buddha are unfortunately obscured within a mass of early literature. The problem of understanding the Buddha's ideas is therefore one of identification: later additions must be distinguished from the earlier teachings, so that both can be understood according to their own logic. But since there has been no break in the Buddhist tradition, and since reliable means of oral transmission were known from the beginning, there is no reason to assume any major loss of teachings. It follows that whatever can be identified as the earliest stratum of teachings can logically be attributed to the Buddha himself.

The Second Council

All Buddhist traditions agree that a Second Council was convened at the northern town of Vesālī, and although there is no general agreement on its date, it can be placed in the period between 340 and 300 BC. This council was an attempt to resolve a dispute which had arisen concerning the practices of this town's Buddhist community: the Pali tradition records ten aberrant customs, of which the drinking of partly fermented liquor and accepting silver and gold from the laity were the most important. That a dispute of this kind could arise is curious, for it suggests that the Buddha created no rules on these points, and this implies that the disciplinary regulations he did leave behind were more limited than those preserved in the extant Vinayas.

This is easy to understand in the case of monetary donations, for coins appear not to have circulated during the Buddha's time. This situated quickly changed in the rapidly developing urban world of the fourth century BC: towns and kingdoms expanded, mercantile activity increased, and it is not surprising that some Buddhist communities adapted to the new economic circumstances. At a later date Buddhist monasteries throughout India eventually came to accept monetary donations. But the Second Council shows that this adaptation was initially rejected, albeit by means of a difficult process of consultation and legal manoeuvring, requiring the judgement of Buddhists from different communities spread across northern India.

It would seem that maintaining communal unity as distinct fraternities began to emerge was still just about feasible, although the geography covered by the various accounts suggests that this would not last long. The Pali tradition reports that after criticizing and then being admonished by the brethren of Vesālī, the mendicant Yasa travelled west to gather support: first to Kosambī, an old centre frequented by the Buddha, but then further west to Mathura before turning south towards the kingdom of Avanti in central India, both of which were new Buddhist centres that did not exist during the Buddha's time. The Second Council thus appears to have been the last major attempt to stem the tides of change, and maintain the old disciplinary unity, in a rapidly changing world.

The council was ultimately resolved on the word of the oldest monk present: Revata, a pupil of Ānanda, is said to have agreed with Yasa's western contingent in concluding that the ten practices of Vesālī were contrary to the Vinaya. But this final decision was reached after a lengthy legal process, one that reflects the proceedings imagined in those parts of the Vinaya dealing with the resolution of disputes. The *Kosambaka* section of the Pali Vinaya reports that after a dispute between the different Buddhist factions of Kosambī had been defused, the Buddha advised that in order to establish concord in spirit and letter, a respected and learned *bhikkhu* ought to be approached and questioned on the case.

In another section on resolving disputes, the Pali Vinaya states that if differences cannot be resolved 'face to face' between the incumbents of a monastery, the virtuous and learned *bhikkhus* of a neighbouring monastery should be asked to make a decision. But if a ruling cannot be reached the case is to be referred to a select committee of virtuous and learned *bhikkhus*, failing which a vote on the matter is to be taken. With these stories we get an idea of how the early Buddhist Sangha conducted its affairs: communal discussions were held at which the judgement of respectable elders was sought, failing which a vote was to be taken as a last recourse. Since the proceedings of the Second Council followed a similar course as this – but were resolved by a learned committee before voting was required – it is likely that certain parts of the early Vinaya had reached a fairly advanced stage of development.

If, indeed, the Vinaya rules for individual mendicants (the *Pātimokkha*) or its commentary (the *Vibhaṅga*) were still relatively open, they would certainly have been altered to disallow the ten practices of Vesālī. For the Vinaya evolved in exactly this way: as situations arose, either new rules were composed or existing rules were refined to accommodate the developments. Since this did not happen at the council of Vesālī, it would seem that a sufficiently complex set of rules must already have existed, no doubt alongside a considerable collection of the Buddha's discourses. Although the Buddhist canon was still open and so able to accommodate the challenges of an increasingly complex urban society, a significant amount of material had already been fixed: parallels between the Pali Suttas and their equivalents preserved in Chinese translation show a far-reaching agreement, which must have been established at an early date.

Early Buddhist Communities

Since the Buddhist Sangha was in possession of a large and still-growing collection of sacred literature at the time of the Second Council, it is likely that many of its communal institutions had already been formalized. Indeed, the arduous and time consuming matter of oral composition and transmission cannot have been carried out by itinerant mendicants: a more settled way of life was required, one which is implied by the accounts of the Second Council. By the end of the fourth century BC, within 100 years of the Buddha's death, the Sangha consisted of distinct communities, for example that of Mathura to which belonged the mendicant Sambhūta Sāṇavāsin, or Revata's community at Soreyya, and also the relatively settled community of Vesālī, which was able to store goods on its premises and accept money.

A fairly settled monastic life differs from the lifestyle of the Buddha. Urban life in the fifth century BC was quite basic: there is virtually no archaeological evidence for buildings of brick or stone dating to this period, and if so the earliest Buddhist centres cannot have contained anything beyond simple huts. The Pali Vinaya mentions dwellings (*vihāra*), probably of wood and bamboo and with roofs of grass, that could be constructed in a single day, and also states that before the First Council could begin, an entire month was spent repairing the community's dilapidated buildings in Rājagaha. If permanent dwellings existed at Buddhist centres before the Buddha's death, these had not been properly maintained because they had not yet been permanently settled, at least by any sizeable monastic population.

But settled monasticism by the time of the Second Council is suggested in the account of Yasa's trip to the west: some of his supporters are called 'wilderness dwellers' (*āraññika*) and 'beggars of alms' (*piṇḍapātika*), designations which indicate that the mendicant lifestyle was not necessarily the norm. Monasticism was therefore developing, with the communities (*āvāsa*) of this period in possession of such things as beds, seats, rugs and bedding, all of which are mentioned in the *Pātimokkha*, along with disciplinary rules on the size of monastic buildings. If the *Pātimokkha* was relatively closed at this time – as it must have been for it to have been consulted but not updated when making rulings at the Second Council – it would seem that

Fig. 4. Cave temple at Bhaja, c.second century BC, *its inward slanted columns a direct copy of earlier structures in wood*

the difference between the early dwellings of the First Council and the more settled residences of the Second Council was considerable.

The development of settled communities does not imply that the itinerant lifestyle was lost. Yasa's mobility indicates that peripatetic Buddhists travelled freely between the emerging monasteries of northern India: the general pattern for Indian Buddhism henceforth was the preservation of the peripatetic habit within the context of settled monasticism.

Although a Vinaya passage which records an extension of the period of retreat during the rainy season (around three months) suggests that monasticism emerged from customs established even during the Buddha's life, no Buddhist texts explain the reasons for the evolution of a new institutional norm. But this can probably be attributed to the practical necessity of adapting to changes in both the Sangha and society. As noted above, the need to meet regularly in order to preserve the Buddha's teachings would have encouraged a more settled lifestyle. Pupils would also have gathered around famous Dhamma teachers, who for ease of instruction would have remained near prominent areas of Buddhist support. This support would have become increasingly substantial as the urban life of northern India developed: pious lay patrons would naturally have offered the Buddhist mendicants new and improved dwellings suitable for a more settled life as their own conditions of living improved in the urban era.

The style of the Buddhist dwellings in the fourth century BC can be inferred from sites dating to the following century. The entrance to the Lomas Rishi caves, donated by Aśoka to the Ājīvikas in the mid-third century BC, consists of a rectangular doorway framed by a horse-shoe shaped roof. A more elaborate version of this style can be seen in the cave monasteries of western India, the oldest of which probably date to the second century BC. Buddhist sculpture of approximately the mid-second century BC is similar: a stone panel from Bharhut depicts two buildings of the Jetavana monastery in Sāvatthī, and both have the same style as the Lomas Rishi entrance that is roughly 100 years older. A simpler version of this style can thus be attributed to the early, wooden, monasteries of the fourth century BC.

Guild Monasticism

If the buildings at Buddhist sites just after the Buddha's death were rudimentary, it means that extensive portions of the surviving Vinayas cannot be taken at face value: although these books claim to report changes that happened during the Buddha's ministry, their contents go beyond what can be deduced from the accounts of the First Council. These books must instead record the Sangha's evolution into a monastic order in the first few centuries of the Buddhist era, a process which involved the extension of the Buddha's pragmatism rather than a rejection of his lifestyle. This can be seen in the trial and error structure of the monastic rules: when new issues arise that require a legal treatment – for example when the order is furnished with a new sort of provision, such as couches or bedding – a ruling is made about what is permissible. But this is not the end of the matter, for when complications arise with the new practice, the rule is then refined according to the circumstances.

The Vinayas thus describe a process of negotiation which always ends with a compromise, in which the conflicting interests of the laity and the monastic community are reconciled and harmony maintained. The concern to maintain good relations with the laity was partly due to practical necessity, but was also a consequence of Buddhist universalism and the recognition that the laity had an important role to play in the Buddha's religious mission. This meant that apart from the fortnightly Uposatha ceremony (celebrated on the days of the new and full moon), when the recitation of the *Pātimokkha* was accompanied by teachings to the laity, specific rules were devised to maintain and further contacts between the lay and monastic communities, for example stipulating that monks were not allowed to farm or cook: self-sufficient monasteries cut off from the world were not an option.

The disciplinary rules of the Vinaya thus form a sort of case law directed by pragmatism rather than idealism. These rulings were not created in the abstract, based on a utopian vision of the perfect spiritual society: they were not an exercise in forcing the world to fit an ideal, but were rather an attempt to refine the ideal according to the demands of the real world. The Vinaya thus navigates a practical course between what was spiritually beneficial, what would have inspired the faith of the laity, and what would preserve and promote the Buddha's mission. These guiding principles emerged from the Buddha's pragmatism and impersonalism: remaining faithful to his advice not to appoint a single head of the order, and instead following his Dhamma as a matter of individual conscience, the Sangha worked its way forward through dialogue and compromise.

The lack of an institutional leader thus required all members of the different Buddhist communities to think for themselves, and take personal responsibility for the Buddha's mission. The Buddha's individualism thus allowed the Sangha to spread across India in the form of local (and localized) communities (*āvāsa*), which functioned in a fashion not entirely different from the mercantile guilds which supported them. Both established a similar position in their own domain within the emerging urban civilization, enjoying considerable autonomy to conduct and regulate their own affairs. If anything, the institutional independence of the Buddhists was greater, for the renunciant groups had no official role in the affairs of the emerging kingdoms.

This distinction of religion from the state was a consequence of renunciant pessimism. Since the renouncers of the Buddha's day saw only pain and difficulty in the world, secular affairs were viewed as an intrinsic aspect of the existential problem to be avoided at all costs; the concept of a state religion was a contradiction in terms. Although the Buddha navigated a middle way between this social and ideological dichotomy, his Dhamma nevertheless remained apolitical, its social engagement confined purely to ethical interaction at the individual level. Even when major state patronage eventually came with the conversion of Aśoka, it did not alter the socio-political distinction between sacred and profane. The Sangha thus institutionalized the religious freedom of the earlier renouncers within a system of guild monasticism: local Buddhist communities were free to pursue their own agendas without interference from a centralized church, and in a culture more or less outside the political powers of the state.

Indian Buddhism was a quite different sort of world religion from Christianity and Islam, both of which positioned themselves at the centre of the socio-political order. The Sangha instead chose to conduct its affairs from the social fringe, with no purpose to direct society let alone manage it. This does not mean that there were no Buddhist kings who applied the principles of the Dhamma to their government; of course there were, the most brilliant example being Aśoka. But it does mean that there was no Buddhist political tradition, or even Buddhist advisors at court. The advantage of this approach was that the Sangha was not tied to any particular ruling house, and so did not suffer the immediate consequences of regime change. But the course of Buddhist history shows that the apolitical approach was also a weakness. Whenever Buddhism was forced to compete with other movements that wished to position themselves at the socio-political centre, such as Brahminism, Confucianism or Islam, it was pushed to the margins and declined.

Was the Buddha a Philosopher?

In a monastic culture made up of autonomous communities, it is not surprising that different interpretations of the Dhamma soon emerged. The canonical discourses contain a few traces of these early developments, which can be explained as an unintended consequence of the Buddha's impersonalism and pragmatic style of teaching. As the Buddha was concerned to use his ideas to benefit whomever he taught, rather than stating them in the abstract, he did not create any such thing as a philosophical system. Because he preferred to adapt according to the context, the Buddha's legacy was a highly diverse set of teachings. When guided to think for themselves, with the Dhamma as their light, the early Buddhists thus developed their master's teachings in a multiplicity of doctrinal formulations.

The Buddha's pragmatism can be seen in the simile of a man shot by an arrow, which states that just as it would be pointless for this man to enquire about the person who shot him (his social class, name, family and height), so too is it pointless for the person afflicted by suffering to ask whether the world is infinite, eternal and so on. What matters in both cases is being healed: the man shot by an arrow should follow the advice of a doctor, whereas a mendicant should apply the Buddha's teachings in order to end suffering, rather than indulging in pointless speculation. The simile of the man shot by an arrow, and that of the raft (p. 17), show that for the Buddha the value of knowledge depends upon the spiritual purpose it serves: the Buddha was a religious teacher first and a philosopher second.

Pragmatism can also be seen in the teaching to Prince Abhaya, where the Buddha states he will only speak what he knows to be true, even if it is disagreeable, so long as it is the correct time to say it, but will not speak an unhelpful truth. It would therefore seem that the Buddha's judgement of spiritual efficacy was more important to him than abstract truths uttered regardless of their effect. But this pragmatic articulation of ideas does not authorize the utterance of any teaching which might have a beneficial result: it instead appears that the Buddha's pragmatism was limited to what he believed was objectively true, and if so it can also be assumed that the Buddha believed in objective truth, and that he had some kind of world-view or philosophy from which his teachings were drawn.

The simile of a leaf points towards exactly this conclusion: by likening the ideas he had revealed (the Four Noble Truths) to a single leaf in his hand and contrasting this with what he actually knew (said to be as much as all the leaves in a forest grove), the Buddha indicated that he had knowledge but was more interested in its pragmatic application. It can therefore be surmised that the teachings of the Buddha are philosophically grounded, even if a comprehensive philosophy was never articulated.

A further indication of this can be seen in the Buddha's refusal to answer questions of an ontological nature. For this silence is charged with philosophical significance: although it shows that the

Buddha was not a philosopher interested in an abstract presentation of certain ideas, a specific philosophical understanding is clearly implied. Philosophical subtlety and pragmatism are indeed combined throughout the early teachings, a clear example being the *Brahmajāla Sutta*. This discourse comes close to explicating the Buddha's ideas about epistemological conditioning, but nevertheless avoids a direct statement of abstract truth and focuses on how wrong beliefs condition a person's entanglement in *saṃsāra*.

All this suggests that the Buddha's Dhamma is profoundly philosophical. Indeed, teachings such as the Four Noble Truths suggest a rational approach more in keeping with the tradition of ancient philosophy; one much closer in spirit and method to Socrates than Moses. But the Buddha's followers extended this philosophical example by attempting to explain what the Buddha had left unsaid: early generations of Buddhist thinkers pondered their master's idea of a radical difference between reality *as it really is* and reality *as it is perceived*, and thus elaborated the Dhamma into a range of philosophical positions and related spiritual practices.

Contemplative Practices

The canonical teachings advise various contemplations as a means of developing the attitude and insights required to follow the path to Nirvana. Most of these focus on developing the necessary attitude of renunciation and letting go, but some work at a much deeper level, dealing with the root problems of attachment, desire and ignorance. In the former category are contemplations of bodily impurities in a negative light, such as the advice to regard the body 'from the soles of the feet up and from the top of the hair down' as full of 'faeces, bile, phlegm, pus, blood, sweat, fat, tears, spit, snot, oil and urine'. A more extreme contemplation is that of the body in its various stages of decay: beginning with its decomposition after one, two or three days, when it becomes 'bloated, livid, and oozing matter', the mendicant is told to imagine it being eaten away by crows, vultures, jackals and worms, until it becomes a skeleton that eventually crumbles into dust.

Two further contemplations tend towards the same negative assessment of the human lot, although at a less gruesome level. First is the simple contemplation of the body in terms of its four constituent elements: earth (or solidity), water (or fluidity), fire (or heat) and wind (i.e. breath or air). The contemplative is here advised to resolve each part of the body into these elements just as a butcher cuts up the carcass of a cow into small pieces. A more important contemplative exercise, while less abstract and reductionistic, similarly emphasizes the idea of individual impermanence:

> Here the mendicant understands: 'Form is thus, its arising is thus, its fading away is thus; sensation is thus, its arising is thus, its fading away is thus; apperception is thus, its arising is thus, its fading away is thus; volitions are thus, their arising is thus, their fading away is thus; consciousness is thus, its arising is thus, its fading away is thus.'

The contemplation of the five aggregates as an impersonal process directs attention towards the underlying structure of conditioned experience. Its purpose is therefore somewhat more ambitious than merely thinking over the idea of bodily impermanence; as the mendicant Khemaka explains, the point of this exercise is to dissolve the sense of an individual 'I' that persists behind the changing world of conditioned experience:

> The noble disciple immerses himself in observing the rise and fall of the five aggregates of attachment: 'form . . . feeling . . . apperception . . . volitions . . . consciousness is thus, its arising is thus, its fading away is thus'. In doing this the conceit, intention and underlying tendency 'I am' with regard to the five aggregates of attachment that had not been destroyed is destroyed.

This thought experiment is therefore presented as a means of deconstructing the state of consciousness in which the 'I' is felt to be a stable entity that persists above and beyond the five aggregates. Khemaka likens the contemplative process to placing a fresh cloth in a scented box so that the smell of the cleaning agent disappears as the cloth is perfumed. This assumes that over an extended period of time, and perhaps along with other spiritual disciplines (although this is not stated), the contemplation of the five aggregates gradually reduces a person's tendency to identify with individual phenomena, the end result being liberation from the notion 'I am'.

This was not the only way in which the Not-Self teaching was understood, however. Whereas Khemaka presumes that the Not-Self teaching takes time to understand, the elders of Kosambī, to whom

Khemaka discloses his ideas, do not. They ask Khemaka whether he sees that the five aggregates are 'not-self', and when he responds that he does, they believe that he must be liberated. This seems to assume that merely understanding the Not-Self teaching effects a person's liberation, regardless of any process of purification achieved over time, through contemplation (and/or meditation). These elders appear to have believed that knowledge liberates, although Khemaka disagrees by denying that he is a liberated saint.

The same belief in liberating knowledge is stated in the *Susīma Sutta* ('Discourse to Susīma'), a discourse in which some mendicants claim to have been 'liberated through insight', apparently without attaining the four stages of meditation. What really matters, according to this text, is understanding the teachings on Not-Self and Dependent Origination: thinking through and grasping Buddhist ideas is enough to be 'liberated by insight' alone. Other texts state the similar idea that the minds of various individuals were liberated simply by listening to the Buddha's teaching, for example Sāriputta, as he stood behind the Buddha, fanning him and at the same time thinking over his teaching.

The idea of achieving an instantaneous liberation through grasping Buddhist truths is quite different from the path schemes studied in the previous chapter. For these schemes imply that understanding fundamental truths is a foundational aspect of the spiritual life rather than its culmination: Right View is the first aspect of the Eightfold Path, which eventually culminates in a state of purified meditation (Right Absorption). But it would seem that some early Buddhists came to a quite different conclusion, namely that they could be 'liberated through insight' without even meditating, as if Right View is itself enough.

It is clear that discourses such as the *Khemaka* and *Susīma Sutta*s also disagree with the philosophy of epistemological conditioning. For this philosophy implies that the very structure of conditioned experience ceases in Nirvana, just like an extinguished flame, an idea quite different from that of liberation through contemplation alone. If so, it would seem that within a few generations of the Buddha's death, some of his followers developed new ideas about contemplation, mindfulness and meditation. And not only this, for in thinking over the Buddha's ideas deeply, based on the belief that this would effect liberation, the actual understanding of the ideas also began to change.

The No Self Teaching

The idea of liberation through knowledge was an unintended consequence of two key features of the Buddha's teachings: the idea that liberation is not achieved in a meditative trance, and the importance assigned to analysing and understanding ideas about the conceptual construction of experience, the insubstantiality of the phenomenal person and so on. The Buddha challenged people to think, and this seems to have led some in the early Buddhist community to think too much, and eventually come to believe in the liberating power of thinking *per se*. This does not mean that meditation was avoided altogether by these early Buddhist contemplatives. But conceptual thought seems to have been the primary concern of some, a focus which led them to a new understanding of the teachings, especially with regard to Dependent Origination and the Not-Self teaching.

The Not-Self teaching (p. 35) is a good example of the Buddha's skill in means, for it does not state that the five aggregates are impermanent and so not-self, but rather invites others to consider the matter and realize its truth by themselves. But this avoidance of philosophical abstraction is also due to the fact that the teaching is based on the philosophy of constructed realism. This can be seen in the content of the five aggregates, which presupposes an embodied person (form) who, upon becoming aware of something (consciousness) and having primary experience (sensation) then conceptualizes it (apperception) and has a volitional response to it (volitions). As a summary of Dependent Origination, the list obviously deals with cognitive processes and constructs (*how* things are), rather than the static world of objective reality (*what* things are).

Indeed, by asking whether a mendicant should regard (literally 'view') the five items *as* one's self, the Buddha speaks in terms of dynamic experience rather than ontology: the five aggregates are not a static complex in which a person searches for a self, but are rather aspects of a person's experiential being to be contemplated *as they happen*. The focus is on epistemological conditioning rather than ontology, but this is not actually stated, for the teaching avoids abstract truth so that others can discover its meaning by themselves. But when the Buddha and his disciples were no longer available to guide the understanding of subsequent generations of Buddhist mendicants, it seems that these later Buddhists decided to fill in the gaps.

An important shift in the understanding of the Not-Self teaching can be seen in question put to Khemaka by the elders of Kosambī: they ask whether he can see a self *in* the five aggregates, rather than whether the aggregates can be considered *as* self. This question suggests a different kind of enquiry, one in which a person contemplates the different aspects of individual being in an attempt to establish whether an entity can be found therein. By replying that he could not see any such thing, Khemaka implies that the self does not exist, rather than merely being a concept ill-suited to conditioned experience.

This different manner of articulating the Not-Self teaching suggests that a major change in its understanding was taking place, from not-self to no self. Clear evidence for this philosophical change is contained in a number of other early texts, the best example being the *Vajirā Sutta*, in which the nun Vajirā states the non-existence of the self to the demon Māra as follows:

> Why do you believe in a living being? Is not this your view, Māra?
> This is nothing but a heap of formations: No being is found here.
>
> When there is a collection of parts, the word 'chariot' is used;
> Just as when the aggregates exist the term 'being' is applied to them.
>
> Only suffering comes into existence and only suffering endures.
> Nothing apart from suffering comes into existence,
> and nothing apart from suffering ceases to exist.

These verses do not presume that the human being is a dynamic complex of experiential factors, as the Buddha had taught, but instead state that an abiding existential principle cannot be found within the various constituents of the human being. This development raises profoundly difficult religious problems. For if there is no real subject of experience, who or what attains Nirvana? The problem is avoided by the philosophy of epistemological conditioning, which considers only two different modes of experience: that which is constructed and can be described in terms of the five aggregates, and its opposite, which is Nirvana, the ineffable cessation of the five aggregates.

According to the Buddha's understanding, the question of who experiences liberation is a misconceived attempt to conceptualize Nirvana. But once Buddhist thought took an existential turn, such problems had to be tackled, even if satisfactory answers could not be found. For when seen in an ontological light, the old similes and metaphors were bound to be misunderstood: in particular, the image of an extinguished flame suggests the complete disappearance of the five aggregates from *saṃsāra*, and hence the annihilation of a liberated person at death.

Reductionistic Realism

The transformation of 'not-self' into 'no self' required only that some thinkers avoided the philosophical presuppositions of the *Brahmajāla Sutta*, and adopted an ontological approach to the old teaching. Aspects of experience originally thought unsuitable to be regarded as 'self' (the five aggregates) thus came to be considered as impermanent existential factors in which no self can be found. Exactly how the new understanding was developed can be seen in the *Mahā-hatthipadopama Sutta* ('Great Discourse on the Simile of the Elephant's Footprint'). This discourse considers the first aggregate of 'form' not as an aspect of experience, but rather in terms of the ontological factors of which it consists (the four material elements of earth, water, fire and wind). To these four elements the Not-Self teaching is applied as follows:

> What, venerable sirs, is the earth element? It might be internal or external. And what is the internal earth element? That which is internal and personal, i.e. that which is solid, hard and materially derivative, such as head-hair, bodily hair, nails, teeth, skin, flesh, sinew, bones, bone-marrow, kidney, heart, liver, membrane, spleen, lungs, bowels, intestinal tract, stomach, faeces, and whatever else is internal and personal, i.e. that which is solid, hard and materially derivative. This, venerable sirs, is said to be the internal earth element. This very internal earth element and the external earth element are simply the earth element, which should be seen with correct understanding as it really is: 'This is not mine, I am not this, this is not my self'. Once seen with correct understanding as it really is, one becomes disillusioned with the earth element, one cleanses one's mind of passion for the earth element.

This teaching does not consider the process of conditioned experience and its conceptual appropriation, but is rather focused on a virtually exhaustive analysis of the physical constituents of a human being and the lack of self therein. All this points towards a new Buddhist philosophy, one that is realistic (since the human being is held to exist in an external world independent of mind) but reductionistic (since the really existent human being is made up of constituent parts which lack self). The simile of the house, found towards the end of the text, makes this reductionistic realism quite clear:

> Venerable sirs, just as an enclosed space is designated 'house' dependent on logs, creepers, grass and clay, so too is an enclosed space designated 'form' dependent on bones, sinew, flesh and skin.

A person's physical being is here said to be a mere accumulation of different parts, located in which, as the text goes on to state, are the 'aggregates' of sensation, apperception, volition and consciousness. The reference to an enclosed space shows that the authors of this text regarded the human being as a structure in space-time, albeit one that lacks self. The truth to be known, according to this perspective, is thus that although the human being really does *exist*, he is an *aggregate* that lacks an intrinsic, abiding identity. The Buddhist contemplative is advised to consider this truth as follows:

> He understands thus: 'Thus indeed is the coming together, collection and accumulation of the five aggregates of attachment'. But the Blessed One has said this: 'The one who sees Dependent Origination sees the Dhamma, and the one who sees the Dhamma sees Dependent Origination'. These very things are dependently originated, that is to say the five aggregates.

As impermanent parts out of which a person is constructed, the five aggregates of this discourse really are 'aggregates'; the term *upādāna* ceased to be the metaphorical 'fuel' which supports a person's conditioned being, and instead came to be understood literally, as the material constituents of a composite entity. This was a major change from the teachings of the Buddha: whereas the Not-Self teaching had originally implied that 'self' is an inappropriate way of designating conditioned experience, according to the new reductionistic realism the self does not exist in the ontological aggregate that is a human being.

Process Philosophy

Apart from the conceptual differences between the *Brahmajāla Sutta* on the one hand and the *Khemaka*, *Vajirā* and *Mahā-hatthipadopama*

Suttas on the other, the fact that the latter are not directly attributed to the Buddha suggests an attempt to distance new ideas from him. The *Mahā-hatthipadopama Sutta* even indicates its status as an exegetical work by framing its formulations within the context of authentic utterances of the Buddha (*buddha-vacana*), through the statement 'The Blessed One has said this'. Furthermore, since this statement occurs in the text's discussion of Dependent Origination, it follows that the early Buddhist reductionists must also have devised a new, realistic understanding of Dependent Origination, a development of the older epistemological conditioning of the *Brahmajāla* and *Madhupiṇḍika Suttas*.

Exactly this is suggested by a number of early Buddhist texts which elaborate Dependent Origination into a twelvefold form; although largely absent from the Dīgha and Majjhima Nikāyas, and very old sources such as the Sutta Nipāta, this teaching is found throughout the Saṃyutta, Aṅguttara and Khuddaka Nikāyas, and became the standard form of the teaching. This elaborated version of the doctrine shows how an experiential being comes into existence in the first place; how, in short, there is 'the coming together, collection and accumulation of the five aggregates of attachment', as stated in the *Mahā-hatthipadopama Sutta*. This form of the teaching thus elaborates the No Self idea to show how individual continuity over time is possible without an underlying substance:

> Dependent on (1) ignorance arise (2) volitions, dependent on volitions arises (3) consciousness, dependent on consciousness arise (4) name and form, dependent on name and form arise (5) the six sense faculties, dependent on the six sense faculties arises (6) contact, dependent on contact arises (7) sensation, dependent on sensation arises (8) thirst, dependent on thirst arises (9) grasping, dependent on grasping arises (10) becoming, dependent on becoming arises (11) birth, and dependent on birth arise (12) old-age, death, sorrow, lamentation, suffering, depression and tribulation: thus arises this entire mass of suffering.

This teaching goes beyond the *Brahmajāla Sutta* in explaining how an embodied being comes together in a former life: at some point in the past, ignorance (1) created the volitions, or karmic potential (2) for another individual consciousness (3) to come into existence, which then developed into an embryonic psycho-physical being (4). These stages precede the teaching of Dependent Origination as stated in the *Brahmajāla Sutta,* which begins with the six sense faculties, stage five in this formulation; this thus looks like an attempt to explain individual continuity before the present. Since stages 1–2 can be logically assigned to a different lifetime in the past, it would seem that the Buddha's teaching of Dependent Origination was expanded to show how personal continuity and rebirth are possible in the absence of a self.

The No Self orientation of this scheme is suggested by the fact that its first four stages (ignorance → volitions → consciousness → name and form) resemble the first phases of creation from the cosmic self in early Brahminic texts, albeit in a negative sense, without mentioning any transmigrating entity. According to the Brahminic accounts, the absolute exists in a state of divine perfection, but then becomes conscious when the urge to cognize something arises, on the basis of which the material world is projected. The first stages in the twelvefold version of Dependent Origination sketch the same creative process in the negative: the initial state before cognition is turned into a state of cognitive indeficiency ('ignorance'), from which arise the mental impulses that fashion the consciousness which lays the foundations for a rudimentary existential entity of mind and matter.

These modifications to the teaching of Dependent Origination resulted in an elegant process philosophy: individual existence was explained as the coming together of a complex series of cause and effect, without there being any substance to 'undergo a transformation'. Early Buddhist thinkers thus proposed a solution to a major problem created by the No Self theory: if there is no self, how can a person continue after death in other modes of individual existence and experience? The teaching of Dependent Origination explains how this is possible despite reductionistic realism.

A fuller treatment of process philosophy is in a discourse which depicts the Buddha in dialogue with the Brahmin Acela-Kassapa. In response to questions about whether or not a person (in a previous life) causes his own suffering (in the lifetimes that follow), the Buddha states that the suffering is caused neither by that very person nor by someone else. For if it were true that the effects of karma were caused by the very same person in a previous life, the person would be eternal, whereas if the results of karma are caused by a different person in a previous life, the original agent of the karma would be destroyed at death:

> O Kassapa, someone who contemplates the distant past and thinks 'the one who acts is the one who experiences', he claims that suffering is caused by the same individual, and thus comes to believe in eternalism. Someone else overwhelmingly concerned with sensation thinks 'the one who acts is different from the one who experiences', he claims that suffering is caused by a different individual, and thus comes to believe in nihilism.

This text therefore proposes the twelvefold version of Dependent Origination as a 'middle' way between eternalism and nihilism:

> Avoiding both these ends, Kassapa, the Tathāgata teaches the Dhamma through the middle: volitions are dependent on ignorance, consciousness is dependent on volitions and so on . . . Thus arises this entire mass of suffering.

The authors of this teaching thus believed that Dependent Origination explains the causal relationship between karmic deed and its eventual retribution, over a series of lifetimes, but without an essential subject of experience. According to this understanding Dependent Origination explains the continuity, but not identity, between successive states of being: individual existence is not a matter of ultimately real substances, but of ever-changing experiential processes within *saṃsāra*. The process teaching to Acela-Kassapa, although attributed to the Buddha, thus presumes philosophical realism and as such disagrees with the philosophy of constructed realism. Both cannot be attributed to the same thinker: process philosophy, and the No Self teaching it presupposes, is probably a realistic development of the Buddha's teachings.

The Mystical Cessationist School

During the same early period in which some Buddhists developed the idea of liberation through knowledge, along with the No Self teaching and process philosophy, other Buddhists developed the Buddha's ideas on meditative absorption. Although the Buddha rejected the notion that altered states of consciousness are sufficient for liberation, he did not deny the benefit of such practices to those who had studied such methods and achieved a degree of accomplishment in them; the Buddha merely adapted them to a different end. The Buddha therefore allowed non-Buddhist meditation to be practised by his followers, especially those states taught by his former teachers, Āḷāra Kālāma and Uddaka Rāmaputta. These probably included element meditation: the practice of concentrating exclusively on the constituent elements of the world (earth, water, fire and wind).

Related to these practices and following in sequence from them are the meditations on space and consciousness, which in early Brahminic texts mark the culmination of the regression through the subtler levels of the cosmos, spheres closest to the cosmic source of all (*brahman*). Early Buddhist sources show that the same practices were continued in the Sangha, who formulated them in lists such as the so-called 'spheres of totality' (*kasiṇāyatana*), a list of ten objects of meditation (earth, water, fire, wind; dark blue, yellow, red, white; space, consciousness), each of which the meditator is said to perceive as 'above, below, across, non-dual, immeasurable'. The Buddha's spiritual pragmatism suggests the possibility that such practices were known among his disciples.

A similar list of meditative objects is the eight 'spheres of mastery'. In the first two of these peculiar and slightly obscure states, the meditator is said to be aware of his own form, but unaware first of 'limited' and then 'unlimited' external forms, both of which are said to be attractive and unattractive; the third and fourth states are described in exactly the same terms, although the meditator is now said to be unaware of his own form. In the final four states the meditator remains unaware of his own form, and focuses successively on blue, yellow, red and white forms; the overall process sketches a gradual refinement of awareness, so that in the end the meditator attains a purified state of absorption in clear, white light, most probably a state similar to the eighth sphere of totality (the colour white):

> Not internally conscious of forms, he sees external forms that are white, with a white colour, appearance and radiance. Just like the white morning star, or white Benares cloth which is smooth on both sides, so he becomes internally unconscious of form(s), and sees external forms that are white, with a white colour, appearance and radiance. He thinks: 'having mastered these, I know, I see'.

Such practices should be understood as Buddhist adaptations of pre-Buddhist meditations – those that flourished in and around early speculative Brahminism. Even if the Buddha sanctioned such practices, their continued use led to changes in how his teachings were understood. This can be seen in a meditative scheme known as the eight 'releases'. The first three releases sketch a progression similar to the eight spheres of mastery, since the third state is an awareness of 'lustrous light' or 'beautiful radiance': the text simply states that the meditator remains focused on the idea ('it is) radiant'. This is then followed by four formless spheres: infinite space → infinite consciousness → nothingness → neither perception nor non-perception. The progression culminates with the state of 'cessation':

> Completely transcending the sphere of neither perception nor non-perception, the mendicant realizes the cessation of perception and sensation: this is the eighth release.

Some accounts suggest that the cessation of perception and sensation was considered a state of insentience, in which bodily functions such as breathing cease. Other texts imply that the state is liberating, even if this is in complete disagreement with the vast majority of early teachings: most detailed accounts of the path culminate in a state of purified mindfulness in the fourth stage of meditation (*jhāna*), and so clearly state that a person attains Nirvana while remaining conscious and objectively aware. But according to what could be called the 'mystical cessationist' understanding, Nirvana is a state similar to the early Brahminic concept of liberation (*mokṣa*), which was thought to be achieved in a meditative trance devoid of awareness and experience. Early Brahminic texts thus claim that in order to realize the divine source of the cosmos (*brahman*), a person must eventually become completely insentient, just like a log of wood; those Buddhists who aimed to achieve 'cessation' seem to have shared this belief.

Meditative Realism

The mystical cessationist school therefore developed the pre-Buddhist practice of meditative absorption, albeit in a fashion contrary to the Buddha's Dhamma. This in turn led to further changes, including the positioning of the formless spheres and cessation above the four stages of meditation in a number of canonical texts. In the hands of these meditators, the four stages of meditation, which encapsulate the Buddha's unique contribution to spiritual practice, came to be seen as preliminary stages of a path leading towards a substantialist, neo-Brahminic understanding of Nirvana. This concept of the spiritual goal can be seen in descriptions of liberation that mirror those found in the early Brahminic texts, for example a famous statement in the Pali *Udāna*, which describes a transcendent absolute:

> There is, mendicants, a sphere where there is no earth, water, fire, wind; no sphere of the infinity of space, no sphere of the infinity of consciousness, no sphere of nothingness, no sphere of neither perception nor non-perception; no this world or the other world, no sun or moon. There, mendicants, I say there is no coming, no going, no persisting, no falling away, no arising; it is unfounded, uninvolved and without support. This is the end of suffering.

This passage reflects the early Brahminic understanding of *brahman* very closely, as can be seen from the following verse from the early Upaniṣads:

> There the sun does not shine, nor do the moon or stars; lightning does not shine, let alone this fire here . . .

According to this, liberation is an actual escape into an eternal, transcendent reality beyond the conditioned world of space-time. The same substantialist understanding of liberation can be seen in a further teaching from the *Udāna*:

> There is, mendicants, the unborn, unbecome, unmade and unconditioned. If, mendicants, there were not an unborn, unbecome, unmade and unconditioned, a release for that which is born, become, made and conditioned would not be discerned here. Because, mendicants, there is an unborn, unbecome, unmade and unconditioned, therefore a release for that which is born, become, made and conditioned is discerned here.

Such evidence suggests that some Buddhists came to believe in the existence of Nirvana as an absolute reality into which a liberated person merges at death. This suspicion is confirmed by a few texts which distinguish between the 'Nirvana realm with substratum' (i.e. the experience of Nirvana in this life) and the 'Nirvana realm without substratum' (i.e. the realization of Nirvana at death), with the latter being described as an unconditioned place that is neither filled nor depleted by those liberated beings who enter it, just as a great ocean is neither filled nor depleted by its rivers:

> Although streams flow into the great ocean, and rain falls down from the sky, not because of this is any deficit or excess discerned in the great ocean. In just the same way, mendicants, although many mendicants attain final Nirvana into the Nirvana realm without substratum, not because of this is any deficit or excess to be understood in the Nirvana realm.

This understanding of liberation corresponds to the early Brahminic notion that liberation is a merging into the infinity of *brahman* at death, a point made in the *Muṇḍaka Upaniṣad* as follows:

> Just as flowing rivers sink into the ocean, abandoning name and form, so the wise man, released from name and form, reaches the divine person, beyond the other world.

If a person is only really liberated by merging into an unconditioned reality beyond *saṃsāra*, it follows that there must be a real difference between the state of this person before and after death. But this is not the case in the Buddha's philosophy of constructed realism, according to which individual existence in space-time is stopped once and for all by a Tathāgata before death, when cognitive conditioning ceases. It was on the basis of this idea that the Buddha, when asked by the Brahmin Upasīva whether consciousness remains for the person liberated after death, replied that even the sage liberated in life cannot be defined (pp. 59–60).

The doctrine of constructed realism implies that the person liberated in life enters an ineffable reality beyond conceptualization. The idea that the liberated sage is not really liberated until he dies differs from this, and must therefore be a later idea, the most likely explanation being that it was an idea of those Buddhist meditators influenced by early Brahminic speculation. For the early Brahminic literature on meditation and liberation is realistic: it assumes that the world of space-time is objectively real, and that liberation consists in escaping the process of rebirth in it, by finally merging into *brahman* at death – a release anticipated in life through the cultivation of meditative insentience.

The early Buddhists who proposed similar ideas were therefore philosophical realists, albeit in a strikingly different sense from the reductionists who denied the existence of the self. Both groups presupposed that existence or non-existence in the world is an objectively real state of affairs. But whereas reductionistic realism tends towards nihilism (since Nirvana is defined negatively as the cessation of continued existence in *saṃsāra*), meditative realism tends towards eternalism (since Nirvana is imagined as an eternal realm beyond *saṃsāra*).

Early Debates

The contemplative reductionists and meditative mystics who proposed differing interpretations of the Buddha's Dhamma most probably emerged in the first century of the Buddhist era. Neither was entirely wrong, but in focusing on contemplation at the expense of meditation, or meditation at the expense of mindfulness, both deviated from the subtle combination of mindfulness and inner absorption that distinguishes the Buddha's path, and both departed from the subtle metaphysic of constructed realism on which this is based.

Since these conflicting ideas were held not by idle philosophers given to disputation in the abstract, but by committed individuals devoted to living the Dhamma and furthering the Buddha's mission, disputes were bound to arise. This was made even more likely by the fact that the different groups certainly attributed new discourses to the Buddha himself. The canonical texts contain evidence for such disputes, and suggest that there were differences between three major orientations: the early mainstream committed to the Buddha's teachings, contemplatives who believed in the non-existence of the self, and meditators who believed that Nirvana must be realized in a state of insentient trance.

A debate between the mainstream and the mystical school can be seen in the account of the disagreement about the meditative state in which the Buddha died: whereas Anuruddha is said to have believed it happened in the state of cessation, Ānanda's view that the Buddha finally died in the fourth stage of meditation was instead accepted. Evidence for a debate between contemplatives and mystics is more abundant, and consists in the first place of texts which record divergent accounts of the Buddha's awakening: whereas some texts imply that this was effected by understanding Dependent Origination (or the Four Noble Truths), others state that the attainment of cessation was the vital factor.

The suggestions of debate contained in these contradictory texts burst into fractious life in other texts which describe outright hostility between the different factions. The *Mahā-cunda Sutta* thus describes a debate between contemplatives devoted to the doctrine, who are said to 'penetrate' the Dhamma without meditating, and meditators who are said to 'touch' the 'deathless realm' with the body – another way of describing the attainment of cessation. In the face of such hostility, this text pleads with both parties to respect each other. Whether or not this advice was heeded, some texts show that a synthesis of contemplative and meditative practices was achieved. Indeed, a number of texts combine the different meditative and contemplative notions of liberation into a single idea of the person 'released on both sides' (*ubhato-bhāga-vimutta*), the two 'sides' being meditative absorption (culminating in cessation) and contemplative insight.

Other texts articulate the same approach of combining the meditative and contemplative streams through different ideas and terminology. A good example is the *Aṭṭhakanāgara Sutta*, in which the Buddha's disciple Ānanda describes how a person should attain higher states of meditation before contemplating that they are 'conditioned and volitionally produced, but what is conditioned and volitionally produced is impermanent and subject to cessation'. The early Buddhists who composed these texts believed that altered states of consciousness could be used to understand important Buddhist ideas. Meditation thus came to be seen as a sort of mental training which sharpens the mind and so enables insight into abstract truths.

While this understanding is not a radical departure from the Buddha's combination of meditation and mindfulness, an important difference is that mindfulness plays virtually no role at all. Also different from the Buddha's teaching is the idea that liberating insight is effected by a contemplation of abstract ideas, rather than a direct, non-conceptual understanding of conditioned experience. The notion that awakening requires first the cultivation of non-conceptual awareness, as well as paying close attention to the structure of experience, was therefore subtly transformed into a scheme in which meditative absorption was followed by intellectual contemplation.

The tendency to imagine the Buddhist path as a combination of inner meditation and insight is found throughout the early Buddhist texts. Many of the most important detailed accounts of the path, which include the four stages of meditation, thus culminate in the knowledge of the Four Noble Truths. Such texts suggest that the point of the fourth meditation is not to establish a purified state of mindfulness, but rather to improve the mind's clarity so that the Noble Truths can be properly known.

A similar understanding is contained in the analysis of the Buddhist path into virtue (*sīla*), inner meditation (*samādhi*) and insight (*paññā*), an analysis which is even applied to the Eightfold Path, even though the only aspects of this scheme that could be taken in the sense of 'insight' are the first two stages of Right View and Right Resolve. What only makes sense as the foundation of the path – the resolve to follow the path based on developing a Buddhist perspective – was therefore taken as its culmination, despite the fact that a liberated person has no further need to resolve for anything. The understanding of the path that emerges from such texts, and which became the norm in the post-Aśokan period, was thus that 'calming' meditation (*samatha*) paves the way for contemplative 'insight' (*vipassanā*). This twofold analysis is barely stated in the early texts, but probably emerged through the synthesis of the different interpretations of the Dhamma which emerged in the first century of the Buddhist era.

Was there a Schism?

The century or so after the Buddha's death was a time of institutional and ideological ferment. The Buddha's refusal to appoint a successor encouraged individual engagement with the Dhamma and personal responsibility for the mission, which soon resulted in a widely dispersed community of diverse spiritual inclinations. With emergent monastic fraternities (*āvāsa*) increasingly free to develop along their own lines, fragmentation was highly likely. To counter this attempts were made to preserve a common spiritual vision, grounded in ethical inclusivism, even when disputes raged. The *Mahā-cunda Sutta* thus urges the disputing meditators and contemplatives to be mutually respectful, on the basis that the Buddha's Dhamma is 'for the benefit of gods and men'.

The canonical texts thus suggest an early awareness of the fact that doctrinal harmony was less important than a common missionary goal; perhaps encouraged by the Buddha's pragmatic example, unity of purpose was apparently considered more important than ideological zeal. If so, the early expansion of the Buddhist mission should have been spontaneous and unplanned, and without formal division. Support for this version of history is found in the epigraphic and literary evidence, which from roughly the first century BC mentions a large number of Buddhist communities spread throughout and beyond India. Against the idea of a relatively harmonious spread of Buddhism, however, are a number of old sources which claim that there had been a schism soon after the Second Council, one that produced the Mahāsāṃghika ('Of the great community') and 'Sthavira' ('Elders') orders.

It is difficult to make sense of these accounts, and not only because it is hard to imagine a schism in a decentralized and widely spread church. A far more serious problem is that the accounts are inconsistent and even contradictory: had there really been a split in the Sangha, a reasonably reliable version of events is only to be expected, given the extreme gravity with which this issue was viewed in ancient times. In its discussion about an old dispute in Ḳosambī, for example, the Pali Vinaya states that any schismatic will be reborn in hell and remain there for the remainder of the aeon. With such an extreme attitude towards the matter, the Buddhist records of the early period would hardly have failed to record a schismatic dispute in considerable detail, if only to cast the others as the party at fault. But this is not the case.

The various accounts of the schism mention two issues: Vinaya differences and the liberated condition of an Arahat. The Pali tradition focuses on the former problem, and identifies the schismatic Mahāsāṃghikas with the monks of Vesālī who were defeated at the Second Council. But this version of events must be rejected, for the Mahāsāṃghika account of the Second Council also condemns the monks from Vesālī: whoever the Mahāsāṃghikas were, they did not come from this community. A different sort of Vinaya dispute is suggested in the Mahāsāṃghika literature: the *Śāriputraparipṛcchā* ('Inquiry of Śāriputra') states that one group, which became the Sthaviras, wished to expand the Vinaya with outside materials, a move which led to a split with another group (who became the Mahāsāṃghikas), after a vote was unable to reconcile the different factions.

Some support for this is contained in the fact that the extant Sthavira Vinayas contain more rules than the Mahāsāṃghika Vinaya.

But these rules concern matters of behaviour and deportment, and belong to the most minor category of disciplinary concerns (the *sekha* or *śaikṣa* section). They are not nearly as contentious as the disciplinary problems dealt with at the Second Council, and as such it is hard to see how they could have provoked a schism: whether a monk can handle gold or silver and how a monk eats are disciplinary infractions of an entirely different order.

The *Śāriputra-paripṛcchā* account should thus be understood as a record of a local dispute concerning the rearranging of the canonical texts: the expansion of the Vinaya with other works of the Buddha was not a matter of monastic discipline. While this was no doubt a contested issue, it was not serious enough to have sown dissension throughout the Indian Buddhist world, especially since textual rearrangement occurred in all orders. Moreover, the text dates the schism after the great Aśokan expansion of Buddhism in the mid-third century BC, and it is difficult to see how a local dispute could have split such a widely dispersed community.

A different sort of dispute is recorded in those accounts which focus on differences of opinion regarding the liberated condition of the Buddhist saint. But these accounts are also historically implausible. According to the Sthavira account of Vasumitra, the proto-Mahāsāṃghikas tried to lower the status of the Arhat by arguing for his susceptibility to sexual desire while dreaming. This would certainly have been a contentious issue, for a liberated person should have eradicated all desire for sensual pleasure, and any opinion to the contrary is harshly criticized by the Buddha in the canonical texts. Notwithstanding the gravity of this idea, the earliest version of Vasumitra's account relates the dispute to a monk called Mahādeva, who belonged to the Buddhist groups of the Krishna river valley, a region which became Buddhist some time after the Aśokan expansion in the third century BC. As in the case of the *Śāriputra-paripṛcchā*, it is difficult to see how a local dispute could have split a widely dispersed community.

Evidence for an early Buddhist schism is therefore late, in more or less complete disagreement, and comes at a time when different monastic congregations had formed quite naturally, through a process of missionary expansion and localization. This is not very good evidence for a schism at all. In fact the best evidence for a major dispute in early times also states that the problem was resolved:

Aśoka's 'schism edicts' state that the Sangha had been forcibly unified, which implies that a serious dispute in the Buddhist community had been resolved by Aśoka himself, with no lasting legacy. The fact that Aśoka's schism edicts are found at the geographically distant sites of Sarnath, Kosambī and Sanchi suggests Buddhist unity throughout a large area of his empire, and certainly the core region of the North.

There is therefore no compelling evidence for a schism, and much that goes against it. Since the evidence for a difference along Mahāsāṃghika and Sthavira lines dates well into the post-Aśokan period, it is more likely that the problem was one of identification and allegiance among the newly emergent sects. Perhaps in the attempt to work out how this general pattern of allegiance had come about, various Buddhist controversies of the age were read back into ancient times. But there is no convincing evidence to suggest any such dispute before the reign of Aśoka.

Chapter V

Buddhist India

> But the victory of Dhamma is considered best by Beloved of the Gods, and has been won repeatedly . . . Even where Beloved of the Gods' envoys do not go, when they hear Beloved of the Gods' statements, ordinances and instructions on Dhamma, they conform to Dhamma and will do so in the future.
>
> Aśoka, Rock Edict XIII

Accounts of the Second Council suggest that within 100 years of the Buddha's death, the Buddhist order had spread across most of northern and much of central India. Lacking possessions and emerging from a peripatetic religious culture, the Buddhist mendicants were natural missionaries, whose travels took them far beyond the Gangetic region in which the Buddha taught. During the same period the kingdom of Magadha expanded across the north: after the retreat of Alexander the Great from northwest India in 326 BC, northern India was dominated by the Magadhan kingdom of the Nandas. But the Nandas were succeeded in around 321 by Candragupta, who extended his Mauryan empire as far as Gandhāra in the northwest, consigning the Indo-Greeks to their extensive territories further west (including Persia and Bactria in Central Asia).

Candragupta was succeeded by Bindusāra and then Aśoka, in about 268 BC, by which time the Mauryan empire covered much of the subcontinent. This empire was administered through centrally appointed princes and ministers, rather than vassal states, and so was able to establish a common socio-political order. The cultural norms of Magadha were thus spread across India, and since Aśoka was a Buddhist convert, the principal gainers in the socio-political transformation were the Buddhists. The Buddhist Sangha became firmly established throughout most of the Mauryan empire, which further enabled Buddhist missionaries to venture into Central Asia and Sri Lanka. It was under Aśoka, then, that Buddhism became the most widely spread and popularly supported Indian religion, and indeed a world religion.

Aśoka

The rise of Buddhism under Aśoka is known not merely through Buddhists records, but also because Aśoka had over 30 edicts inscribed on rocks and pillars across his empire, in dialects of Prakrit that in some places closely resemble Pali. These inscriptions are remarkable for their content, for rather than exaggerate his imperial might, Aśoka instead describes the sorrow he felt after the bloody defeat of the Kaliṅgas (of modern-day Orissa), his subsequent conversion to Buddhism, and his aim to spread Dhamma throughout the empire. In recording this Dhamma in monumental form, the edicts were a key element in the implementation of Aśoka's socio-cultural policies.

Aśoka's Dhamma consisted of promoting certain moral ideals alongside a simple programme of state action, involving such things as having wells dug, trees planted along the roads, rest-houses made for travellers, and medicinal herbs and roots imported and grown. Aśoka also established a class of Dhamma ministers to help various needy groups (the poor, the aged, religious groups, prisoners, etc.), to make charitable gifts, and – most importantly – to promote his moral ideals. The basic aspects of the latter are respect towards one's parents, friends, acquaintances, relatives, servants and religious specialists (both renouncers and Brahmins), and the promotion of ethical norms such as non-violence, kindness, generosity, gentleness, truthfulness, moderation and so on. These ideals can be seen in Rock Edict IX, in which Aśoka draws a distinction between Dhamma thus defined and the general belief in ritual magic:

> Beloved of the Gods, King Piyadasi, speaks thus: people perform various ceremonies, for those who are ill, at the marriage of a son or daughter, when children are born, or when someone is away on a journey. For these and other such occasions, people perform all sorts of ceremonies; women, indeed, often perform many kinds of lowly and pointless ceremonies. Even if these ceremonies are to be performed they have little reward, whereas the ceremony

> of Dhamma yields a great reward. This involves correct conduct towards slaves and employees, respect for teachers, restraint towards living beings, and generosity towards ascetics and Brahmans. These and other such things constitute the ceremony of Dhamma.

Although these ideals were commonly accepted among the various renunciant sects of the time, it is almost certain that Aśoka learnt of them through his contact with Buddhism. This is suggested by the extensive correspondence between the edicts and canonical teachings. For example, the categories mentioned in Rock Edict IX are close to those mentioned in the Buddha's advice to Sigāla (see p. 18), which refers to: father and mother; teachers, wife and children; friends and companions; slaves and servants; and ascetics and Brahmins. Virtually the same categories are found in Rock Edict XI (servants and employees; mother and father; friends, companions and relations; ascetics and Brahmins) and Rock Edict III (mother and father; friends, acquaintances and relatives; ascetics and Brahmins). This close correspondence suggests that the categories used by Aśoka were derived from the Dhamma instruction he claims to have received from the Buddhist Sangha (as recorded in Minor Rock Edict I).

Apart from this extensive correspondence, Aśoka's edicts often articulate an inner dynamism that is entirely in keeping with the Buddha's psychological approach to matters of morality. This can be seen in Aśoka's advice to his ministers at Tosali, that impartiality in judgement is hindered by 'envy, wrath, cruelty, haste, deliberation, laziness and fatigue', to ward off which Aśoka advises 'You must resolve, "may these dispositions not develop in me".' The Buddha speaks to his disciples in a similar vein in the *Brahmajāla Sutta*, where he points out that they should not become angry if anyone speaks ill of him, the Dhamma or Sangha, since this would be a hindrance to an impartial and correct understanding of what is true and untrue. In both cases the psychological approach – to be aware of inner faults, in order to judge the situation impartially and correctly – is the same.

The inscriptions elsewhere state (Pillar Edict I) that '(happiness) in this world and the next is difficult to obtain without the highest love for Dhamma, or without the highest self-examination, obedience, fear (of evil), and endeavour'. The religious life for Aśoka therefore follows the Buddhist vision of a spiritual path, one focused on moral introspection and the cultivation of pure mental states. This introspective tendency is well described in Pillar Edict III:

> Beloved of the gods, King Piyadasi, speaks thus: a person considers only his good and thinks 'I have done this good deed', but does not similarly consider his evil, thinking 'I have done this evil deed', or 'This, indeed, is corrupting' (*āsinave*). Although self-examination is difficult, a person should reflect as follows: 'These lead to corruption: violence, cruelty, anger, pride and envy. Let me not ruin myself by just these deeds.' In particular, a person should reflect 'This deed of mine pertains to the present world, whereas this pertains to the future world'.

A constant feature of Aśoka's edicts is that inner zeal is required to live a pure moral life, an understanding which follows a distinctly Buddhist vision of the spiritual path. As Rock Edict VII points out, the person who makes many religious gifts (*dāna*) without restraint, inner purity, gratitude and firm commitment is 'certainly contemptible'. It follows

Fig. 5. The Southern gateway of the great stūpa *at Sanchi, with the stump of the Aśokan pillar in the bottom right*

that when Aśoka claims his Dhamma teachings express the 'essence' of all religions (Rock Edict XII), the essence he had in mind was a distinctly Buddhist understanding rather than the religious ideas of the other renunciant religions, such as the amoral transcendentalism of the Jains and early Upaniṣads.

If Aśoka's Dhamma was inspired by Buddhist ideals, we might expect him to have made similar efforts to promote Buddhism in general. This is exactly what Buddhist sources claim, and is supported by the evidence of Rock Edict XIII, in which Aśoka claims that his 'Dhamma victory' has been achieved both within his empire and beyond, 'even where his envoys have not travelled'. This choice of words implies that Aśoka's Dhamma victory was achieved largely by means of his imperial envoys, a fact confirmed by the Pali chronicles of Sri Lanka, which describe how Buddhist missionaries (including Aśoka's son Mahinda) arrived there together with Aśoka's imperial envoys. The Dhamma victory of Aśoka cannot therefore be separated from the spread of Buddhism.

The archaeological record supports the notion of a significant Buddhist expansion during the Mauryan period, the monumental remains of which established Buddhism as the dominant religion in India for the next 500 years. But this does not mean that Aśoka attempted to establish Buddhism as the official religion of empire. His intervention to purify the Sangha of fractious *bhikkhu*s, as recorded in his 'schism edicts', suggests a close relationship between Sangha and the Mauryan court, but not to the extent of elevating Buddhism to the position of a state religion. The edicts instead present Aśoka as a pious devotee: Buddhism is only mentioned in the edicts where Aśoka addresses the Sangha directly, as a lay disciple, but there is no explicit connection between these and the edicts which outline Aśoka's Dhamma policies.

The distinction between Aśoka the Buddhist and Aśoka the emperor reflects a general cultural separation of religion and the state. Buddhism thus emerges from the edicts as the first religion among equals, with the Sangha receiving the most support within the context of a pluralistic and apolitical religious culture. As the Buddhist Sangha had no direct involvement in the Mauryan polity, either symbolically (as a source of ritual legitimation) or actually (with learned Buddhist monks advising the Mauryan court), Aśoka benefited from his support of Buddhism in other ways. By filling his empire with

Buddhist monks, nuns, monasteries and *stūpas*, Aśoka promoted a single ideology and material culture around which the disparate regional identities of India could be united. At the heart of this religious culture were universal ideals, and an ethos that promoted an ethical engagement with the world as a means of progressing towards salvation.

Post-Mauryan India

The Mauryan dynasty succumbed to that of the Śuṅgas in about 185 BC, roughly 50 years after Aśoka's death in around 230 BC. The first Śuṅga king was the Brahmin Puṣyamitra; Hindu records state that he murdered the last Mauryan emperor, and inscriptional evidence shows that he celebrated Vedic sacrifices. Some Buddhist texts also state that Puṣyamitra instigated a series of Brahminic reprisals against the Sangha. These stories may well be exaggerated, but they probably contain some truth, such as the destruction of the main Buddhist monastery in the Magadhan capital of Pāṭaliputta, the Kukkuṭārāma, which is a common factor in the records.

Further support for the anti-Buddhist policies of the Śuṅgas is suggested by the extensive damage inflicted on the great *stūpa* of Sanchi in this period, an event which coincided with a serious decline in activity at the site. Since the decline at Sanchi was reversed in the second century BC, it would seem that the Śuṅgas were ultimately unsuccessful, probably because they did not wield power at anything near the level of the Mauryas. Instead it would seem that the Śuṅgas had little control over the numerous semi-independent kingdoms that emerged with the demise of the Mauryas, whose centralization of power did not survive long.

The ongoing prosperity of the Sangha after the Mauryan empire disappeared is to be explained by the fact that Buddhist ideals and institutions had already been widely disseminated before Aśoka. Based on these foundations, the Buddhists benefited from imperial support without depending entirely upon it. Indeed, inscriptions from some of the small vassal kingdoms near to the core Śuṅga region in the north show a high level of Buddhist support beyond royal circles: donations from merchants, bankers, administrators, scribes, craftsmen, masons, weavers, dressmakers and so on easily outnumber the donations made by members of the local ruling elite. That a large section of the newly urbanized population was sympathetic to the Buddhist mission is further shown by the augmentation of Buddhist monuments during the Śuṅga period: the Mauryan legacy could not be so easily undone.

At the same time that Puṣyamitra succeeded the Mauryas, the Indo-Greeks of Bactria created a large kingdom in the northwest. Aśoka claims to have sent his Dhamma-ministers to the Greeks, whom he calls 'Yonakas', and the Pali chronicles state that one of the missionaries to the Yonakas was a Greek called Yonadhammarakkhita: 'the Ionian protected by the Dhamma'. There is also evidence for Greek participation in Buddhist devotional activity during the Indo-Greek period, since a reliquary inscription records the establishment of Buddha relics in a *stūpa* by the Greek ruler Theodorus, 'for the prosperity of the many'. But the most fascinating evidence for the Indo-Greek interaction with Buddhism is found in the *Milinda-pañha* ('Questions of Milinda'), a Pali text which records an extensive dialogue between the Indo-Greek general Menander and the Buddhist monk Nāgasena.

This dialogue cannot easily be explained as an attempt to fabricate major support, since the Indo-Greek kingdom was relatively short-lived, and a dialogue with a king from a more prominent royal house would have made for better propaganda. A significant encounter between Milinda and Nāgasena is likely, even if the authenticity of much of this dialogue is doubtful. Regardless of its historicity, the dialogue at least suggests how the Buddhists of this period imagined their appeal. It is revealing that the book opens with the monk Āyupāla telling Milinda that Buddhism is a religious path for both laymen and gods, and not just Buddhist mendicants. But Milinda is not impressed by this universalism, since he believes it implies that liberation does not require renunciation, and thus renders monasticism pointless. In the next part of the story an alternative way of winning round the disappointed general is therefore presented, with Nāgasena introducing the Buddhist philosophy of personal identity to Milinda, who becomes interested and is drawn into a lengthy dialogue. Even if this did not actually happen, the *Milinda-pañha* shows a Buddhist awareness that different aspects of their system could be utilized to achieve support depending on the circumstances.

Most of the northwest remained under foreign rule after the Indo-Greeks were eventually usurped by invading Iranian tribes from Central Asia in the late second century BC (the Asian Scythians, or Śakas, and Parthians, or Pahlavas). Despite maintaining their ancestral Iranian traditions, there is much evidence that these foreigners supported Buddhism and contributed to its growth in the northwest and west. Further Buddhist patronage in the northwest was provided by the powerful Kuṣāṇas, who succeeded the Śakas and Pahlavas; one inscription records that Huviṣka, the successor of Kaniṣka (early–mid-second century AD), had 'entered the Mahāyāna', a minority movement within Buddhism throughout the first half of the first millennium AD. The origins of the Kuṣāṇas are obscure, but it appears that they migrated south from the Central Asian steppes, and had arrived in Bactria by the first century BC, before subsequently establishing an extensive empire stretching all the way from Mathura to the edge of the Tarim Basin, home of the city states of the Silk Road. Kuṣāṇa support thus opened up the East to Buddhist missionaries, who finally reached China in the first century AD.

Besides these developments in the north, Buddhism had also spread further south and east under the Mauryas. The lower number of Mauryan *stūpa*s in these regions indicates no significant presence until the second century BC, with some of the monastic settlements along the east coast dating back to this time. The Sātavāhana dynasty, which dominated the Deccan region of central India from the first century BC until the third century AD, were important patrons of the Sangha, as were the Īkṣvākus who later replaced them in the Andhra region of the southeast, in particular around the Krishna river valley, where Buddhism flourished especially from the first century BC onwards. Buddhist remains from post-Mauryan India have also been found further south, and northeast, in the old Kaliṅga country corresponding to modern Orissa.

If the *Milinda-pañha* suggests that the ideological appeal of Buddhism was an important factor in its spread, the archaeological record suggests other ways in which migrant Buddhists were able to win support in new lands. Throughout India the remains of Buddhist monasteries and *stūpa*s are often located within or adjacent to ancient megalithic burial sites; it even seems that some of these sites, such as that adjacent to the large Buddhist complex at Amaravati, were still in use when the Buddhists arrived. Because of their expertise in mortuary matters, expressed in the form of funerary rituals, *stūpa* devotionalism, and sophisticated ideas about karma, rebirth and the various realms of the cosmos, it is easy to imagine that the Buddhists convinced local populations that filial piety could be directed towards a more rewarding destiny in the new Buddhist cosmos.

Mythic Buddhism

The meditative and speculative traditions inspired by the Buddha were not the only, or necessarily most significant, aspects of the Dhamma. It is more likely that devotionalism and ethical commitment were more fundamental to the ultimate success of Buddhism, at the popular and even monastic level. Buddhist devotionalism in India was focused on the cult of the *stūpa*, funerary cairns which originally contained only the Buddha's remains, and which the Buddha stated should be located at the places of his birth, awakening, first teaching and death. But *stūpa*s were not confined to just these four sites: the *Mahā-parinibbāna Sutta* states that immediately after his death the Buddha's remains were distributed among the most prominent states and tribes in the region, and as the Buddhist movement spread across India, *stūpa*s were used to demarcate the religion's sacred space. But the practice of pilgrimage to the four main *stūpa* sites remained important to the cult, and was promoted by Aśoka. In his edict at Rummindei, Aśoka states that he went to Lumbinī, the Buddha's birthplace, on pilgrimage, 20 years after his consecration, and relieved the town's tax burden.

Apart from the spiritually beneficial mental states generated through devotionalism, the canonical texts offer more concrete rewards for the performance of simple rituals at *stūpa*s. The account of the Buddha's death – in which the psychological reason for building *stūpa*s is outlined – also states that the person who visits sacred Buddhist sites and dies there will go to heaven. Pilgrimage and devotionalism at *stūpa*s was thus articulated in terms of simple religious goals from the very earliest period: being in the presence of a *stūpa* was believed to confer mystical spiritual benefits. Further evidence for the extension of the cult is contained in Aśoka's Nigali Sagar edict, which states that in the fifteenth year of his reign he had the *stūpa* of the Buddha Konākamana doubled in size, and that in the 21st year of his reign he visited the *stūpa* himself, having a stone pillar erected there.

According to the canonical texts Konākamana is the fifth of six past Buddhas, the Pali texts giving the full list as Vipassin, Sikhin,

Vessabhu, Kakusandha, Konāgamana and Kassapa. The early Buddhists thus came to consider their founder as the most recent figure in a remarkable religious lineage, its members reappearing from age to age to reveal Buddhist truths and establish the Dhamma once again. According to this myth, the Buddhist dispensation (*sāsana*) is not just one sect within the Indian religious landscape, but is a recurring phenomenon. The myth thus exaggerates Buddhism into a uniquely significant movement, and turns the historical Buddha into a predestined religious hero of cosmic stature. The *Mahāpadāna Sutta* ('Great Discourse on Karmic Retribution') even states that the Buddha's knowledge of former Buddhas is due to his penetration of the 'dhamma realm' (*dhamma-dhātu*), the implication being that the cosmos has a sacred order that Buddhas 'touch', thus allowing them to understand and reveal the Dhamma, and know facts about other Buddhas who have done so.

Aśoka's edicts allow us to date these ideas to around 100 years after the Buddha's death. Some of the Buddhist texts which develop the myth of the former Buddhas must therefore have been composed by this time, even if in a more rudimentary form than the extant literature. Foremost among these texts is the *Mahāpadāna Sutta*, which outlines the identical religious career of each of the seven Buddhas based on the story of the first Buddha, Vipassin. Later legendary accounts of the historical Buddha's life are based on this myth: other canonical texts do not state that Gotama lived a sheltered life in his father's palace, provided with all types of sensual pleasure, eventually realizing the unpleasant reality of existence upon seeing certain unpleasant sights (of a sick man, an old man and a dead man) on his trips outside the palace. This legend is first worked out in association with Vipassin, but is ascribed to Gotama since the religious career of all Buddhas is thought to follow the same course.

The *Mahāpadāna Sutta* outlines the career of a Buddha-to-be, a 'Bodhisatta', the one 'devoted (*satta*) to awakening (*bodhi*)', as follows. First is the descent from the Tuṣita heaven to the human realm, where the Bodhisatta will assume his last existence within *saṃsāra*; at the moment of descent into his mother's womb, immeasurable light shines through the 10,000 worlds of the cosmos. The conception is therefore miraculous, and perhaps even virginal, for the text states that at the time of conception the mother of a Bodhisatta has no thought of sexual pleasure, and that she cannot be violated by an impassioned man. Infinite light and the other miraculous events accompany the Bodhisatta's birth, who is then said by soothsayers to possess the '32 marks of a great man'.

The *Lakkhaṇa Sutta* ('Discourse on Auspicious Characteristics') states that these supernatural marks are the karmic result of religious practice in the Bodhisatta's former lives: through perfecting a number of spiritual virtues in the past, such as non-violence, generosity, honesty and so on, the Bodhisatta is said to have accumulated a huge mass of good karma. This karma is the spiritual basis which enabled him to attain awakening, and so realize the supernatural body of a Buddha. The 32 marks are therefore the somatic expression of the awakening, and emphasize the fact that a Buddha is not just a man, but an incomparably sacred being.

The various spiritual adventures of the Bodhisatta as he followed his spiritual path were outlined in Jātakas and Avadānas, texts of roughly the Mauryan period which very often focus on the heroic and selfless deeds that mark him as a special kind of spiritual aspirant. This mythological development was bound to heighten the significance of visiting *stūpa* sites and undertaking devotional acts at them. Since the focal points of the *stūpa* cult were believed to contain the last remnants of the Buddha's supernatural body, they came to be regarded as uniquely sacred spaces, and not just places that could inspire faith. To visit a *stūpa* was therefore to be in the presence of the holy reality revealed through the Buddha's body.

Imagining the Buddha

According to the Buddhist legend of Aśoka, relics of the Buddha were distributed in thousands of *stūpa*s across his empire. This claim is not just a fiction invented by pious Buddhists, for a large number of Buddhist sites and monumental *stūpa*s date to the Mauryan period: at this time, a major attempt was made to institutionalize the religion at an unprecedented level. Sanchi is the best preserved site from this period, although most of its finely carved sculptures and bas-reliefs were added in the Śuṅga period and afterwards. The grandeur of these remains, as well as those from Bharhut in the north and Amaravati in the south, and many others which did not survive or have been partially preserved (or remain undiscovered), was unmatched in India for many hundreds of years.

Fig. 6. View of the Western gateway from the great stūpa *at Sanchi*

The art of Sanchi is found on the pillars, gateways and architraves that surround its *stūpa*s, and is slightly later and more developed than that of Bharhut. But its carvings are earlier than the more elaborate reliefs from Amaravati, the intricacy and rich decoration of which anticipate the later Buddhist art of Southeast Asia. Also surviving from the Śuṅga period are carvings from the palisade surrounding the Aśokan shrine at Bodhgaya, a compound which contains the Diamond Throne that marked the spot of the Buddha's awakening; this is now adjacent to the Mahābodhi temple, which was added later on in the late Gupta period. Despite subtle differences in date, style and construction, the artistic themes of all these sites are the same. The most important subject is the legend of the Buddha: there are numerous depictions of key events in Gotama's life as well as those from his previous lives, as described in the Jātaka tales.

Early Buddhist sculpture also depicts various supernatural figures (*nāga*s, *yakṣī*s, etc.), as well as the elaborate devotional activity which took place there; the general impression evoked is one of a cosmic religious order, comprising humans, gods and various spirits, centred

Fig. 7. Aniconic art from Sanchi: the Buddha's footprints bearing the imprint of thousand-spoked wheels, one of the marks of a 'great man'

on the Buddha and his Dhamma. But given this artistic expression of mythic ideology, one feature of the early art is both surprising and mysterious: the lack of any depiction of the Buddha himself. Although scenes from the Jātakas contain images of the Buddha in his former lives as various animals, depictions of scenes from his actual life as Gotama are not found. The Buddha is instead marked by an empty space, a feature which has led some to view early Buddhist art as aniconic.

Not all the reliefs lacking the Buddha can be understood in this way, for many examples probably depict contemporary worship at such shrines, rather than events in the life of the Buddha: scenes of worship at the Bodhi tree in Bodhgaya, or of the Buddha's footprints carved onto stone, need not be taken as aniconic references to the Buddha. These depictions rather added to the religious atmosphere at newly established sites by invoking the Buddhist devotion of the old centres of Magadha. This does not, however, explain the total absence of Buddha images at these sites. Why do scenes of events in Gotama's life prior to the awakening fail to depict him? Given the mythology of past Buddhas and their predestined religious career, it is surely surprising that the Buddha's supernatural body was not depicted in art.

Perhaps depictions of the Buddha were thought unnecessary because the relics within the *stūpa*s were deemed devotionally sufficient. A significant amount of literary and epigraphic evidence shows that Indian Buddhists believed Buddha-relics to be somehow 'alive' with the Buddha's religious essence. The lack of Buddha images seems less significant against this ideological background, according to which the Buddha continued to be present within the *stūpa*. It is also possible that a knowledge of the Buddha's impersonalism, as well as his teachings on the ineffability of the awakened condition, were also important factors: an enigmatic statement such as 'He who sees the Dhamma sees me' could have influenced an early aniconic tendency.

Whatever the truth, the oldest images of the Buddha date to the first century AD, being produced in the northern city of Mathura and in the kingdom of Gandhāra in the far northwest. The iconography of the images produced in these two regions was quite different: whereas the Gandhāran Buddhas show a Greco-Roman influence, a consequence of the previous Indo-Greek kingdoms of this region, those from Mathura follow an indigenous style close to that of Jain statues of Mahāvīra, made in the same location, naked images of whom date back to the second century BC. The early appearance of Jain images raises the possibility of an earlier date for the first iconic depictions of the Buddha. But even if so, the use of Buddhist icons did not become widespread until the late first century AD, when images were established at important sites by prominent monks and nuns, rather than pious laymen and women. Inscriptions on large Mathuran images from the important centres of Sāvatthī, Kosambī and Sarnath show that they were endowed by the monk Bala and his associate, the nun Buddhamitrā.

Monasteries and Cave Temples

The Pali chronicles of Sri Lanka add literary support to the archaeological evidence for a considerable expansion of monastic Buddhism in the post-Aśokan period. The *Mahāvaṃsa* records that at the foundation of the 'great stūpa' (*mahā-thūpa*) in the ancient capital of

Fig. 8. Medieval Buddha statue from Sanchi (temple 45)

Anurādhapura, as part of the celebrations of Duṭṭhagāmaṇi's victory over the Coḷa ruler Eḷāra in the first century BC, delegations were sent from 14 Indian monasteries. At least six of these monasteries had developed from the parks donated in the Buddha's life: the Isipatana of Sarnath (the site of the Buddha's first sermon), the Jetavana of Sāvatthī, the Kūṭāgārasālā of Vesālī, the Ghositārāma of Kosambī, the Bodhi-maṇḍa vihāra of Bodhgaya and many from the general region of Rājagaha.

Some of the other monasteries mentioned go back to the Mauryan period or just afterwards: the Aśokārāma/Kukkuṭārāma of Pāṭaliputta (built by Aśoka in his capital city), the Vindhya forest monastery to the south of Magadha, the Dakkhiṇāgiri of Ujjenī, established as Buddhism spread southwest from Magadha towards the Deccan – a development that also led to communities in Vanavāsa (probably the Konkan coastal region of southwest India), a delegation from which is also said to have visited Sri Lanka. A similar date can be attributed to the Buddhist communities of Kashmir, the western Himalayas

(Kelāsa) and the northwest frontier region, although the delegations said to have come from the Pallava region and the Greco-Bactrian city of Alexandria-under-the-Caucasus should perhaps be considered as belonging to a later phase in the spread of Buddhism. It would seem that after the Aśokan expansion of Buddhism, the monasteries remained in regular contact, allowing ideas and texts to be exchanged across a vast area of South Asia. It was in this period, for example, that the text of the *Milinda-pañha* was brought from the northwest to Sri Lanka and preserved in Pali.

The Buddhist movement of this period had changed significantly since the time of the Buddha. Accounts of the Second Council suggest that more or less permanently settled monastic communities had emerged even during the fourth century BC, but the large monasteries that emerged in the post-Aśokan age were more firmly embedded in society than the Buddha could have imagined. The books of monastic law (Vinaya) show that attempts were made to maintain the old peripatetic ways, for example by forbidding the practice of reserving lodgings beyond the rainy season. But Buddhism had developed into a religion of permanently settled monasteries, receiving donations of land from at least the first century AD, as well as the labour of local villages to maintain them, which in some places turned the Buddhist Sangha into a feudal landlord.

No later than the first century BC, Buddhist monasteries were being built in stone rather than wood. A record of the early monumental architecture is preserved in the cave temples of the Western Ghats, where monasteries were carved directly out of cliff faces. Early sites such as Bhaja and Kondana replicate the earlier monastic architecture in wood, their façades being elegant replicas of the horse-shoe shaped structures known from early Buddhist sculpture; the *stūpa* at Thanale lacks such a façade, although the monastic complex built around it still copies the wooden structures of the time. So faithful were these sites to the wooden Buddhist monasteries that attempts were made to carve inward-sloping columns and roof-beams into the ceiling, and even to chisel quadrangles of monastic cells into the cliff face. The early *stūpa* halls (*caitya-gṛha*) at Bhaja and Kondana even had wooden beams fitted into the dome-shaped ceiling, some of which still exist, and which were probably connected to a wooden façade similar to that found in stone at sites such as Karla and Bedsa.

The most spectacular Buddhist cave site is that of Ajanta,

Fig. 9. Ruined cave temple at Kondana containing some of its old wooden beams

probably excavated first through the patronage of the Sātavāhanas in the first century AD, and then during the reign of the Vākāṭaka king Hariṣena in the fifth century. Ajanta is famed for the fine paintings which adorn the walls of its shrines and cells, which are still a spectacular sight even if they are now in a somewhat fragmentary condition. But this unusually elaborate site should not be taken as a general model for Buddhist monasticism in the early centuries AD. A more typical guide to the Buddhist monasticism of this period, especially across the Deccan, is the site of Thotlakonda on the coast of northern Andhra Pradesh. Occupied for roughly 500 years between the third/second centuries BC and the second/third centuries AD, this hill-top site probably emerged as a retreat for monks from the adjacent hill monastery of Bavikonda, before developing into an independent site of its own.

The situation of a series of related sites along the northern coast of Andhra, such as Thotlakonda, Bavikonda and Pavurallakonda, suggests that they were involved in long-distance trade. Nevertheless, most of the remains at Thotlakonda are of local provenance, with the coins found there coming from the nearby Sātavāhana empire

Fig. 10. Elaborate façade of the cave temple at Karla

to the south, indicating close links with inland trading networks and local agriculture. The numerous cisterns carved out of the hillside of Thotlakonda – a feature of Buddhist sites across the Deccan, indicating an advanced knowledge of water management systems – also suggest a close connection with local agriculture. It is possible these features of Buddhist sites in the Deccan were connected to the Mauryan dissemination of new methods of irrigation and rice cultivation.

It would thus seem as if Thotlakonda and other nearby Buddhist centres were maintained primarily by local communities, rather than the support of regional kingdoms (the Sātavāhana kingdom to the south and the Kaliṅga kingdom to the north). Although periodic suzerainty to these centres of power was inevitable, they were distant enough to minimize major royal support, which probably explains the fact that only a single inscription has been found recording a royal donation. More important than royal support was the ability to forge close connections with local communities, for which sake the Buddhist knowledge of other-worldly realities was vital. Thotlakonda lies in close proximity to megalithic sites which were apparently still in use, indicating the adaptation of the *stūpa* cult and the doctrine of karma towards very old forms of ancestor worship.

The secluded location of the monastery atop Thotlakonda hill – a feature of many Deccan sites, especially that at Karla – shows that the Buddhists chose their locations carefully, to highlight their sacred detachment from the world. The layout of the site also shows a clear distinction between the quadrangular monastic quarters and the kitchen/refectory, although this detachment is tempered by the central position of the main devotional area, including an apsidal shrine (*caitya-gṛha*) and large *stūpa*, as an area of lay and monastic interaction. The site is thus an excellent example of a sedentary monasticism which neither escapes the world nor is situated within it, being both a secluded sanctuary for Buddhist monks and yet within reach of the laity, who were able to fulfil their ritual and devotional wishes. The settled Buddhist sites of the middle period should thus be regarded as a further adaptation of the Buddha's skill in means, placing the Sangha as mediators between the sacred and profane in the societies to which Buddhism spread.

Buddhism and Indian Society

In the post-Mauryan period, and especially during the second half of the first Buddhist millennium (i.e. 0–500 AD), Buddhist monasteries dominated the religious landscape of India. The old peripatetic style of life was still important, but now followed a circuit mapped out by monasteries which housed permanently settled monastic communities, usually led by an abbot, and where temporary lodging could be gained. Deccan sites such as Bhaja and Thotlakonda probably housed up to 50 or 60 monks, although larger sites such as Ajanta could have supported more than 100, as would the major centres in the core region of Magadha.

The archaeological remains of these old monasteries usually reveal a major *stūpa* at the site's centre, around which the remains of a large number of smaller *stūpa*s are randomly spread. It would seem that these minor *stūpa*s served no votive function, but were rather funerary cairns containing the remains of pious monastics and local laity within the site, preferably as close to the main *stūpa* as possible. For it was believed that proximity to the sacred space demarcated by the major *stūpa*, with its holy remains, would be beneficial, even in death, based on the notion that the religious virtue of a holy man could be preserved in his physical being. Buddhist *stūpa*s were thus believed to contain the spiritual qualities of Buddhist saints: the virtue, understanding, meditative achievement and so on accumulated during a life of spiritual practice, and in the case of the Buddha, over many such lifetimes.

Fig. 11. Stūpa *graveyard at Thanale, Maharashtra*

This change in the understanding of a *stūpa*'s religious function implies that external forces, and not just the karma for which a person is directly responsible, were believed to play an important role in a person's fate after death. Such a development in karmic Buddhism was mirrored by the early adoption of the general Indian belief that the karmic efficacy of a good deed is somehow dependent on the virtue of its recipient. Instilling in faithful laymen and women the idea that the Buddhist Sangha is the purest 'field of merit' was a way of encouraging donations. Although this compromised the original stress on personal responsibility, it placed an even greater focus on the monastic purity of the Sangha, and resulted in a sort of economy of merit, which helped maintain monastic purity and the flow of donations required for the upkeep of the monasteries.

It could be argued that this deviation from the Buddha's teaching was a form of religious exploitation. But the economy of merit only worked if monks and nuns exemplified Buddhist virtues, and if so it would seem that this deviation from the Buddha's Dhamma ultimately strengthened its core values. A further departure from the Buddha's karmic individualism probably had a similar effect. Many inscriptions recording donations to Buddhist monasteries articulate the belief that religious merit could be transferred from one person to the next, in particular to a donor's deceased parents. A good example is an inscription dated to the mid-second century AD from Mathura:

> On this date an image of the Blessed One Śākyamuni was set up by the monk Buddhavarman for the worship of all Buddhas. Through this religious gift may his Preceptor Sanghadāsa attain Nirvana, (may it also be) for the cessation of all suffering of his parents . . . (and) for the welfare and happiness of all beings.

Apart from articulating the old idea that good karma advances a person to Nirvana, this inscription also states that one person can gain from another's good deeds, and so violates the principle of individual responsibility. But this was an unintended consequence of the Buddha's definition of karma as intention: some early texts state that it is possible to participate in another person's virtuous thoughts, simply by empathizing with that person's good deeds. When somebody performs a devotional act at a *stūpa*, for example, another person who observes this pious display can participate in it, mentally, and if so it could be said that the devotee's virtuous mental states are transferred to the observer. This idea was extended as Buddhism spread among peoples who valued filial piety, for example those who maintained ancestor worship at the megalithic sites where Buddhist missionaries placed their *stūpa*s. The incoming Buddhists thus accommodated local forms of ancestor worship, by teaching the new audience a revised form of the old doctrine of merit transference.

Another similar adaptation of the karma doctrine was the idea that the continued use of an item donated to the Sangha accrues merit to its donor, even after death. This belief encouraged the donation of larger gifts, such as the art and sculpture found at major sites, as well as objects and images found in shrine rooms, other artifacts of daily religious use, and even the monastic dwellings and monasteries themselves. The use of such things long after an individual's death therefore functioned as an ongoing gift to the most pure 'field of merit', large donations of villages and land by kings being the best way of ensuring this. A similar way of achieving the same end was to create permanent endowments, in the form of capital to be lent out at interest by the Sangha to merchants and businessmen. Such donations gradually turned Buddhist monasteries into feudal landlords and merchant banks, and so bound them closely to local socio-economic affairs.

Apart from these economic matters, Buddhist monasteries fulfilled an important role in health and welfare, especially for aged Buddhist supporters. Early Buddhist texts refer to infirmaries for sick Buddhist mendicants; these were probably centres in which the medical tradition of ancient India was practised, this being originally related to the renunciant circles that flourished in and around Magadha, but which was later absorbed into the Vedic tradition of *āyur-veda*, the 'science' of 'life' or 'longevity'. Buddhist monasteries were also centres of education. For the most part this consisted of scriptural study and related subjects, but in early medieval times the large monasteries of Bihar, such as Nāḷandā and Vikramaśīla, grew to become monastic universities, the greatest seats of learning in the medieval Asian world, with a broad curriculum including medicine, mathematics, logic, grammar and astrology besides the core learning of Buddhist texts.

Women in Indian Buddhism

The Buddha's analysis of the human condition is gender neutral, since the psychological factors that 'corrupt' a person – greed, hatred and delusion – occur equally in men and women. This means that men and women have the same capacity to do good and follow the Buddhist path, even to its highest achievement: according to the Buddha's analysis, women are just as able as men to attain Nirvana. If the Buddha's Dhamma was practised in accordance with these universal principles, the role of women should have been just as prominent as that of men. The historical evidence does not quite give this impression of sexual equality, but it does show that Buddhist women occupied a far more important position than that generally allotted to them in the patriarchal society of ancient India.

Gender equality is suggested in a wide range of canonical texts; at the simplest level these include those texts which report that the Buddha taught his Dhamma to create a fourfold community of monks, nuns, laymen and laywomen. More important, perhaps, than texts expressing Buddhist universalism in terms of gender are those texts which claim that equal numbers of men and women had attained advanced spiritual states (such as 500 male and female Arahats, and more than 500 male and female non-returner laymen and laywomen). No doubt this is religious hyperbole, but it exemplifies a general understanding of equality articulated by the nun Somā: 'When the mind is absorbed and understanding activated, for the person seeing the Dhamma correctly what does the state of being female matter?'

Not all texts conform to these ideals: some qualify the principle of gender equality, for example those which state that a woman cannot become a fully awakened Buddha. This inequality is reinforced by the fact that in the Jātaka tales of the Buddha's past lives, the Bodhisatta is never female, even when reborn as an animal or god, and by the fact that all former Buddhas before Gotama are male. Even in later Buddhist texts this understanding is not challenged, and there is a general acceptance that although a person can be female at the lower stages of the path, when a spiritual aspirant nears Buddhahood the rebirth will be as either a male human being or god.

Since the distinction between Buddha and Arahat was introduced only as the Buddha was mythologized, this notion of female inferiority cannot be attributed to the earliest period. Nevertheless, the mythological demotion of women was mirrored by the formal position allotted to them in the emerging institution of Buddhist monasticism. According to the account of the foundation of the order of nuns in the Pali Vinaya, the Buddha was reluctant to assent to Ānanda's request that nuns be admitted into the Sangha, which he made on behalf of the Buddha's stepmother, Pajāpatī. The Buddha eventually gave permission only as long as the nuns observe eight special rules which place them at a lower status to monks; he finally added that because of creating an order of nuns, the Dhamma will decline and disappear after 500 rather than 1,000 years.

This account is historically problematic, and like much of the Vinaya does not go back to the Buddha, but instead reflects the institutional changes necessitated by the development of the Buddhist order of wanderers into a community of sedentary monastics. These changes further involved the Sangha in social life and its norms, and so required an increasing level of deference to cultural convention. Since a major concern of the Vinaya was to cause no offence to the laity, so as not to minimize support and thus endanger the Buddhist mission, it would seem that the order of nuns was made to conform to the gender assumptions of the time.

These social concerns can be seen in the account of the Buddha's response to Pajāpatī's requests to relax the first of the eight special rules, according to which all nuns are inferior to monks – a rule which required them to rise respectfully to monks regardless of official monastic seniority (which is usually measured by the length of time since ordination). The Buddha is said to have denied this request not because the principle is incorrect, but rather because such a practice is not allowed by other sects, so how could the Buddhists allow it? Buddhist ideals were necessarily compromised by the cultural standards of the time.

A case could be made that this approach to gender norms was in agreement with the Buddha's pragmatism: perhaps a better outcome for women was achieved by not pushing an ideological case for sexual equality, but rather by creating the best possible outcome for women within what was conventionally feasible. Exactly this attitude can be seen in the *Mallikā Sutta*: in response to king Pasenadi's unhappiness at the birth of a daughter, the Buddha outlines various benefits in having a virtuous daughter, including the fact that a son born to her could become a mighty and just king. Although the Buddha does not argue that a daughter is as good as a son, he works within the gender conventions of the time to change the king's attitude.

Despite this relatively positive approach to women, other Buddhist texts have very negative depictions of femininity. Such texts demonize women as the most serious threat to male celibacy, and are clearly the work of monastics struggling to overcome their sexual urges. But even these texts do not fail to note that the problem is really about male susceptibility to sexual desire, rather than blatant female provocation, suggesting that even in these more negative appraisals of women, the Buddhist ideal of personal responsibility was known to be the key issue, rather than conventional views of gender.

Inscriptional evidence indicates that women played an important role in Indian Buddhism up until about the fifth century AD. But after this the proportion of nuns and laywomen mentioned in the donative inscriptions falls drastically, a decline in fortunes which agrees with observations made by Chinese pilgrims to India. Gender attitudes within the Buddhist community cannot have been responsible for this decline, the most likely cause of which was the emergence of classical Hinduism in this period, after strong Gupta support for Brahminic culture. This social change was not good news for women, the position of whom in Brahminic texts is notably inferior to that of men: there is virtually no such thing as female independence in Hinduism, and hardly any role for women in it.

The reduced role of women in Buddhism at this time corresponds with the beginning of a long process of Buddhist decline, culminating eventually in its disappearance from India by about the twelfth century. This coincidence suggests that the ancient prediction about the eventual disappearance of the Buddhist order because of admitting nuns was wrong: rather than female involvement in Buddhism bringing about a more speedy decline, it would seem that the lack of female practitioners was an important factor in the eventual disappearance of Indian Buddhism.

Schools and Sects

As Buddhism established itself as the dominant religion of the Indian subcontinent, a number of different intellectual and monastic traditions developed. These groupings are recorded in the epigraphic and literary sources from roughly the first century BC onwards: 18 is the number usually given in literary sources, although there is considerable variation in the different lists. Many of these different traditions appear to have been schools of thought – ideological rather than monastic groupings that required no formal membership apart from philosophical consent, such as the Lokottaravādins, Prajñaptivādins, Sautrāntikas and so on. But other groups seem to have been monastic fraternities or sects – in other words institutions with their own collections of sacred literature, membership of which was formally recognized by initiation into a distinct ordination lineage.

Eight of the groups mentioned in the lists can probably be counted as sects in this sense: the Mahāsāṃghikas, Vātsīputrīyas/Sāṃmatīyas, Kāśyapīyas, Dharmaguptakas, Sarvāstivādins, Mūlasarvāstivādins, Mahīśāsakas and Theravādins (also called Theras, Theriyas and Tambapanniyas). These sects were not formed through ideological conflict and schism, but developed naturally through a process of geographical dispersal that accelerated in the post-Aśokan age. Most formed monastic networks extending out from a particular geographical location: the Sarvāstivādins in Kashmir, the Dharmaguptakas in Gandhāra, the Theravādins in Sri Lanka and South India, the Sāṃmatīyas in western India and so on. Although regional locations are clear for these groups, this is not the case for others, such as the Mahāsāṃghikas, who appear to have been widely spread across much of India.

Identifying the geographical location of the sects is complicated by the fluidity of Buddhist institutions in India: sects could evolve and migrate, such as the Mūlasarvāstivādins from Mathura to Kashmir, the Sarvāstivādins and Dharmaguptakas from the northwest into Central Asia and beyond, and the Mahāsāṃghikas from northern India to Andhra and the southeast. Within these shifting networks, the decisive factor in sectarian affiliation was monastic observance: only monks who shared the same Vinaya could carry out the fortnightly Uposatha ceremony together, for this ceremony required commitment to a particular set of *Pātimokkha* rules. But no ideological commitment was specified in these rules: specific ideologies and dogmas floated above the network of monastic fraternities, although the distinction between sect and ideology occasionally disappeared, as when a Vinaya sect became strongly associated with a particular dogma.

This can be seen in the case of the Sarvāstivādins. This term refers to those who affirm (*vādin*) that things exist (*asti*) in all (*sarva*) three times, and so refers to a school of thought. But since the major thinking on this subject took place in the monasteries of Kashmir (and Gandhāra), this Vinaya group or sect was identified with the idea to such an extent that it was named after it. A Sarvāstivādin monk was not required to accept this scholarly dogma, however, for sectarian identification was determined by observance of the sect's Vinaya. This is demonstrated by the fact that the Mūla-Sarvāstivādin fraternity – literally the 'root' or 'original' Sarvāstivādins – probably used this term of identity not in a dogmatic sense, but because they believed the Vinaya of the Kashmirian Sarvāstivādins was derived from their own. They therefore claimed to be the 'original Sarvāstivādins' in the sense of monastic discipline, rather than in the philosophical sense of ownership of or major contributors to a Buddhist idea.

The relation between schools (of thought) and (Vinaya) sects was therefore fluid, this being a consequence of Buddhist decentralization, with local centres enjoying a considerable degree of institutional autonomy within any given monastic network. It is likely that some of the well-known groups mentioned in literary and epigraphic sources were originally minor centres within the eight major groupings; if such centres never managed to achieve complete independence through establishing their own Vinaya, they would remain as sub-sects formally committed to the parent institution. Many of the Mahāsāṃghika groups located in the Andhra region, such as the Pūrva and Apara Śailas, were probably traditions of this kind. These local fraternities did not develop their own sets of monastic rules, and remained formally within the Mahāsāṃghika fold without ever attaining complete institutional independence; in practice, however, they were free to develop ideas and institutions as they pleased.

Whereas the Pūrva and Apara Śailas groupings were identified by location ('of the "Eastern" or "Western" mountain'), other southern Mahāsāṃghika groups were identified through doctrinal commitment, for example the Caitikas ('those with a doctrine on shrines', *caityas*) and the Prajñaptivādins ('those who espouse the doctrine of conceptualization'). These philosophical traditions were schools of thought which perhaps emerged around lineages of prominent teachers, and since they did not develop their own monastic codes (Vinaya), it is possible that they too were sub-sects of the Mahāsāṃghikas, with semi-autonomous monastic networks just like the Pūrva and Apara Śailas (with whom they perhaps overlapped).

The evidence for monastic groups in post-Aśokan India thus conflates a small number of major sects with a large number of sub-sects and schools of thought. The situation is further complicated by the fact that allegiance to particular ideas and practices did not necessarily alter sectarian identity, and by the fluidity that escapes the historical record: different groupings would have flourished in different periods, e.g. the Dharmottarīyas or Bhadrayānīyas of western India, and it is entirely possible that a sub-sect or school of thought could have developed into a sect proper before disappearing or falling back to a smaller grouping within a major sect and leaving no trace of this. At the present level of understanding it is difficult to distinguish these historical subtleties.

Abhidhamma

The scholastic work conducted in the Buddhist monasteries of India developed from the 'higher' or 'further' teachings of the Abhidhamma (S: Abhidharma), which forms the final 'basket' (*piṭaka*) of the Buddhist canon. The only complete Abhidhammas to have survived are those of the Theravādins (in Pali) and Sarvāstivādins (in Chinese), both of which contain seven separate books. The similarities between some of these books indicate that the Abhidhamma project originated in the pre-Aśokan period, although the considerable differences between the two collections imply that these pre-Aśokan beginnings were greatly elaborated in the following centuries.

The Abhidhamma-piṭakas present the Buddha's Dhamma systematically, in terms of its ultimate truth, rather than through the conventions used by the Buddha as he communicated his ideas at particular times and places. This project is therefore an attempt to state the absolute truth of the Dhamma devoid of the idiosyncrasies that characterize the Buddha's skill in means style of teaching. To achieve this philosophical aim, conditioned experience is reduced to its fundamental aspects, which are termed *dhammas* (S: *dharmas*).

The Theravādin system lists 82 *dhammas*: consciousness, 52 mental factors (*cetasikas*: 25 wholesome states, such as faith and compassion; 14 unwholesome states such as greed and hatred; and 13 neutral states such as sensation and apperception), 28 classes of physical reality (e.g.

the elements earth, water, fire, wind and space), and Nirvana, the only unconditioned *dhamma*. The Sarvāstivādin Abhidharma is similar but has only 75 *dharmas*: 72 conditioned *dharmas* (consciousness, 46 mental factors, 11 physical *dharmas*, and 14 that are neither mental nor physical, such as life, birth and name) and three unconditioned *dharmas* (space, and two different types of Nirvana distinguished according to the manner of its achievement: the 'cessation of the defilements achieved through contemplation', *pratisaṃkhyā-nirodha*, and that achieved without it, *apratisaṃkhyā-nirodha*).

These classificatory systems emerged from the various lists of psycho-physical phenomena contained in the canonical discourses, such as the five aggregates, the 18 'spheres' (*dhātus*: six senses, six sense objects and six resulting types of consciousness), and especially the group of various lists later termed the 37 Factors of Awakening (*bodhi-pakkhiya dhamma)*: the Four Establishments of Mindfulness, Four kinds of Right Effort, Four Bases of Success, Five Faculties and Five Powers, Seven Limbs of Awakening and the Eightfold Path.

Such lists enumerate the various phenomena that make up the totality of experience, including the mundane states that comprise ordinary reality and the more advanced states which Buddhist teachings locate on the path to Nirvana, the ultimate reality. The creation of such lists ultimately goes back to the Buddha's psychological approach to religious matters: his focus on conditioned experience, the definition of karma as mental states, and the emphasis on developing virtuous thoughts and eradicating unwholesome ones. Whether or not the pre-Abhidhamma lists of experiential realities all go back to the Buddha himself, they at least show that his followers maintained his analytical methods as they explored the Dhamma.

As Buddhist thinkers considered the different states and factors of experience contained in these canonical lists, and the intricate relations between them, it seems they came to think of the separate items as *dhammas*. This was a fairly straightforward development, for besides the regular meaning of 'teaching' or 'doctrine', the canonical discourses also use the term *dhamma* to denote mental objects and states. It can be assumed, then, that the foundations for the Abhidhamma project were laid when Buddhist thinkers of the pre-Aśokan age drew up more complete lists of the various mental states and objects mentioned in the teachings, and listed these *dhammas* in the simple sense of 'factors of experience'.

But this *dhamma* analysis of conditioned experience does not nearly explain the nature of Abhidhamma systems. For Abhidhamma thought does not merely analyze the totality of experience according to its different aspects, but also reduces it to these parts and nothing more: the various *dhamma* lists are not just enumerations of the limits of all possible experience, perhaps as a useful guide to the Buddhist contemplative, but also present experience entirely in terms of various combinations of impersonal mental states and factors, without the requirement of a self or soul. Why is this?

This approach to Buddhist thought only makes sense as a philosophical elaboration of reductionistic realism. The canonical discourses show that some time in the first century of the Buddhist era, certain thinkers came to believe that the human being is made up of various parts which lack self, and that really understanding this point is the vital knowledge which effects liberation. The Abhidhamma is a more detailed exploration of this approach to the Dhamma: the reduction of a person to his constituent parts, as stated in texts such as the *Vajirā Sutta* and especially the *Mahā-hatthipadopama Sutta*, was taken to a much more subtle degree of analysis through using the various lists of psycho-physical phenomena.

It would seem that in their contemplation of the 'No Self' teaching, early Buddhist thinkers pushed their reductionistic analysis as far as it would go. Lists of *dhamma*s were thus an attempt to guide a contemplation of the entirely impersonal workings of experience. This exploration of the Buddha's teachings cannot be regarded as abstract philosophy, for it was a rational enquiry motivated by religious concerns: the purpose of looking deeply into the workings of experience, in order to see the impersonal level of conditioning that operates without any self or soul, was ultimately to achieve freedom from the psychological forces that bind a person to *saṃsāra*.

The various canonical lists of psycho-physical phenomena were therefore utilized by contemplatives to help them in their reductionistic enterprise; the end result of this enquiry was the *dhamma* explorations of the canonical Abhidhamma books. The basic theory was then given a more philosophical elaboration in the Sarvāstivādin than in the Theravādin tradition. Whereas the latter did not define the exact ontology of a *dhamma*, the Sarvāstivādins (writing in Sanskrit) took the *dharma*s to be irreducible substances (S: *dravya-sat*), in contrast to which they regarded the composite entities made up by them as conceptually real (S: *prajñapti-sat*). This distinction notes the difference between, say, a house and the complex of physical *dharma*s of which it is made up, or between a person's sense of self and the different psychological *dharma*s from which it is derived.

Abhidhamma thought brings into sharp focus the problem of reductionistic realism, namely the removal of the person as a category of religio-philosophical discourse. For what is the point of a religion if it claims that there is no ultimate subject of salvation? Perhaps in order to offset such criticism, the Abhidhamma systems present Nirvana as a knowable reality (*dhamma*) that is unconditioned and eternal. Even if this sidesteps the problem of nihilism, by making the system finally culminate in a really existent spiritual state, it is a solution that comes at a price. For this presentation of Nirvana gives it the appearance of a transcendent absolute similar to the Upaniṣadic *brahman*, and this understanding caused an important change to the karma doctrine: if Nirvana is transcendent and unconditioned, it must be beyond both good and bad karma, and if so, the Abhidhamma would seem to undermine the soteriological function of Buddhist ethics.

Buddhist Scholasticism

The Abhidhamma analysis laid the foundations for all future Buddhist philosophy. Whether or not its reductionistic analysis was accepted, it provided the intellectual framework within which thinkers henceforth explored the Buddha's teachings. The most pressing problem raised by the analysis is the lack of an experiential subject: this raises the problem of the lack of a subject of salvation, but also creates difficulties in explaining personal continuity within the present life, as well as karmic continuity beyond it. How an act can have an effect in the future when the act itself has ceased to exist, and when there is no ultimate subject of continuity, was a major problem faced by all Buddhist schools.

One book of the Theravādin Abhidhamma, the *Kathāvatthu* ('Points of Controversy'), said to have been composed during the so-called Third Council of Pāṭaliputta just before the Aśokan missions, indicates that a number of approaches to these Abhidhamma problems had arisen by this time. One approach is termed *sabbatthi-vāda*, and was later developed into the *sarvāstivāda* doctrine (*vāda*) that *dharma*s exist (*asti*) in all (*sarva*) three times (past, present and future). The proponents of this idea tried to explain karmic continuity by claiming that *dharmas* which have passed away, as well as those which have yet to come into being, must still exist in some sense.

Various ways of understanding this idea were proposed by Sarvāstivādin theorists, the most influential of which was the formulation of Vasubandhu. In his *Abhidharmakośa-bhāṣya*, a major scholastic treatise of the fourth century AD, he argues that the difference between existence in the present and existence in the past or future is a matter of 'activity' (S: *kāritra*): whereas *dharmas* in the present are active, past and future *dharmas* are inactive and so exist latently. This theory provides an answer to the problem of personal continuity in the absence of a self, for it implies that rather than going out of existence after a single moment, a person's past *karma* still exists to exert its retribution. Karmic continuity is therefore explained, but this solution to the problem of connecting evanescent psycho-physical events without an underlying substance suggests that *dharmas* are eternal, and so subverts the key Buddhist doctrine of impermanence.

Vasubandhu's commentary (*bhāṣya*) on his authoritative exposition of the Sarvāstivāda Abhidharma is in fact critical of the idea of existence in all three times. It expresses a Sautrāntika perspective, this being the approach of those who regarded the Sūtras rather than Abhidharma as the authoritative word of the Buddha. The Sautrāntika critique thus presents a simplified system by proposing a continuum of consciousness in which all *dharmas* have a momentary existence in the present. Although any karmic act is therefore radically impermanent or momentary (S: *kṣaṇika*), it is said to create a subsequent causal series of impermanent *dharmas*, a process figuratively described as a 'perfuming' (*vāsanā*) of the stream of consciousness, the final result of the series being the eventual retribution of a good, bad or neutral experience.

An earlier rejection of *sarvāstivāda* metaphysics was achieved by those who termed themselves Vibhajjavādins: 'upholders of the analytical teaching'. This philosophical identity was inherited by the Theravādins of Sri Lanka, as well as related Indian schools such as the Mahīśāsakas, Dharmaguptakas and Kāśyapīyas. But the attribution of the *vibhajja-vāda* to a number of different Vinaya sects makes it difficult to pinpoint any specific metaphysic to those who accepted it. According to Vasubandhu's *Abhidharmakośa-bhāṣya*, the term denotes those who accept the existence of present karma as well as all past karma which has not yet yielded its retribution, but this idea is rejected in the Theravādin *Kathāvatthu*. These differences suggest that the term does not denote any particular school of thought: the Vibhajjavādins were instead analysts who rejected various Abhidharma ontologies, such as the *sarvāsti-vāda*.

One of the philosophical positions rejected by the Vibhajjavādins and Sarvāstivādins was termed *pudgala-vāda*: the doctrine of the 'person' (*pudgala*), the most controversial Buddhist philosophy that emerged in the Mauryan period. This idea goes against the reductionism of the Abhidhamma by declaring that a person is not merely an aggregate of different parts, but can in fact be said to truly exist in an ultimate sense. The origins of this school are probably to be located in the early substantialist tradition of meditative realists who believed the state of the 'cessation of perception and sensation' to be liberating; indeed, the Pudgalavādins accepted the idea of absorption into the Nirvana-realm at death, a key idea of the early meditative realist tradition.

Since this idea was adapted from meditators influenced by the Brahminic idea of union with *brahman*, it is not surprising that the Pudgalavādins also accepted a principle of personal identity, which was believed to be a transmigrating entity and sometimes termed 'self' (*ātman*). Also suggestive is the Pudgalavādin likening of the 'person' to fire, for early Brahminic texts use fire as a symbol for the self, and liken its absorption into *brahman* at death to an extinguished flame, which disappears into the cosmic ether. It is not difficult to see how some Buddhists came to think in this substantialist way, for the Buddha also compared the liberated person to an extinguished flame: interpreting the metaphors used by the Buddha in the Brahminic sense of the liberated person's final release at death, rather than the liberation achieved in life, was a simple development, even if it turned the Buddha's metaphor of 'extinguishing' (*nirvāṇa*) into a statement of philosophical realism.

A more sophisticated position is attributed to the Pudgalavādins in Vasubandhu's *Abhidharmakośa-bhāṣya*. According to this mature doctrine, although the person is ultimately real, it is neither a primary existent (*dravya*, like the Sarvāstivādin *dharmas*) nor a conceptualization (*prajñapti*, as in the Abhidharma). This perspective is illustrated by a different application of fire imagery: just as the flame is neither entirely identical with nor different from its fuel, so too did the later

Pudgalavādins claim that the person is neither entirely identical with nor different from the fuel of the five aggregates. This position thus states that the 'person' has an ineffable (*avyakta*) relationship with both the five aggregates and Nirvana, an idea not so far removed from the early teaching of the ineffability of the liberated person (even if the Buddha took this idea of ineffability to its logical conclusion by refusing to designate any kind of person or thing).

Whatever its origins and development, the *pudgala-vāda* at least avoided some of the philosophical and ethical problems raised by Abhidhamma reductionism. For the idea of an ultimately real person avoids problems of individual continuity and moral responsibility, charges which could both be levelled against the reductionists. In general, however, neither the Abhidhamma reductionism nor the personalism of the Pudgalavādins can be regarded as a more correct interpretation of the Buddha's teachings. For both traditions assume that a person's perceptions of the world represent a mind-independent reality in which the human being exists, whether with or without the ghost in the machine. Although the substantialist (*Pudgalavādin*) and reductionist (Abhidhamma) interpretations of the Dhamma stand at opposite ends of the philosophical spectrum, both are founded on the same realistic presuppositions.

Chapter VI

Debate, Adaptation and Extinction

> The virtuous universal monarchs, born before the age of discord . . . abided by the path of the ten virtuous actions. These kings who loved their people protected society just as they would protect a beloved son. But now kings born in the age of discord rely on the evil nature of their own opinions and are obsessed by their desire for wealth. They take as authoritative treatises that agree with harmful practices and reject those that agree with virtuous practices. In this way, these kings who have no compassion devastate this world, just as if it were a hunting ground.
>
> Candrakīrti, *Catuḥśatakaṭīkā*

The religious culture disseminated by the Mauryans favoured the Sangha without turning Buddhism into a state religion. The Buddhists instead flourished as the most successful group within a pluralistic religious culture, achieving influence through their close association with the urban centres and their mercantile orders. There was therefore no symbiosis between monarch and Sangha, and so no such thing as a purely Buddhist civilization, even if the religious and ethical norms of the social order revolved around Buddhist values. The Buddhists were rather the main cultural force in an open society, with a positive ethos that avoided the escapist concerns of other groups, and which thus helped bridge the gap between the sacred domain of the renouncers and the profane world of the towns.

The Aśokan expansion of Buddhism had required the Buddhist Sangha to revise and update its institutional norms, a process which continued in the post-Mauryan age. But not all Buddhists approved of the settled monasticism that emerged from this process of change: some believed that an increased level of worldly involvement threatened the spiritual purpose created by the Buddha. Such dissenters, opposed to the post-Mauryan level of worldliness, were free to follow the Dhamma according to their own inclinations, however, according to the Buddha's advice to be 'a light unto yourself'. Buddhist individualism thus supported the creation of new imaginary worlds, especially among secluded mendicants meditating in lonely retreats.

The middle period of Indian Buddhism was thus marked by varying degrees of creative tension within the Sangha. But more serious tensions were building beyond the monastic walls and urban centres, as rival religious forces emerged to threaten the predominant position of the Buddhists. This challenge from without was an unintended consequence of Buddhist individualism: although the Sangha flourished as spiritual advisors and charitable agents at the edge of the urban world, the open society it assumed and encouraged allowed space for other cultural forces, not all of which were favourably disposed to the Buddhists, or even to urbanization. Between the second century BC and the third century AD, a religious culture that could compete with Buddhism was formulated within the Brahminic community, one based on an entirely different vision of society. To survive in India, the Buddhist Sangha would have to deal with a reformulated and resurgent Brahminism, which in the Gupta period began to approximate classical Hinduism.

The Great Vehicle

The myth of the Buddha's past lives elevated Gotama to the status of a religious superhero, and so placed the goal of Buddhahood beyond the reach of most pious Buddhists. This was, indeed, the very point of the myth: turning the Buddha into a religious figure of cosmic stature, with an achievement well beyond that of ordinary disciples, was a way of inspiring fervour among the faithful as well as winning converts. But even if the myth was meant to win new followers and inspire commitment in them, this could not prevent some from trying to imitate Gotama's incomparable path. A new mythic movement thus emerged, led by self-designated 'Bodhisattas' following the example of Gotama's long path to perfection.

When the first Bodhisattas appeared is unclear. An origin in the third century BC is possible, and perhaps even likely, since the myth of Gotama's past lives was given an elaborate treatment in Jātakas and Avadānas of this time. Bodhisatta groups must have appeared no later than the first century BC, for new texts concerned with the Bodhisatta ideal, presented as teachings of the Buddha in the old Sutta style, were almost certainly composed at this time. The oldest surviving examples of this literature are preserved in Chinese translations of the mid-second century AD, but since these texts appear in an advanced stage of development, their transmission and revision over many generations can be assumed.

The Buddhist composers of this new literature were not attempting to articulate anything remotely like a new movement. These Bodhisattas rather made up just another trend within a diverse Sangha composed of numerous monastic guilds, in which a wide variety of ideas and practices flourished. In a religious culture lacking centralization, the early Bodhisatta compositions unsurprisingly contain no indication of belonging to a co-ordinated tradition. It was only much later that the Bodhisattas came to regard themselves as belonging to a distinct and momentous phenomenon in Buddhism, which they termed *mahā-yāna*: the 'Great Vehicle'. But the virtual absence of this term in the early literature implies that the earliest Bodhisattas regarded the mythic path as another spiritual option among many.

In its incipient phase, and indeed for all of its history in India, Mahāyāna Buddhism was thus no sort of sectarian movement with its own monastic institutions. There is no evidence of any attempt to form a distinct Bodhisatta fraternity, with a separate book of monastic discipline: the Bodhisatta ideal was instead accepted by individuals who continued to operate within established Vinaya groupings. If, for example, Sarvāstivādin and Mahāsāṃghika monks took the Mahāyāna vow to attain full awakening for the benefit of all sentient beings, they did not cease to be members of the Sarvāstivādin or Mahāsāṃghika sects. They rather incorporated the Bodhisatta ideal, and a range of beliefs and practices required by it, within an already established set of Buddhist ideas, practices and identities.

Early Mahāyāna texts such as the *Ugra-paripṛcchā Sūtra* ('Discourse on the Inquiry of Ugra') show that those who emulated the way of the Bodhisatta included monks and laymen, with a particular concern to practise the perfection of giving. Other texts suggest that early Bodhisattas followed a more disciplined lifestyle in forest retreats – ascetics probably regarded by the mainstream as inconsequential idealists. The Buddhist mainstream must have regarded such Bodhisattas with a mixture of amusement and suspicion, for what could be more ridiculous than trying to mimic the monumental career of the Buddha himself? But even if so, with their forest lifestyle and ascetic prestige, these Bodhisattas were well situated to offer a critique of developments in the mainstream, a constant if not exaggerated feature of the early Mahāyāna literature. As long as the Buddhist movement prospered, these isolated quietists would not have caused much trouble: the Bodhisattas either criticized sedentary monasticism from the religious fringe, in which case they were marginalized, or else their ideals were absorbed into the monastic mainstream, in which case they were domesticated.

Epigraphic and art-historical evidence suggests the Mahāyāna was nothing more than a minority concern for most of the middle period: the material remains do not amount to much before the late fourth century AD, and are not widespread until the fifth and sixth centuries onwards, when Buddhism was already in serious decline in much of India. During these centuries the Mahāyānists constituted small but vigorous pockets of spiritual creativity, gradually expanding into the mainstream despite their most controversial innovation: the composition of new texts. The early Mahāyānists took the extremely contentious step of composing texts as if they were authentic discourses of the Buddha, even though they eventually came to use Sanskrit rather than a dialect of Prakrit more closely related to the language of the Buddha – a change that turned the word 'Bodhisatta' into 'Bodhisattva' and 'Sutta' into 'Sūtra'.

There is no simple explanation for the failure to distinguish the new Bodhisattva literature from the canonical teachings, perhaps as a separate genre of post-canonical literature. For this is more or less what happened in the Theravāda tradition of Sri Lanka, the post-canonical literature of which contains texts (such as the *Buddhavaṃsa* or *Cariyāpiṭaka*) which celebrate the Bodhisatta's strivings in a manner similar to the early Mahāyāna texts. But the fact that the Buddhist canons were built up over a number of centuries, with new discourses and minor texts being added as late as – and perhaps beyond – the first century BC allowed space for innovation. The composition and redaction of canonical texts in the post-Mauryan period must have encouraged Bodhisattvas to imagine a similar status for their works, which they regarded as authentic utterances of the Buddha.

The Bodhisattvas were certainly aware of the problems involved in passing off new works as the word of the Buddha, for some Sūtras go to great lengths to justify their authenticity, indicating that attributing new works to the Buddha, in the old Sūtra style, was controversial and had the potential to split the Sangha. The fact that this did not happen was probably due to the reluctance of the Mahāyānists to form a new sect, as well as the general impossibility of splitting an acephalous religious organization: monastic guilds were generally free to do more or less as they pleased, without any interference from a central office (which did not exist).

The system of guild monasticism thus allowed space for new developments, and some took advantage of this to reformulate old ideals, often in response to institutional and ideological change. The reactionary tendencies of much early Mahāyāna literature suggests its authors rejected the post-Aśokan evolution of the Sangha, and instead proposed a return to the forest ideals of the Buddha and his followers. The problem was not so much that the mainstream had degenerated into an 'inferior' path (*hīna-yāna*) focused on the selfish goal of individual liberation. The Bodhisattvas were more concerned with institutional change: large-scale, sedentary monasticism, with all the worldly compromises it required, and the scholastic curriculum followed at the expense of pursuing the supreme goal.

Meditation Among the Bodhisattvas?

That some Buddhists decided to emulate the Buddha myth raises a peculiar problem. Since it took many lifetimes of spiritual struggle for Gotama to achieve complete awakening, did the aspiring Bodhisattvas imagine that they must do likewise, rather than simply attempting to attain Nirvana in the present life as taught by the Buddha? And should they even try to avoid becoming 'stream-attainers', a quite basic level of attainment which guarantees a person eventual release? Some of the Bodhisattva literature suggests that for some this was indeed the case. A late but telling example is the *Bodhicaryāvatāra* ('Entry into the Conduct Leading to Awakening'), a classic work on the Mahāyāna path written in the seventh century AD by Śāntideva, a resident of the monastic university of Nāḷandā. This text is peculiar in that it has nothing much to say about meditation, its chapter on absorption consisting of basic advice for the Bodhisattva: places suitable for meditation, the dangers to be encountered and so on.

Since the *Bodhicaryāvatāra* offers no substantial advice on how to cultivate inner absorption, it is reasonable to suppose that Śāntideva was not a meditator. While this might seem contrary to the entire point of being a Buddhist monk, the Jātaka tales on which the Bodhisattva ideal is based focus on the development of moral virtues: if there is little place for meditation in the myth of the Buddha's past lives as a Bodhisattva, why should a Bodhisattva following in Gotama's footsteps bother with it? To do so might lead to the unfortunate reward of attaining Nirvana too quickly, before the cultivation of the Bodhisattva virtues, and if so a preferable course would be to focus on Mahāyāna ethics, and on trying to understand Mahāyāna philosophy, both of which form the focus of Śāntideva's most important work.

An earlier and more basic indication of this non-meditative orientation is contained in the schemes of Bodhisattva perfections (*pāramitā*), mentioned in both the mainstream and Mahāyāna literature. Six are usually listed in the latter: giving, morality, patience, endeavour, meditation and understanding. The order of these perfections gives the impression that a Bodhisattva should not master meditation and understanding too soon, before the accumulation of the requisite merit to finally become a Buddha. The fact that many early Mahāyāna texts advocate 'ascetic practices' (S: *dhūtaguṇa*), such as begging for alms, living in the forest or open air, and sleeping in the sitting position without lying down, only reinforces this impression, since the aim of these practices is to cultivate correct attitudes and moral qualities, and not meditation *per se*.

Even if the cultivation of Buddhist virtue was the basic focus of early Mahāyāna, too much should not be read into the scant treatment of meditation in the *Bodhicaryāvātara*. For meditation is prominent in two important genres of early Mahāyāna literature: that focused on the final Bodhisattva perfection of understanding (*prajñā*), and that focused on the practice of visualization. The latter developed from canonical descriptions of the fabulous worlds of mythic figures, such as the lengthy description of the capital city of the legendary King Sudassana in the Pali *Mahā-sudassana Sutta*. This discourse provided the basis for the similar description of the Buddha Amitābha's Pure Land of 'Sukhāvatī' in the larger *Sukhāvatī-vyūha Sūtra*: in both cases, the lengthy descriptions of fabulous worlds look like a template for visualization, rather than just a teaching to be heard (or read) and mastered.

A further canonical starting point for visualization was a practice known as 'recollection' (P: *anussati, S: anusmṛti*): of the Buddha, the Dhamma, the Sangha as well as morality, generosity and the gods. In an ideological world focused on Bodhisattva mythology, such recollections of the Buddha no doubt included the visualization of his supernatural body, as described in canonical texts. The contemplation of such ideas would have led, in turn, to visions of new Buddhas outside the lineage of seven masters to which Gautama belonged, some of whom were believed to exist in the present and so could be contacted. Texts such as the *Pratyutpannabuddha-saṃmukhāvasthita-samādhi Sūtra* ('Discourse on the Absorption of Direct Contact with Buddhas of the Present') thus direct the practice of Buddha recollection towards the Buddha Amitāyus (i.e. Amitābha), and advise the devotee not only to recollect Amitābha's pure realm of Sukhāvatī, but also his supernatural body.

Although the extant literature does not permit a detailed historical reconstruction, a general development of early visionary Mahāyāna Buddhism can be sketched. Starting with canonical contemplations, and building on a general elevation of the historical Buddha into a cosmic religious hero, some Buddhists developed mythic aspects of the Buddhist mainstream. In visualizations inspired by mythic texts these Bodhisattvas encountered other Buddhas and various celestial beings, experiences which inspired the composition of further visionary texts, around the sacred pantheon of which a distinct Mahāyāna identity began to be fashioned.

The Perfection of Understanding

Visionary Bodhisattvas were not the only early Mahāyānists interested in meditation. An entirely different tradition is formulated in another corpus of Mahāyāna Sūtras: those concerned with the 'perfection of understanding' (*prajñā-pāramitā*). The earliest text of this class, the *Aṣṭasāhasrikā-prajñāpāramitā Sūtra* ('Perfection of Understanding in Eight Thousand Lines'), was among the first Mahāyāna texts translated into Chinese in the late second century AD, a translation of such complexity that it implies an initial composition in perhaps even the first century BC. Along with other texts in the Perfection of Understanding corpus, the *Aṣṭāsāhasrikā-prajñāpāramitā* contains much material on meditation, although generally not of the visionary kind.

Prominent among these meditations are those said to be 'without object' (*animitta*), 'without direction' (*apraṇihita*) and simply 'emptiness' (*śūnyatā*), a triad already contained in the canonical discourses. This interest in advanced states of meditation reflects the primary focus of this corpus on the higher Bodhisattva perfections (*pāramitā*), which culminate in liberating gnosis (*prajñā*). Thus the opening chapter of the *Aṣṭāsāhasrikā-prajñāpāramitā*, which constitutes the earliest layer of what may well be the oldest Mahāyāna text, has nothing much to say about the lengthy Bodhisattva path, and instead focuses on the attainment of complete awakening in the present. The Bodhisattva is thus to 'course in the perfection of understanding' so as to attain Buddhahood quickly.

It seems that the Bodhisattva composers and transmitters of this text, or at least its earliest layers, were interested in attaining the full awakening of a Buddha not in the remote future, but as soon as possible, preferably in this very life. If so it can be supposed that these thinkers understood the term 'bodhisattva' in its original adjectival sense, of 'being devoted to awakening', rather than as a mythic title. This does not mean that the *prajñā-pāramitā* corpus lacks mythic elements, even in its earliest layers. Indeed, in the *Aṣṭasāhasrikā*, the Bodhisattva is thus advised to develop his meditation in such a way that it does not yield the karmic fruit of spiritual progress: in such a context 'skill in means' refers not to advanced proficiency in spiritual communication, but rather to the ability to practise meditation and yet stall its soteriological effects. This peculiar idea is in keeping with the Mahāyāna aim of following the long Bodhisattva path, rather than realizing the final Bodhisattva perfection of understanding immediately.

The presence of mythic elements alongside the general focus on perfecting understanding is an historical problem, for the predominant interest in advanced states of spiritual realization (of the latter) is mitigated by the advice not to progress too far in meditation (of the former). These conflicting interests suggest divergent concerns among those responsible for transmitting these texts. A possible solution is that the texts are made up of various chronological strata, with the mythic elements being an attempt to moderate an original focus on liberating understanding in the here and now. But even this does not distract attention away from these texts' zeal to grasp the awakened gnosis, which is presented as a response to two forms of philosophical realism: that on which the Bodhisattva myth and path is based, and Abhidharma reductionism.

Abhidharma thought, with its presumption that ultimate reality is within the scope of language, was particularly important in pushing the *prajñā-pāramitā* thinkers to define more clearly what the Buddha meant by his charismatic silence. An attempt to negate the Abhidharma realism can be seen in the opening chapters of the *Aṣṭasāhasrikā*. In a mainstream setting, the Buddha asks the Bodhisattva Subhūti to explain how a Bodhisattva should practise ('go out into it') the perfection of understanding. But Subhūti, responding from the perspective of ultimate reality, states that he does not see any *dharma*s termed 'Bodhisattva' or 'perfection of understanding'. This wording is crucial: Subhūti does not state that these two things are unreal, but rather points out that they are not to be conceived as ultimate realities (*dharma*s) in the Abhidharma sense. To emphasize the point, Subhūti then states that even the resolution to attain Buddhahood should not be taken too seriously: a true Bodhisattva would not think in this manner, which implies a naive realistic understanding.

The *Prajñā-pāramitā Sūtra*s extend this dialectic to the entire imaginative world of Buddhism: apart from traditional rejection of the person as an ultimate real existent, the collection of aggregates is said to be an 'illusory person' (*māyā-puruṣa*), and all traditional categories – the Four Noble Truths, the Eightfold Path and so on – are negated as ultimately true, since they presume a conceptual understanding. The point of this is not to rubbish traditional Buddhism, but rather to show that the canonical categories are not ultimately real entities, according to the standards of philosophical realism. Such teachings thus point towards the radical deconstruction of conceptualization required to realize the way things really are.

The paradox of the perfection of understanding is that language had to be employed in a rather elaborate fashion in order to negate conceptuality. To point towards the quiescent true nature of things, the *Prajñā-pāramitā Sūtras* texts thus state that all phenomena (*dharmas*) are conceptual constructs 'empty' (*śūnya*) of their own-identity (*sva-bhāva*), and so only as real as a magical illusion. The clearest and most radical example of this dialectic is the negation of Nirvana as a really existent 'thing' (*dharma*) in the second chapter of the *Aṣṭasāhasrikā*:

> Addressed thus, venerable Subhūti said this to those heavenly scions: 'All *dharmas*, O heavenly scions, are like an illusion, like a dream! The stream attainer and his religious attainment are like an illusion, like a dream; likewise the once-returner and his religious attainment, the non-returner attainer and his religious attainment, the Arhant and his religious attainment, the solitary Buddha and his religious attainment, and a completely perfect Buddha as well as complete, perfect Buddhahood: all are like an illusion, like a dream.'
>
> Then the heavenly scions said this to venerable Subhūti: 'You say that even a completely perfect Buddha, venerable Subhūti, is like an illusion, like a dream? And that even the state of complete, perfect Buddhahood is like an illusion, like a dream?'
>
> Subhūti said: Even Nirvana, heavenly scions, is like an illusion, like a dream, let alone any other *dharma*!
>
> The heavenly scions said: 'You say that even Nirvana, venerable Subhūti, is like an illusion, like a dream?'
>
> Venerable Subhūti said: Even if, heavenly scions, there were any other *dharma* superior to Nirvana, I would say even that is like an illusion, like a dream.

Such radicalism was intended as a challenge to realistic interpretations of the Dharma, and hence is easily misunderstood. But it is important to note even in this, the most charged statement of the entire *prajñā-pāramitā* corpus, Subhūti only negates the understanding that Nirvana is a *dharma*. This is not a curious case of Buddhist nihilism, therefore, and instead a pointer towards the early apophatic understanding that Nirvana cannot be conceived as an ontological existent.

Neither Realism nor Idealism

Some help in understanding the *prajñā-pāramitā* teachings on emptiness is provided by Nāgārjuna's *Mūlamadhyamaka-kārikā* ('Fundamental verses on the Middle Way'), perhaps the single most important work of Buddhist philosophy. But this work, composed in the second century AD, most probably in a Mahāsāṃghika monastery of the Krishna river valley (modern Andhra Pradesh), is also difficult: cryptic and elusive, and consisting of extremely succinct but memorable aphorisms entirely in verse, it can be explained quite differently according to the perspective of the interpreter. Luckily, a further aid to understanding Nāgārjuna's 'middle way' (*madhyamaka*) philosophy is provided by a canonical discourse: the Pali *Kaccāyana-gotta Sutta* (*'Discourse to Kaccāyanagotta'*), a Sanskrit version of which is cited by Nāgārjuna in the fifteenth chapter of his verses on the middle way.

The Buddha's interlocutor in this canonical discourse is his disciple Kaccāyana, the same person to whom is attributed the clearest account of epistemological conditioning in the early texts (the *Madhupiṇḍika Sutta*). While this suggests that the *Kaccāyana-gotta Sutta* deals with the philosophy of constructed realism, its presentation of ideas is unusually developed, and stylistically different from similar formulations that can be assigned to an earlier period of thought. If the text is a few generations beyond the life of the Buddha, it should be considered an elaboration of an old idea, most probably in response to other elaborations of the early teachings (such as reductionistic realism and process philosophy). Whatever the case, this discourse states the Buddha's teaching as follows:

> This world for the most part depends on a duality, Kaccāyana, of existence and non-existence. But for the person who correctly sees the origin of the world, as it really is, the notion of non-existence in it (*loke natthitā*) does not arise. And for the person who correctly sees the cessation of the world, as it really is, the notion of existence (*loke atthitā*) in it does not arise.

This difficult statement seems to refer to different ways of understanding conditioned or constructed experience. For in early Buddhist teachings the term 'world' (*loka*) often refers not to the objective realm of space-time, but rather to a person's world of experience, which is unsatisfactory (*dukkha*). This experiential sense of the term *loka* is made clear in the *Kaccāyana-gotta Sutta* through the following point:

> He has no doubt or perplexity that only suffering (*dukkha*) arises and comes into being, and only suffering ceases and goes out of being: just so is his private understanding.

If the origin and cessation of the 'world' (*loka*) is thus equivalent to the origin and cessation of suffering (*dukkha*), the Buddha's original formulation must refer to the 'world' of individual experience. This means that the teaching presumes an experiential understanding of the world rather than an ontological one, and if so the original formulation of the Buddha can be understood as follows. The correct understanding of the world's cessation is that only experiential construction ceases, rather than individual existence, leading to the realization that the notion of individual existence in the world (*loke atthitā*) is just a delusion. By the same logic, when it is understood how any world of experience arises – through the objective functioning of the laws of karma – the notion of going out of existence in a mind-independent realm (*loke natthitā*) also ceases.

This teaching on suffering and its cessation thus draws out the fact that conditioned experience is governed by objective laws (Dependent Origination in its twelvefold form), while at the same time denying that this experience occurs in any objectively real world. In short, the text asserts conditioned experience as a middle way between philosophical realism and idealism: the objective reality of experiential conditioning is accepted, and yet this reality is not to be considered in terms of existence and non-existence in the world; that is to say, philosophical realism. The Buddha thus concludes the teaching by explaining Dependent Origination as a 'middle way' between the notions 'everything exists' and 'everything does not exist':

> 'Everything exists': this is one extreme, O Kaccāyana. 'Everything does not exist': this is the second extreme. Avoiding both extremes the Tathāgata teaches the Dhamma through the middle: from ignorance arise mental constructions, from constructions arises consciousness (and so on) . . . thus arises this entire mass of suffering. But with the complete and utter cessation of ignorance, mental constructions ceases, and with the cessation of constructions consciousness ceases (and so on) . . . thus ceases this entire mass of suffering.

The notions 'everything exists' and 'everything does not exist' appear to be two ways of understanding a person's experience: either by the theory that the totality of individual experience has an existence beyond a person's mind, and so is objectively real, or that the things of experience do not exist in an objectively real sense, and so exist only in the mind. Since this explication of Dependent Origination as the middle ground between philosophical realism and idealism is the only text actually cited by name in Nāgārjuna's *Mūlamadhyamaka-kārikā*, his philosophy should elaborate a similar middle way between realism and idealism. We should therefore expect Nāgārjuna to follow the

Buddha in negating philosophical realism without asserting idealism, thus pointing towards the ultimate ineffability of reality.

Nāgārjuna's Verses on the Middle Way

Since next to nothing is known about Nāgārjuna it is difficult to be sure of the authenticity of the many works attributed to him. But his authorship of the most important and famous exposition of his philosophy, the *Mūlamadhyamaka-kārikā*, is beyond doubt. Building on the Buddha's insights into the nature of experience, and its radical expression in the Perfection of Understanding literature, in this work Nāgārjuna fashions arguments to prove the philosophical impossibility of the world as an objective reality. This basic perspective is indicated when Nāgārjuna refers to the Buddha's teaching to Kātyāyana (P: Kaccāyana):

> Intrinsic identity and extrinsic identity, being and non-being: who sees these does not see reality in accordance with the Buddha's teaching. In the discourse to Kātyāyana, both existence and non-existence were rejected by the Blessed One through his perception of being and non-being. (XV.6–7)

This verse introduces the basic elements in Nāgārjuna's thought: intrinsic identity (*sva-bhāva*, literally 'own-being') and extrinsic identity (*para-bhāva*, literally 'other being'), being (or 'a being' in the sense of an individual existent: *bhāva*) and non-being (or 'a non-being/non-existent': *abhāva*), existence (*asti*) and non-existence (*nāsti*). The rejection of these ideas, and citation of the Discourse to Kātyāyana, suggests that Nāgārjuna's philosophy develops the constructed realism of the Buddha. But a close examination shows that although this is indeed the case, this is achieved by employing an entirely different method: through philosophical argumentation, Nāgārjuna does not merely articulate the Buddha's distinction between reality as it is and reality as it is perceived, but also attempts to prove that perceived reality is philosophically impossible.

The text is thus made up of a series of arguments which negate the objective reality of such things as causality (I), time (II, XIX), the sense faculties and their objects (III), karma (VIII, XVII), suffering (XII), bondage and liberation (XVI) and even Buddhist teachings such as the Four Noble Truths (XXIV). These various critiques are based on a single, simple idea: that the individual identities of things are mental constructs, which means that things do not have their 'own-being', this being instead supplied by the thoughts of the observer. The identification of one object as 'table' and another as 'chair', for example, is a mental construction which does not denote any essential core of the things beyond the observer's thoughts. Nāgārjuna points out that the same idea applies to anything which depends upon causes and conditions: all identities refer not to 'own-being' – some essence which objects really are or possess – but are ideas imposed upon the coming together of different causal factors. This reasoning leads Nāgārjuna to the radical conclusion that the existence or non-existence of anything is logically impossible:

> The origination of intrinsic identity from conditions and causes is not logical, for an intrinsic identity created from conditions and causes would be constructed. But how could intrinsic identity be constructed? Intrinsic identity must be unconstructed, and without dependence on something else. But in the absence of intrinsic identity, how could there be extrinsic identity? For extrinsic identity is said to be the intrinsic identity of another being. And apart from intrinsic and extrinsic identity, how could 'being' be possible? For being is only established when there is intrinsic and extrinsic identity. But if being is not established, non-being cannot be established, since people describe non-being as a change in being. (XV.1–5)

Nāgārjuna here draws out the deeper implications of the fact that the individual identity of any causal product is a mental construct. It must therefore lack intrinsic identity, its 'own-being' – something about it that is not a label attached to it from without. But if nothing within the world of causality can have its own, inherent identity, it follows that nothing can logically exist, for without individual identity what can actually be said to exist? And if no individual thing in the realm of causality can exist, it means that non-existence also makes no sense, since the two concepts are mutually dependent. It also follows, inevitably, that concepts such as time (IX.6) must be an illusion. Thus the experiential world of existence and non-existence in the mind-independent reality of space-time is logically impossible.

The negation of non-being indicates that this philosophy is not intended to be nihilistic. Indeed, rather than assert that the mentally constructed world is non-existent, Nāgārjuna's point is rather that the understanding of the world in terms of existence and non-existence is misconceived. Against opponents who accuse him of nihilism, Nāgārjuna counters with the point that philosophical realism is really nihilistic. The argument here is that if a thing were to be ontologically rather than nominally real – to be actually 'out there' regardless of its identification by a perceiver – it would have to be outside the nexus of causality, for only when a thing is not a product of causes and conditions could it be said to have an identity that is not constructed. Nāgārjuna thus argues that philosophical realism negates the causal world and the Buddhist teachings about it:

> If you perceive the true reality of individual existents in terms of intrinsic identity, you must believe that individual existents are beyond causes and conditions. You deny cause, effect, the agent, his activity and action, as well as arising, cessation and karmic retribution. (XXIV.16–17)

Nāgārjuna's rejection of an ontological understanding of conditioned reality means that he must also reject any interpretation of Dependent Origination based on philosophical realism:

> Since the existence of individual things which lack intrinsic identity is not found, the statement 'When this exists, that comes into being' does not pertain. (I.10)

Nāgārjuna here cites the formulaic summary of Dependent Origination ('When this exists, that comes into being') alongside his conclusion that the reality of things considered in terms of intrinsic identity cannot be proved. If so, his point is not that Dependent Origination is wrong, but rather that it should not be taken in a philosophically realistic sense. Nāgārjuna instead claims that Dependent Origination deals with the causal world of conceptual construction:

> We assert that Dependent Origination is emptiness: it is conditioned conceptualization, and that alone is the middle way. Since no *dharma* is found to arise without a cause, there is no *dharma* that is not empty. (XXIV.18–19)

The assertion that Dependent Origination is emptiness (*śūnyatā*) or 'conditioned conceptualization' (*prajñaptir upādāya*) implies that causality involves factors of experience (states of mind, sensations, concepts and so on) rather than substances. And if all that is conditioned is entirely nominal, it follows that *dharmas*, the ultimate entities of the Abhidharma analysis, are not ontologically real. In both the Perfection of Understanding literature and Nāgārjuna's thought, the rhetoric of 'emptiness' (*śūnyatā*) is not a mere device to indicate that an existent lacks some quality (is 'empty' of it): the implication of an entity being 'empty' is that it lacks substance, is not ontologically real, and so is just like an apparition or mirage. If 'things' do not actually 'exist', as discrete, substantial objects in a mind-independent realm of space-time, the world of conditioned experience must therefore be like an illusion or dream:

> Arising, enduring and then dissolution are said to be just like an illusion, a dream, or a city of Gandharvas. (VII.34)
>
> Form, sound, taste, touch, smell and mental objects: these six objects of passion, aversion and delusion are conceptualizations. All forms, sounds, tastes, touches, smells and mental objects are like a city of Gandharvas, a sparkle of dust in the air, a dream. (XXIII.7–8)

These statements do not deny the reality of the various aspects of experience *per se*, but instead indicate they are not real in an ontological sense, as is normally presumed. The phenomenal world of *saṃsāra* thus consists of the causal continuity of conceptual construction, the cessation of which is Nirvana, the exact opposite of all that is conditioned:

> Not abandoned, not attained, not cut off, not eternal, not a cessation, non-arisen: this is said to be Nirvana.
>
> The teacher advised the abandoning of being and non-being, therefore it is not proper to say that Nirvana is either being or non-being. (XXV.3,10)

At the core of Nāgārjuna's philosophy is this understanding of two modes of experience: the conventional reality of conditioning and causality, in which everything is conceptually real and lacks intrinsic identity, existence and non-existence; and the opposite of this, in which there is no such conceptualization, and hence also no existence or non-existence. Nāgārjuna terms these two experiential states the 'two realities':

> The Dharma instruction of the Buddhas depends on two realities (*dve satye*): the conventional reality of the world, and the reality that accords with the supreme purpose. Those who do not understand the difference between these two realities do not understand the profound truth of the Buddha's teaching. (XXIV.8–9)

Comprehending the difference between *saṃsāra* and Nirvana is crucial to Nāgārjuna's philosophy. Rather than take the former in a philosophically realistic sense, as ongoing reincarnation in an objectively real world of space-time, Nāgārjuna develops the Buddha's point that it consists of modes of experience, and so is only epistemologically rather than ontologically distinct from Nirvana. The notion of an epistemological rather than substantial difference between Nirvana and *saṃsāra* helps explain Nāgārjuna's most difficult statement:

> There is no deviation between *saṃsāra* and Nirvana, and no deviation between Nirvana and *saṃsāra*. Nirvana and *saṃsāra* share the same threshold: there is not even the slightest difference between them. (XXV.19–20)

If Nirvana is not an actual stopping of ongoing existence in the mind-independent reality of *saṃsāra*, and if there is therefore no separate reality into which a person disappears upon release, there can be no ontological distinction between the two realities. Since both Nirvana and *saṃsāra* cannot be said to exist or not exist, at the level of ontological analysis they are therefore indistinguishable. This epistemological rather than ontological distinction of Nirvana and *saṃsāra* is, of course, equivalent to the Buddha's teaching of liberation in the present life, according to which Nirvana is not a disappearance from the realm of existence into a transcendent state beyond it, but rather a realization of ineffability in the present. Exactly this understanding is stated by Nāgārjuna as a way of introducing his identification of Nirvana and *saṃsāra*:

> Beyond death, it is not said that the Blessed One exists, does not exist, both exists and does not, or neither exists nor does not exist. Even while the Blessed One remains it cannot be said that he exists, does not exist, both exists and does not, or neither exists nor does not exist. (XXV.17–18)

The conjunction of verses 17–18 and 19–20 in chapter XXV suggests that the ineffability of the Buddha is Nāgārjuna's ultimate riposte to philosophical realism: the idea that the Buddha's liberated reality is not a separate realm or place (v.17–18) implies that there is no ontological difference between *saṃsāra* and Nirvana (v.19–20). To make this point absolutely clear chapter XXV of the *Mūlamadhyamaka-kārikā* concludes by reiterating the point that there are only two experiential realities – conceptual proliferation and its quiescence – and no such thing as the *dharma*s of the Abhidharma or the realm of space-time in which they are held to abide:

> The auspicious (*śiva*) quiescence of all acquisition and conceptual proliferation: the Buddha did not teach any *dharma* to anyone, anywhere. (XXV.24)

Nirvana is therefore not an escape from this world, some kind of merging into a Nirvana realm as imagined by meditative realists, or an unconditioned *dharma* as held by Abhidharma thinkers, but rather an experiential reality in which the delusion of existence and non-existence ceases:

> But those dullards who see the existence and non-existence of individual things, they cannot perceive the auspicious (*śiva*) quiescence of all objectification. (V.8)

This clarification of the relationship between Nirvana and conditioned experience explains the underlying soteriological purpose of the *Mūlamadhyamaka-kārikā*. It is significant that Nāgārjuna describes the cessation of conceptualization as an auspicious state: this is perhaps the only suggestion of a positive religious understanding in the entire text, which indicates that Nirvana is a true and meaningful reality rather than a mere nothing. When understood in the context of his arguments against ontology, Nāgārjuna's point is that philosophical realism is not just an intellectual error, but a deeply ingrained cognitive disposition that maintains suffering.

Beyond their bold statement of anti-realist Buddhist philosophy, Nāgārjuna's verses on the middle way are presented as a remedy to a person's disastrously misconceived understanding of reality. The direct, aphoristic, form of the verses is intended to draw a person into a profound contemplation of reality, and so function as a sort of philosophical shock therapy. Nāgārjuna's negations of ontology must thus be considered an attempt to induce an intuitive sense of the Buddha's perspective in the thoughts of the reader or listener. The final aim of this more philosophically advanced formulation of the Buddha's teaching is thus to point the way out of all views and conceptualization and advance a person towards liberation:

> Since all existents are empty, where, of what, which and from what will views concerning eternalism and so on arise? I bow down to Gautama, who out of compassion taught the true Dharma for the abandonment of all views. (XXVII.29–30)

Representation Only

The negation of Nāgārjuna and his followers was meant to undermine the philosophical foundations of Abhidharma thought. For Abhidharma thinkers, however, the doctrine of emptiness must have seemed a perverse exercise in nihilism. But the differing perspectives of the Ābhidharmikas and Mādhyamikas do not exhaust all possible ways of approaching Buddhist reductionism and its anti-realistic negation. It is possible to imagine, for example, that Nāgārjuna's anti-realism appealed to some Buddhist thinkers without leading them to abandon their prior scholastic interests in the Abhidharma. Perhaps scholars of this inclination, although impressed by Nāgārjuna's radicalism, preferred rather to present anti-realist thought more positively, in a way that avoided the anti-scholastic agenda raised by the *via negativa* dialectics of the Mādhyamikas.

It can thus be supposed that some thinkers decided to elaborate the conceptual simplicity inherent in a system that negates rather than asserts. For Nāgārjuna's reduction of Buddhist thought to two realities – constructed/conceptual and unconstructed/non-conceptual – is hardly informative, even if essentially faithful to the Buddha. For scholar-monks who wished to articulate this basic understanding in more positive terms, the Abhidharma tradition, with its intricate analysis of individual existence in *saṃsāra*, was the ideal resource. Why should the Abhidharma analysis not be utilized without subscribing to its philosophical realism, in order to form a clearer picture of constructed reality and its cessation?

A school of this kind emerged in the form of the Vijñaptimātra or Yogācāra tradition. Since the latter term denotes a person devoted to spiritual practice (*yoga*), its association with a school of thought indicates that these thinkers were deeply interested in meditation.

Indeed, early portions of the *Yogācāra-bhūmi*, a large and heterogeneous work assembled in the fourth century AD, and one of the school's foundational texts, propose a solution to the problem of how a meditator can emerge from the unconscious meditative state of 'cessation' (*nirodha*). It is claimed that this is due to the fact that a person has a substratum consciousness (*ālaya-vijñāna*) – a sort of subconsciousness similar to the Sautrāntika idea of a stream of consciousness – within which all karmic impressions are contained, and from which new states of consciousness and experience can be activated.

While this scholastic interest in the philosophy of meditation also suggests an Abhidharmic background, the term *vijñapti-mātra*, 'representation only', indicates an interest in anti-realist philosophy, a fact supported by the other names of the tradition: 'mind-only' (*citta-mātra*) and 'the doctrine of consciousness' (*vijñāna-vāda*). An anti-realist influence can indeed be seen in another foundational text of the tradition, the *Saṃdhi-nirmocana Sūtra*, also composed or assembled in approximately the fourth century AD. This text begins with *prajñā-pāramitā* themes before describing a third turning of the wheel of Dharma (Chapter 7), to supplement the first two turnings (the canonical teachings and the perfection of understanding literature). Since this Sūtra supplements (in Chapter 6) the anti-realist idea of emptiness with the doctrine that all *dharma*s can be understood in terms of three 'aspects', or 'realities' (*svabhāva*), only one of which is the lack of intrinsic identity (*svabhāva*), its composers appear to have believed they were advancing Buddhist thought into a new phase.

The various starting points of the emerging tradition were brought together in the works of Asaṅga and his half-brother Vasubandhu (author of the *Abhidharmakośa-bhāṣya*), with perhaps some contribution from a certain Maitreyanātha. The texts attributed to Asaṅga include the *Abhidharma-samuccaya*, which presents the scholastic thought of the Abhidharma from an anti-realist perspective, but a more succinct and influential exposition of the school is contained in the works of Vasubandhu. Besides his commentary on the *Madhyānta-vibhāga-kārikā* ('Verses on Distinguishing the Extremes from the Middle', attributed to Maitreyanātha), Vasubandhu's Yogācāra works include the *Viṃśatikā* ('Twenty verses') and its commentary, the *Triṃśikā* ('Thirty verses') and the *Trisvabhāva-nirdeśa* ('Exposition of the three realities'). Vasubandhu's scholastic background is evident in all these works, especially the *Triṃśikā*, which begins with an Abhidharma-style analysis of three modes of consciousness:

> Metaphorical uses of the terms 'self' and *dharma* are multifaceted, and function with regard to the transformation of consciousness. This transformation is threefold: resultant, that called 'thinking', and the representation of an object. Therein, resultant is the consciousness termed 'substratum', which contains all seeds. (v.1-2)

Since the seeds (*bīja*) mentioned here are the mental impressions created by intentional acts, the substratum (*ālaya*) or resultant consciousness is therefore the sum total of a person's karma. These seeds continue in a subconscious mode until eventually yielding their experiential retribution, a process which Vasubandhu likens to a torrent of water (v.4). Exactly how a volitional act is connected to its retribution is explained as follows:

> Consciousness, indeed, consists of karmic seeds: its transformation is instigated by the mutual influence (of the seeds), by which means this and that mental construction (*vikalpa*) is generated. When a prior karmic result has disappeared, karmic impressions, along with the latent impression of conceptual duality, generate another karmic result. (vv.18–19)

The substratum consciousness is therefore the essential aspect of individual existence in *saṃsāra*, being that by which experiential continuity is maintained. Vasubandhu also explains that it must cease in order for liberation to be attained:

> Its devolution (*vyāvṛtti*) occurs in Arhantship. The consciousness termed 'mind' functions in dependence on it, and is supported by it; its essence is thinking. (v.5)

Although morally neutral (just like the substratum consciousness), 'mind' or 'thinking', the second transformation of consciousness, is the source of – or an ultimate point of reference for – the deluded view of self (v.6). The substratum consciousness is not only that which enables individual continuity, therefore, but is also that which allows for a person's sense of subjectivity. The third transformation of consciousness is objective experience:

> This (mind) is the second transformation (of consciousness); the

> third (transformation) is the perception of six kinds of objects, which is either morally good, bad, or neither. (v.8)

Objective awareness or the 'representation of a sense object' (v.2: *vijñaptir viṣayasya*) therefore occurs at the end of an entirely subjective process of mental transformation. Vasubandhu claims that the experience which finally results from the transformation of a person's karmic seeds exists only in the mind, and has no external reality:

> This transformation of consciousness is (a process of) construction, but what is constructed by this (process) does not exist: therefore all this is merely representation (*vijñapti-mātraka*). (v.17)

The karmic process thus generates new experiences which are no more real than an illusion or a dream. This direct statement of Buddhist anti-realism is given a lengthy treatment in Vasubandhu's *Viṃśatikā* and its commentary, the latter containing his major arguments for the non-existence of the external world. Vasubandhu first deals with three key objections to the idea that all experience does not refer to an objectively real world (v.2): that there appears to be an objective order operating in the apparently external world of experience ('restriction as to time and place'); that experiences are shared and so cannot take place in a single mind ('non-restriction to a single continuum of consciousness'); and that the things experienced in dream have no effect (no 'performing of a function') in the real world.

Vasubandhu responds to the first and last of these objections by pointing out that even in a dream things appear to follow an objective order, so that real effects can be achieved (such as the experience of sexual pleasure). With regard to the second objection, he refers (v.4.) to the Buddhist belief in hell, according to which guardians of hell inflict pain on its denizens, as a result of their bad karma. The argument here is that since an individual is born in hell to experience intense pain, as a result of bad karma, then how can the guardians of hell, who inflict rather than receive pain, be real? Vasubandhu thus concludes that they are a mind-created manifestation of individual karma, and if so it follows that objective delusions can be shared.

These arguments are not, perhaps, convincing to those who do not subscribe to basic Buddhist beliefs. But the point that dream experiences appear to have a convincing representation of an objective order is important. For if a dream feels real, why should an enhanced sort of dream-like experience, in which the representation of an apparently objective order is felt to be even more real, not be possible? Vasubandhu thus raises the possibility that the difference between dreaming and waking experience might be one of order rather than kind, and so prepares the way for more subtle arguments against the objective reality of the world. Chief among these is his argument against atomism.

Vasubandhu claims that the notion of an atom as an irreducibly small piece of matter with spatial extension is illogical. He explains that the atomic view is based on the idea that tiny bits of matter connect up with other tiny bits of matter, a process of aggregation that eventually yields the manifold things of the world. But for this to be the case an atom cannot be an irreducibly small thing as claimed, for the formation of atomic aggregates requires each atom to have logically distinct spatial points, which come into contact with the logically distinct spatial points of other atoms. Vasubandhu imagines an atom connected to six other atoms (v.12), and states that in such a case the atom must have six parts. Since an atom can be logically analyzed into even smaller pieces, it cannot be irreducibly tiny. This leads to the conclusion that an irreducibly small substance must have no spatial extension, but if so, how could the objective world of material forms be possible? For the aggregation of things without spatial extension is illogical.

This argument against substance supports Vasubandhu's thesis that the objective world is an illusion. But the affirmation of consciousness in this way does not mean that Vasubandhu's *vijñapti-mātra* can be reduced to simple idealism. For a basic point of the *Triṃśikā* is that the ongoing transformation of consciousness, which consists of the projection of experience from karmic seeds, ceases with a person's liberation (v.5). The cessation of consciousness in liberation does not mean that the system ends in nihilism either, for the doctrine of three aspects or realities (*sva-bhāva*) grounds these ideas in an affirmation of what is ultimately real. The *Triṃśikā* explains the three aspects as follows:

> Whatever 'thing' (*vastu*) is constructed by whatever (process of) construction, that is merely the constructed aspect, which does not exist. The dependent aspect is mental construction (*vikalpaḥ*), which is (the process of) coming into being through causes. The

> perfected (aspect) is the (dependent aspect's) state of being void, always, of the preceding (the constructed aspect). (v.20–21)

What is here termed the 'constructed aspect' (*parikalpita svabhāva*) is the non-existent illusion of external objects of experience, which is produced by a real process of mental construction termed the 'dependent aspect' (in other words the transformation of consciousness from subconscious karmic seeds). But the constructed and dependent aspects cannot be completely distinguished, since apart from the definition of v.21, the *Triṃśika* also defines mental construction as the entire 'transformation of consciousness' (v.17), comprising karmic seeds as well as the illusion of objective experience, and which thus includes the subconscious substratum, mind (subjectivity) and the representation of objects (i.e. the three transformations of consciousness). Moreover, it is also stated (v.3) that the substratum consciousness – the essential part of the dependent aspect – consists of 'subconscious representations of mental states such as anger etc.' (*asaṃvidita-kopādi-sthāna-vijñaptika*). This implies that the constructed and dependent aspect are closely related and not substantially distinct: the former is the inevitable result of the latter, and only differs from it in being the fully known, objectively projected phase in the process of mental transformation or construction.

This understanding of karmic continuity, in which the largely subconscious and subjective functioning of consciousness is more real than the objective world of experience, is a bold statement of Buddhist anti-realism, one that subverts common-sense assumptions about the human condition. But it is not a final statement of the way things ultimately are, for Vasubandhu reformulates the doctrine of emptiness in order to undermine the ontological reality of the dependent aspect. A trace of this can be seen in v.21 of the *Triṃśikā*, which defines the perfected aspect as the dependent aspect's 'state of being void' (*rahitatā*) of the constructed aspect. To be empty of the constructed aspect implies that the dependent aspect is ultimately devoid of the structuring of experience into subject and object. But since the very notion of a thing's existence depends on the duality between subject and object, it follows that the dependent aspect, when seen as it really is, is not an existing thing, and so can be nothing other than the perfected aspect.

In other words once the reality of the constructed aspect is negated, it follows that the dependent aspect must also be negated, as an individual existent, and if so the dependent aspect must ultimately be nothing other than the perfected aspect. The same point is suggested in v.19 of the *Triṃśikā*, which states that the transformation of subconscious karmic seeds into conditioned experience – the process of change that is the dependent aspect – depends on the 'latent impression of perceptual duality' (*grāha-dvaya-vāsana*). It follows from this that the dependent aspect cannot function as a separate thing apart from the constructed aspect of objective experience: the negation of the one implies the negation of the other, thus indicating that the process of karmic continuity is ultimately unreal, and so identical with the perfected aspect. These ideas are similarly stated in the *Trisvabhāva-nirdeśa* as follows:

> That which appears is the dependent (aspect, which is so called) because its state of activity depends on causes; the manner of its appearance is the constructed (aspect, which is so called) because of its state of being merely imaginary. The perfected reality ought to be understood as that appearing thing's (the dependent aspect) constant state of not being found to exist, because of its state of not being otherwise. Therein, what appears? The construction of the non-existent. How does it appear? In terms of duality. What, therefore, is its non-existence? The nondual ultimate reality of phenomena therein. (vv.2–4)

The conclusion of this complex statement suggests an identity between the perfected aspect and the dependent aspect, for the former is defined as the nondual ultimate reality of phenomena (*advaya-dharmatā*) in the latter (*tatra*), which is earlier termed the 'construction of the non-existent' (*asat-kalpa*). In other words, the dependent aspect, a process of karmic continuity that is more or less completely subconscious, becomes manifest ('appears') in experience as the constructed aspect, which is the illusion of objective experience. But the subconscious karmic basis of the illusion is not a truly existent thing, and so is not distinct from the liberated state, the non-dual ultimate reality of phenomena. The three aspects are therefore identical, an idea stated as follows in the *Trisvabhāva-nirdeśa*:

> Because of its state of essentially being the non-existence of duality, the constructed (aspect) should not be considered categorically distinct from the perfected (aspect), (for the latter) is the essence of non-duality. (v.19)

> Because of its state of essentially being that which lacks existence, the perfected (aspect) should not be considered categorically distinct from the aspect termed 'dependent', (for the latter) is non-existent according to the mode of its appearance. (v.20)
>
> Because it lacks essence according to the mode of its appearance, the dependent (aspect) should not be considered categorically distinct from the perfected (aspect), (for the latter) is the essence of non-existent duality. (v.21)
>
> The three aspects are each categorically non-dual and ungraspable: because of the non-being of (the constructed aspect), because of (the dependent aspect's) not being like that, and because (the perfected aspect) is the essence of that non-being. (v.26)

Although an extremely difficult formulation, Vasubandhu's overall presentation of the three aspects can be more simply understood as an elaboration of Nāgārjuna's thinking on Nirvana and *saṃsāra*. The idea of ultimate reality as an ineffability beyond ontology is equivalent to Nāgārjuna's understanding of Nirvana, whereas Vasubandhu expands Nāgārjuna's discourse on conventional reality – or the process of Dependent Origination – into conscious and subconscious aspects. Both thinkers also identify conditioned continuity in *saṃsāra* with the ultimate, liberated, reality through the doctrine of emptiness. Vasubandhu, however, asserts this in more positive terms, primarily through his general preference for assertion rather than negation: this is particularly apparent in the idea of three 'realities' (*sva-bhāva*), a formulation which is obviously meant to go against Nāgārjuna's negation of intrinsic identity (also termed *sva-bhāva*). Thus the statement of ineffability which concludes the *Triṃśikā* is stronger than anything in the *Mūlamadhyamaka-kārikā*. Vasubandhu states that the 'devolution' of the 'basis' – that is to say, the cessation of the substratum consciousness – is a state of 'supramundane cognition beyond consciousness and perception' (v.29), a liberated condition which he defines as follows:

> That very essence is beyond, unthinkable, good and constant. It is the blissful body of release, and is called the *dharma* of the great sage. (v.30)

Further Developments in Mythic Buddhism

Both the Madhyamaka and Vijñaptimātra systems emerged from the Buddha's insight that reality perceived is different from reality as it actually is. But two other major streams of Buddhist thought and practice existed from the earliest times: the reductionistic realism that developed into the various Abhidharma schools, and the meditative realism that was initially associated with the Buddha's teachers, and was subsequently elaborated into the mystical cessationist and Pudgalavāda traditions. The philosophical and spiritual heritage of Indian Buddhism consisted of developments within these three streams: anti-realism, reductionistic realism and meditative realism/personalism. But a fourth stream was probably more important than them all, for its influence pervaded the Buddhist world beyond the virtuoso concerns of Buddhist gnostics. This was the mythic Buddhism which, based on the legend of the Buddha's life as a Bodhisattva, came to include such developments as the Mahāyāna visions of multiple Buddhas of the present and their blissful abodes.

Although lacking the philosophical sophistication of the other varieties of gnostic Buddhism, mythic Buddhism formed a broader sort of religiosity, one that included such things as devotional activity at the apotropaic and karmic levels. At its higher, gnostic, levels, mythic Buddhists were less interested in articulating philosophical truths than in speculating about the superhuman nature of a Buddha, with all the miraculous abilities this was thought to involve, and aspiring to realize such an elevated spiritual state. Already in the pre-Aśokan period, mythic speculation had advanced as far as the idea that the Buddha's superhuman powers included the ability to attain virtual immortality. For the Pali *Mahā-parinibbāna Sutta*, a text rich in mythic elements, has the Buddha inform his disciple Ānanda that he could remain in existence until the end of the current aeon, if only this were to be requested. Unfortunately Ānanda did not realize the significance of this statement, and the moment passed without the request being made.

This episode is a relatively straightforward defence of the Buddha as a mythic hero with immense supernatural powers: the fact that the historical Buddha had actually died, when he could have lived on indefinitely, was blamed on Ānanda. The necessity of making such excuses inevitably decreased over time, and at a later point, when the

Buddha legend was the central item in the imaginary world of Indian Buddhism, it became possible for mythic Buddhists to go as far as to deny the Buddha's death. The *Saddharma-puṇḍarīka Sūtra* ('Discourse on the Lotus of the true Dharma') thus claims that the Buddha's death was an example of his skill in means, since it exemplified the major themes of the canonical teachings (impermanence and suffering). In claiming that the Buddha remains in the world until the end of the aeon, the Lotus Sūtra therefore extended, and even corrected, the mythic ideas of the *Mahā-parinibbāna Sutta*.

The Lotus Sūtra also went much further than the mainstream ideas, and even further than most Mahāyānists, by claiming that the goal of mainstream Buddhism – the Nirvana achieved by a Buddhist saint – is only a provisional stage on the path to complete awakening, there being only one Buddhist path (*eka-yāna*) to the goal of complete Buddhahood. Although the Lotus Sūtra does not explain how all Buddhists are on a path leading to Buddhahood, even without realizing it, its tentative answer to this problem set the agenda for a further trend within mythic Buddhism: the simile of a poor man who does not realize a valuable jewel has been stitched into his clothing suggests that every person has the innate spiritual potential to become a Buddha. Although not further explored in the Lotus Sūtra, this idea inspired a further trend in mythic Buddhism: the 'Buddha-nature' (*tathāgata-garbha*) tradition.

The *Tathāgata-garbha Sūtra*, probably composed in the third century AD, uses a number of simple images, similar to that of the jewel hidden in a poor man's clothing, to show that a Buddha abides within every person, such as the description of a Buddha image within, seated in meditation. In a particularly magical part of the text, lotuses are said to emerge from the pavilion in which the Buddha is meditating, rising into the sky to create a canopy, with a seated Buddha, cross-legged, emitting hundreds of thousands of rays of light from the calyx of each lotus. Although the petals then putrefy and become disgusting, the Buddhas continue to emit light, which the Buddha explains as follows:

> Sons of good family, just as these unsightly, putrid, disgusting and no longer pleasant lotuses, supernaturally created by the Tathāgata, and the pleasing and beautiful form of a Tathāgata sitting cross-legged in each of the calyxes of these lotuses, emitting hundreds

> of thousands of rays of light, are such that when they are recognized by gods and humans, these latter then pay homage and also show reverence [to them], in the same way, sons of good family, also the Tathāgata, the Honourable One and Perfectly Awakened One, perceives with his insight, knowledge and tathāgata-vision that all the various sentient beings are encased in myriads of defilements, such as desire, anger, misguidedness, longing and ignorance. And, sons of good family, he perceives that inside sentient beings encased in defilements sit many tathāgatas, cross-legged and motionless, endowed like myself with a tathāgata's knowledge and vision.

The idea of a Buddha within is a powerful statement of the idea that a spiritual aspirant need only be rid of spiritual defilement to achieve awakening. Although without much intellectual sophistication, the text presumes philosophical realism: the image of a Buddha abiding inside the calyx of a lotus suggests that the Tathāgata within is an entity within a person's physical being. The text also implies that the Buddha within is a transmigrating substance, one that has always been contained in a person's individual incarnations. This is not to say that it is a sort of soul or self, as in the Hindu tradition, for the Upaniṣadic *ātman* is an impersonal, abstract essence, whereas the *tathāgata-garbha* is a fully formed Buddha, conceived in terms of the mythic idea of a superhuman somatic state. This ultimate religious goal must thus be understood as another expression of the eternalist tendency within mythic Buddhism: to become a Buddha with all its supernatural majesty, power and longevity.

A mythic direction different from the philosophical realism of the *Saddharma-puṇḍarīka* and *Tathāgata-garbha Sūtra*s is contained in the earlier *Lokānuvartana Sūtra*. The extant Chinese and Tibetan translations of this text, as well as the surviving Sanskrit fragments, have a proto-*prajñāpāramitā* orientation: roughly half of it is devoted to stating the fact that *dharma*s are empty of 'own-being'. This fits its ascription to the Pūrvaśaila sub-sect of the Mahāsāṃghikas, a group among whom perfection of understanding ideas appear to have flourished. But the text also applies the idea of emptiness to less abstract themes, so that all acts of Buddhas are said to be just a show: although they appear to eat, wash, sleep and teach, they abide in a 'supramundane' (*lokottara*) state beyond appearance. This doctrine of transcendence in the here and now is also equated with the Buddha's supernatural body, said to be golden, ever-clothed and with uncut black hair.

This obscure Sūtra thus brings mythic ideas within the orb of anti-realist/proto-*prajñāpāramitā* thought. Its anti-realist application of mythic ideas is further extended to include the historical Buddha's career as a Bodhisattva, when it is stated that ever since his encounter with the former Buddha Dīpaṃkara, the Bodhisattva had been 'devoid of thirst'; this statement assumes the Bodhisattva's liberation at the very beginning of his mythic career, and so suggests that all rebirths ending in the life of Gautama were a supernatural display that did not really happen. An anti-realist reading of the historical Buddha's career would seem to negate, rather than merely adapt, mythic Buddhism, and if so the *Lokānuvartana Sūtra* can perhaps be understood as a polemic against the realistic presuppositions of the Buddha myth. This was, perhaps, a forerunner to a similar critique of early anti-realist Mahāyāna: the *Aṣṭasāhasrikā-prajñāpāramitā Sūtra*, for example, constantly criticizes those who take the Buddha myth literally, as if resolving for awakening, accumulating merit, progressing towards awakening and then realizing it actually denote real happenings in an objectively real world.

The idea of the historical Buddha as a supernatural emanation of an already awakened being was developed further in later anti-realist circles. The *Mahāyānasūtrālaṃkāra* ('Adornment of the Mahāyāna Sūtras'), attributed to the Vijñaptimātra thinkers Maitreyanātha and/or Asaṅga, thus articulates a doctrine of three Buddha-bodies, as an attempt to make sense of three levels of reality comprehended by a Buddha, albeit from an anti-realist perspective: his awakened state of cognition, the supernatural somatic reality he realizes upon awakening, and his mundane physical form which is born and dies. In the *Mahāyānasūtrālaṃkāra*, these are termed *dharma-kāya*, *saṃbhoga-kāya* and *nirmāṇa-kāya* respectively: the 'Dharma body', 'enjoyment body' and 'emanation body'.

The first two of these bodies restate standard Buddhist ideas. In the discourses of the Pali canon, the term *dhamma-kāya* is applied to the Buddha metaphorically: in explaining that his followers should refer to themselves as his 'sons', since they have been 'born' from his Dhamma, it follows that the Buddha has the 'Dhamma as his body', so to speak. But the term *kāya* ('body') can also be used in the sense of 'category' or 'collection', and in post-canonical Sarvāstivādin literature the term *dharma-kāya* refers not to a body, but rather to the 'collection (*kāya*) of qualities (*dharma*) unique to a Buddha'. The term seems to have both meanings in early and middle Mahāyāna sūtras, where it is used to denote the collection (*kāya*) of qualities or teachings (*dharma*) of the Buddha, or else it is used metaphorically to equate such things with the Buddha (his 'body' in the sense of what is most important about him). Against this textual background it is not surprising to find that the term *dharma-kāya* has a metaphorical sense in the three-body theory of the *Mahāyānasūtrālaṃkāra*, where it is equated either with the realm of ultimate reality of phenomena (*dharma-dhātu*), or else the devolution of the substratum consciousness; that is to say, the state of awakening as termed in Vijñaptimātra thought.

Whereas the *dharma-kāya* is not literally a body as such, but is rather a designation for the indefinable state of cognition to which Buddhas awaken, the second body in the system refers to the supernatural body achieved by Buddhas, replete with its characteristic marks. The *Mahāyānasūtrālaṃkāra* explains that this body is termed the 'enjoyment body' (*saṃbhoga-kāya*) for two reasons: first because it is the individual reward of accomplishing Buddhahood, and so is the form in which the bliss of the Dharma is fully realized by a Buddha; and second because it is through this body that a Buddha brings about direct enjoyment of the Dharma for those beings abiding in their blissful Buddha fields. The final body in the scheme is the emanation body (*nirmāṇa-kāya*), of which numerous types can be created by Buddhas in order to help other beings accomplish spiritual fulfilment; such emanations are examples of a Buddha's skill in means, and include various categories of rebirth, including that in which a Bodhisattva might seem to attain Nirvana.

The Yogācāra scheme of three Buddha bodies achieves multiple aims. Its most basic function is to clarify thinking about the nature of Buddhas: Vasubandhu's commentary on the *Mahāyānasūtrālaṃkāra* states 'the entire collection of bodies of the Buddhas should be understood in terms of these three bodies', and so suggests a scholastic attempt to systematize the mass of Mahāyāna speculations on Buddhas, their supernatural abilities and modes of cognition. But the scheme was more than an attempt to provide a systematic Buddhology, for in developing the idea of emanation bodies, and placing this idea and that of supernatural enjoyment bodies below the cognitive goal of Vijñaptimātra thought, the scheme looks like an attempt to place anti-realist Buddhist thought at the heart of the diverse world of Indian Mahāyāna.

Tantra

Between the third and twelfth centuries AD, and especially from the eighth century onwards, Indian Buddhism was increasingly dominated by texts that came to be called 'Tantras'. These broadly Mahāyāna compositions are concerned not with explaining the nature of insight or understanding (*prajñā*), or even the various other Buddhas and Bodhisattvas that can be contacted in the present, but rather focus on a particular type of skill in means. The earliest Tantras use the expression 'mantra method' (*mantra-naya*) to define this skilful action, indicating their focus on magically potent formulas (*mantras*) which were believed to effect various worldly and spiritual ends. The earliest texts of this type are termed 'Action' (*kriyā*) Tantras, and are concerned with apotropaic aims such as protection, prosperity, the destruction of enemies and so on. For these purposes they came to present various mantras for use in rites conducted in front of elaborately patterned geometric diagrams painted on the ground (*maṇḍalas*), within which deities were to be visualized.

Spiritual goals increasingly dominated Tantric Buddhism in the texts which appeared after the Kriyā Tantras. Starting with the Caryā Tantras and continuing with the Yoga Tantras, between roughly the sixth and eighth centuries AD, visualization and ritualism were promoted as the most effective soteriological method. Both the Caryā and Yoga Tantras focus on the Buddha Vairocana, but outline visualizations and rituals dealing with four other cosmic Buddhas (Akṣobhya, Ratnasaṃbhava, Amitābha and Amoghasiddhi) and their retinues of supernatural beings (Bodhisattvas, goddesses and so on). Mahāyoga Tantras emerged out of the Yoga Tantras in roughly the eighth century, and focus on Akṣobhya, rather than Vairocana, as the central deity of the *maṇḍala*. These texts also introduce transgressive rites into Buddhism, such as the consumption of impure substances (alcohol, blood, urine, faeces and semen) and sexual rites, with the five cosmic Buddhas of the *maṇḍala* visualized in sexual union with female partners.

The rites described in such texts sometimes involve copulation with a partner and the ingestion of sexual fluids, both of which were included in the initiation rituals required for a person to undertake the Tantric systems of these texts. Transgressive practices became even more prominent in the Yoginī Tantras, which emerged in the final phase of Tantric composition beginning around the ninth century AD. These Tantras are so called because their rituals involve a *maṇḍala* dominated by female deities called Yoginīs (or *ḍākiṇīs*): wrathful and ferocious, decked in human and animal skins, wearing jewellery made of human bones and with garlands of severed heads, they are visualized drinking blood from human skulls while standing in sexual union with male deities of a similar appearance.

The composition of transgressive Mahāyoga and Yoginī Tantras indicates that some Buddhists in the early medieval period performed rituals incompatible with basic Buddhist values. But the transition to this strange state of affairs was subtle, involving gradual shifts over long stretches of time. Even before the advent of Tantra, some Mahāyāna texts had expanded the scope of skill in means to include morally improper acts, such as killing or lying, these being justified on the grounds that they could be spiritually beneficial in certain circumstances. Indian Buddhism had also never been entirely lacking in supernatural and apotropaic aspects, or visionary practices (as described in the visualizations of the canonical and Mahāyāna texts). The idea of protective chanting had also been elaborated in the Mahāyāna literature, in the form of strings of words (*dhāraṇīs*) believed to contain the essence of the Dharma in magically efficacious formulas. Such elements paved the way for the adoption of additional magical ideas and practices, and eventually transgressive elements.

As long as they satisfied the needs of wealthy patrons and secured the future of the Sangha, magical practices of some kind could be justified by appealing to the pragmatic Buddhist sensibility. But whereas this more or less explains Tantra at the institutional level, it is more difficult to understand how Tantric ritualism was adopted at the individual level of spiritual practice. Even if kings desired magical rituals to be performed for their benefit, why did Buddhist practitioners believe that the visualization of ferocious deities and the ingestion of faeces would advance a person more rapidly to the Mahāyāna goal of complete awakening? Why, from the middle of the first millennium AD, did Mahāyānists increasingly imagine their path as the Vajrayāna, the way (or 'vehicle', *yāna*) of the 'thunderbolt' (or 'diamond': *vajra*) that would quickly destroy all spiritual impediments?

A single explanation cannot be expected for an Indian Buddhist world which was highly diverse and localized. Instead, a number of diverse factors must have contributed to the advent of Buddhist Tantra, of which four can be broadly identified: the gradual broadening of apotropaic Buddhism in order to secure royal patronage; the pervasive influence of Hindu Tantrism; the adaptation of mythic Buddhism to the fragmented world of early medieval India; and the trauma of the Buddhist experience in this period. These forces, buttressed by the pragmatic tendency of Buddhists to adapt to social conditions, stimulated a long process of change which eventually resulted in an unexpected esoteric reformulation of the Dharma.

The shift towards Tantrism began simply enough, with the extension of certain apotropaic aspects of the Mahāyāna: the ritual canon was thus expanded, especially to meet the demands of kings in a period of feudal conflict. An important influence in this were Hindu Tantras, especially those devoted to the god Śiva, which codified the rituals by which kingship was imagined in divine terms. In Buddhist hands such ideas and rituals were adapted to the consecration of the king as a 'wheel-turning' (*cakra-vartin*) 'righteous king' (*dharma-rāja*). Although the Cakravartin was originally imagined in terms of a benevolent monarch establishing a polity based on Buddhist ethics, it was easily adapted to the feudal world of early medieval India, when the goal of kingship was to construct a political 'circle' (*maṇḍala*) of vassal states around the monarch's own central domain, in a fashion not entirely dissimilar to the ideal of kingship as imagined in canonical texts such as the Pali *Cakkavatti-sīhanāda Sutta*.

This pragmatic development had unintended consequences. Since the Cakravartin was originally a secular counterpart to the Buddha, being endowed with the same supernatural body replete with 32 marks, and hence a kind of spiritual figure within the secular domain, the Tantric adaptation of the idea placed the religious ideals of Buddhism within the range of apotropaic ritualism and kingship. Even if Buddhists did not initially draw the simple conclusion that apotropaic means could effect gnostic ends, the internalization of the entire ritual/mythic complex, as a new metaphor for the spiritual path, is easy to understand. For in the fractious world of early medieval India, old sources of Buddhist support had declined and the survival of the Sangha was in serious doubt: Buddhist communities began to disappear, and the disturbing possibility emerged that the Buddha's mission was drawing to a close.

Buddhist Tantra thus emerged in a Brahminic culture defined by relations of power, as a spiritual vehicle in which magical potency and protection were prominent. The Tantric adept was a self-styled spiritual Cakravartin at the centre of a mythic *maṇḍala* containing various deities – just as the medieval monarch claimed lordship over neighbouring kingdoms in the feudal *maṇḍala* surrounding him – whose powers could be controlled and redirected for the sake of protection and welfare, and ultimately the persistence of the Buddhist mission in the most difficult circumstances. In short, Buddhist spirituality was feudalized in the form of Tantra, which was imagined as a new means of sacralizing a fragmented world, in the first place so that a Buddhist monarch could rule it, but also so that a Buddhist adept could pursue Buddhist goals within it, both for himself and the community to which he belonged.

This was not the only response to the difficulties faced by the Buddhist Sangha at this time. Alongside institutional Tantra, the Buddhist trauma became manifest in an individualistic guise, in a new form of Buddhist sainthood: the Siddha ('accomplished one'). The origins of Buddhist Siddhas are poorly understood, although inspiration appears to have come from wizards (or warlocks: *vidyā-dhara*, 'wielders of magical power') and various ascetic followers of Śiva, such as the Kāpālikas ('skull-bowl bearers') and Pāśupatas ('followers of Śiva, the Lord of animals'): in Indian lore, all such figures are associated with the fringes of the civilized world, frequenting such places as cremation grounds and tribal centres to pursue their nefarious ends. It was the Siddhas who developed the more antinomian aspects of Buddhist Tantra, drawn primarily from – or at least inspired by – Śaiva Tantras, and expressed in the Mahāyoga and Yoginī Tantras as well as various other genres of Tantric literature.

As a social phenomenon the Buddhist Siddhas can therefore be explained as a consequence of Buddhist disenfranchisement: as old sources of patronage disappeared, and new regional centres of power emerged, the Buddhist elite of defunct communities began to fashion a novel means of maintaining the Dharma in a new world. The sense of cultural collapse thus led some to move beyond the disappearing – and perhaps discredited – traditional vehicles for the Dharma and seek solutions from the religious fringe. Such Buddhists appropriated the outsider figure of the Siddha, and utilized features of tribal ritual, in the process Buddhicizing alternative means of psychological transformation, such as spirit possession; other innovations included the use of tribal 'naturalness' as a literary trope for the innate (*sahaja*) and nondual spiritual potential which abides within a person. These Buddhists were naturally attracted to successful ascetic models of the period, such as the wrathful Śaiva ascetics who fitted more easily into the warring world of early medieval India. It would seem that in these difficult times the Tantric combination of apotropaic and gnostic religiosity was the most appealing path to pursue, as a means of protecting and maintaining the Buddhist mission and seeking its ultimate salvific purpose.

The mature phase of Buddhist Tantra, from the ninth century AD onwards, emerged as institutional Tantrism was synthesized with the individual Tantrism of the Siddhas, in the process becoming an object of monastic scholarship. Although Tantric Buddhism gradually came to dominate the dwindling monastic centres, it is likely that transgressive aspects were only ever practised by the few. While some Buddhist authors explicitly permit it, they also add various provisos such as that the monk should first attain a provisional insight into emptiness: such a strategy of legitimation would not have been devised unless monks really did break the monastic code of celibacy. The mainstream view, however, seems to have been that sexual yoga was not permitted for monks, for the Buddhist Tantra of the northern Indian monasteries transmitted to Tibet in the eleventh century adhered closely to the monastic curriculum.

The Vajrayāna

Meditation in Indian Vajrayāna, as outlined especially in the Tantras, was focused on visualization, aided by the sacred space of the *maṇḍala*: the Tantric practitioner was taught to visualize a particular awakened deity within the *maṇḍala*, which was actually laid out in front of him at the time of initiation, at the same time reciting *mantra*s to invoke the deity and then partake of its liberated qualities. Tantric Buddhists who engaged in such practices believed them to be the most rapid means of attaining the Mahāyāna goal of complete awakening. But in dealing with powerful beings and substances, and so advancing rapidly towards Buddhahood, this path was believed to be more dangerous than the arduous Bodhisattva path of accumulating virtues over numerous lifetimes. It therefore required the guidance of a Vajra master (*guru* or *ācārya*) to 'empower' the practitioner (*sādhaka*) through various initiations into a specific Tantric system.

Each individual Tantra has its own number of initiations, but the most esoteric systems generally require more: Mahāyoga and Yoginī Tantras often require around six or seven, whereas fewer are prescribed in Kriyā, Caryā and Yoga Tantras. An initiation would typically begin with the blindfolded initiand being told to cast a flower into the *maṇḍala* to determine the Buddha family to which he will belong, after which the guru would lead him through a complex visualization of the *maṇḍala*'s central deity and the recitation of its mantras. Further initiations involving different ritual implements – a crown, bell, vajra and so on – were then performed before the pupil received a Vajra name and was finally empowered to practise the ritual system of the Tantra alone.

Initiation into higher Mahāyoga or Yoginī Tantras required more controversial initiations. In the secret initiation, the initiand's sexual partner was required to copulate with the Vajra guru, after which the initiand then had to ingest some of their sexual fluids (which were equated with the *bodhicitta*, a Mahāyāna term originally indicating the resolve to attain awakening) before copulating with the female partner himself in the 'understanding' (*prajñā*) initiation. The process of initiation culminated with a final empowerment in which the guru explained the real nature of the four types of bliss experienced in sexual congress: these are said to arise through the union of understanding (*prajñā*: this being equated with the female consort) and means (*upāya*: this being equated with the initiand himself).

Post-initiatory Tantric practice in India had two general phases. First was the preparatory period in which the practice as a whole was grounded in Mahāyāna norms: reflecting on the goal of full awakening, the Bodhisattva virtues required to reach this end, and the Great Vehicle's philosophical aspects. The meditative phase that follows involved the practitioner's mental generation of the *maṇḍala* out of nothing, and then the visualization of himself as the presiding Buddha at the centre of the *maṇḍala*, surrounded by a retinue of lesser deities. The identification with the *maṇḍala*'s awakened deity was believed to help cultivate and maintain the liberated consciousness of a Buddha.

To such visualization practices, Tantras from the eighth century onwards added a 'completion phase', focusing on the manipulation of vital energy (*prāṇa*, which also means breath) by concentrating on the powerful nodes (*cakras*) at which the three channels of the subtle body intersect. The general aim was to focus the *prāṇa* within the central channel and direct it towards the *cakras*, in order to manipulate the blissful drop of white semen (the *bodhicitta*) believed to be located in the crown *cakra* at the top of the head. These subtle yogic practices also had a sexual element: in order to accelerate their own path to liberation, Siddha practitioners would use sexual congress as a means of forcing energy into the subtle channels (although the white drop of semen was supposed to be retained rather than emitted in orgasm). The point of this practice was to achieve a series of four states of bliss, the culmination of which, 'innate (*sahaja*) bliss', was held to be identical with the complete awakening of a Buddha.

The End of a Civilization

The travel account of the Chinese pilgrim Faxian, who visited India at the beginning of the fifth century AD, shows that a number of old Buddhist sites – such as Kapilavatthu, Sāvatthī and Bodhgaya – had by then been more or less abandoned. Indeed, donative inscriptions at Buddhist sites declined sharply in this period, and when the Chinese pilgrim Xuanzhang visited India in the late seventh century, he observed a greatly depleted and demoralized Sangha, the lax standards of which he was strongly critical. Many more old sites of Buddhist support, dating to the Mauryan period and before, such as Kusinārā, Vesālī and Pāṭaliputta, were in ruins, and the Buddhist Sangha was in decline across much of India. This evidence suggests that the fortunes of Buddhism changed dramatically under the Guptas (*c.*320–550 AD) and then the early medieval period that followed. Despite the odd medieval success, such as the esoteric Buddhist culture of the Pāla dynasty, which flourished between the late eighth and twelfth centuries in an area that stretched east, and sometimes west, from Magadha, Buddhism gradually retreated and disappeared from India.

The basic causes of this long process of decline can be traced to the rise and fall of the Mauryans. When the Mauryans rose to power (in the fourth century BC) and then established their imperium (in the third century), they spread the socio-political norms of Magadha throughout most of civilized India, establishing an imperial system administered by centrally appointed bureaucrats. If this meant that matters of governance were confined to Magadhan appointees, rather than disseminated among local elites, the collapse of empire would have placed the urban centres in the hands of local rulers with little experience of rule on the Mauryan scale. A gap in statecraft would have ensued, in other words – one that presented an opportunity for the Brahmins, the only educated elite able to provide a comprehensive cultural and legal framework for the new rulers, as well as a powerful means of legitimation through their ancient rites and rituals.

Brahminism had already spread beyond its historical heartland – the doab between the Ganges and Yamunā rivers – even before the Buddha, but it achieved a more enduring presence after the Mauryan demise. Sanskritised inscriptions from the first century BC chart the spread of Brahminism towards the south, the immigrant Brahmins being enticed to the new kingdoms by the offer of tax-free settlements. Since the Brahmins imagined themselves as the purest recipients of religious donations, they were in direct competition with Buddhists for royal patronage. But they were also a self-contained community bound by endogamy, not open to outsiders, and more or less entirely dependent on the goodwill of kings for their survival. Buddhism, on the other hand, was a missionary religion open to all, and apparently supported by a wide section of urban society. As long as this urban support did not fail, and as long as the Brahmins did not find a means of winning popular support, the predominance of the Buddhists was guaranteed.

Unfortunately for the Sangha, the spread of Brahminism changed cultural conditions to such an extent that it affected the foundation of Buddhist support in both these areas. During the first half of the first millennium AD, popular theistic elements of Brahminism gained in prominence, so that by the time of the Guptas a culture of what could loosely be called temple Hinduism had emerged. According to the travel account of Xuanzang, there were more Hindu temples than Buddhist monasteries in the seventh century, a highly significant fact even if most of the temples were much smaller than Buddhist institutions. It would seem as if the devotional forms of ancient Magadha, originally spread across India by the Buddhists, had by this time been appropriated by Brahmins and adapted towards a theistic expression.

In this more accommodating guise, Brahminism was capable of attracting devotees at the popular level.

At the same time the urban support of Buddhism was gradually eroded by the establishment of an agrarian socio-political culture, one based on the hierarchical distinction of four social classes: Brahmins, rulers, merchants/farmers and slaves, all of whom were distinguished by decreasing levels of ritual purity (maintained by endogamy). This alternative cultural vision gained in prominence as Brahminism gradually spread across India, eventually thriving under the Guptas. The urban civilization which had flourished since the time of the Buddha was effectively shut down, for an open society, with its unpredictable individualism, wealth and dissemination of power could not be so easily controlled, unlike the closed world of Brahminic ideology which replaced it. Buddhist texts of this period show the influence of this new cultural settlement: Sanskrit began to be used as the language of choice, rather than the non-Brahminic Prakrits close to the Buddha's language, and the Buddhists accepted the idea of social class distinguished by ritual purity. The disappearance of women from the donative record shows how deleterious these changes were for Indian Buddhism: the lack of female independence in Brahminism had a significant impact on the practice of Buddhism.

A reflection of these difficult times can be seen in some of the Buddhist literature of this period. While the early version of the Mahāyāna *Rāṣṭrapāla Sūtra* (translated into Chinese by Dharmarakṣa in the late third century AD) makes a rather gentle case for a reversion to a more ascetic life and the Bodhisattva ideal, the Sanskrit version of the sixth century is virulently critical of what it believes are corrupt monastic standards. The later version of the text indicates a tradition under the strain of transformed cultural circumstances; in this fractious state, the Buddhist Sangha became increasingly vulnerable to political and economic change. The benefit of historical hindsight allows us to view the disturbed tones of the later *Rāṣṭrapāla Sūtra* as a sign that the survival of Buddhism itself was at stake.

The course of history began to turn against the Buddhist Sangha in the late fifth century. First, the Gupta empire was severely affected by Hun invasions from the northwest; the economic damage, shown by the demise of the monetary economy and devaluation of Gupta coins, must have upset Buddhist patronage from the mercantile community. Partly because of this, and partly because the Brahminic vision of life is essentially agrarian, the urban centres of northern India declined and were eventually abandoned. Things deteriorated further with the demise of the Gupta empire in the north and of the neighbouring Vākāṭaka empire across the Deccan, for the early medieval period which followed was one of political fragmentation and an increasingly martial ethos.

The Buddhists, with their virtue ethics and pacifist ideals, had little to offer this world. Brahminism, on the other hand, offered support and even encouragement to kings embroiled in war. According to the system of four classes, waging war is not just the prerogative of the warrior class (*kṣatriyas*): it is also their divinely ordained duty, as shown in the complex arguments justifying war formulated in sacred texts such as the *Bhagavadgītā*. The conflicts of this period were therefore good for Brahminism, as it created demand for a class of educated priests who could offer a supportive ideology, ritual legitimation and ministerial advice.

These martial circumstances also explain the popularity of forms of Tantric Brahmanism dominated by the wrathful Hindu god Śiva. Early medieval inscriptions frequently eulogize the military prowess of the king, and compare him to the similarly violent figure of Śiva. The testimony of Candrakīrti, a Buddhist philosopher who lived in the Andhra region during these difficult times (*c.*550–650 CE), highlights the problems faced by the Buddhist Sangha. In a period when the Buddhist-supporting Viṣṇukuṇḍis of Andhra were threatened and eventually ousted by the Śaivite Cālukyas, Candrakīrti criticizes kings for being puppets of power-broking Brahmins, who justify war by invoking the words of the *Bhagavadgītā*.

The pacifist advice of Candrakīrti shows that Buddhism had little chance of surviving in this world, for he states that if a king cannot rule righteously, in accord with Buddhist ethics, it would be better for him to renounce the world. While this suggests that many Indian Buddhists realized that the game was up, others disagreed with this appeal to non-violence: it is notable that the only Buddhist success of this period was achieved in the east and northeast of India, in an esoteric guise which could compete with the martial ethos of Tantric Śaivism. But once the Pāla supporters of Tantric Buddhism fell with the Islamic attacks of the late twelfth and early thirteenth century, Buddhism disappeared more or less completely from India.

Chapter VII
Guild Monasticism in the East

> He who has left the household life is a lodger beyond the earthly world, and his ways are cut off from those of other beings . . . Kings and princes, though they have the power of preserving existence, cannot cause a preserved creature to be without woe . . . This is why the monk refuses homage to the Lord of the Myriad Chariots and keeps his own works sublime, why he is not ranked with kings or princes and yet basks in their kindness.
>
> Huiyuan, 'A Monk does not bow down before a King', 404 AD

General Features of Buddhism in Asia

As Buddhism spread throughout Asia the broad religious culture established by the Buddha made for an easy assimilation in different societies. With a plurality of practices based around an inclusive soteriology, it was easy enough for Buddhist missionaries to find a place for the deities and spirits of local animistic cults, so long as the ethical principles of the Dhamma were not violated – or if they were, to turn a blind eye. The spread of Buddhism involved a complex process of mutual adaptation between the host societies and the incoming Dhamma, although this did not alter the fact that the various kinds of Buddhism established in Asia were recognizably Indian. Local customs and traditions were absorbed and adapted, but were always rooted in the religious aesthetic and devotional forms that originally flourished in ancient Magadha: incense, garlands, offerings of flowers and vividly decorated temples were, and still are, the norm throughout the Asian Buddhist world.

Within this common religious culture, the transformation of Buddhist ideologies and practices depended on local conditions.

Where the indigenous intellectual tradition was strong, Buddhist speculation was redirected into new, dynamic avenues. This was most clearly the case in China, where Buddhist thought was initially expressed in a Daoist idiom which laid the foundations for a creative fusion of Indian and Chinese ideas. But Buddhist creativity was no less dynamic in lands without any strong intellectual tradition. While the forms of Buddhism that emerged in Tibet and Southeast Asia did not venture beyond the intellectual framework of the Indian tradition, new ways of interpreting it were devised, as well as new forms of ritual and meditation.

It is normal to classify Asian Buddhist traditions into either Theravāda or Mahāyāna schools, the former being found in Sri Lanka and mainland Southeast Asia, the latter being represented by the Buddhist traditions of Tibet and the Far East. But this categorization is based on differences which are unclear, and does not reflect the very significant ideological and institutional traditions held in common. The distinction between Theravāda and Mahāyāna is, moreover, based on a comparison of fundamentally different aspects of the Buddhist tradition.

Although the term *thera-vāda* means 'teachings of the "elders" (*thera*)', it does not denote any specific ideology, but rather identifies the discourses and monastic rules of the Pali canon, and hence the monastic lineage based on them. The term *mahāyāna*, on the other hand, denotes an ideology rather than a monastic lineage: the Bodhisattva vow to attain full awakening has always been open to any individual Buddhist, regardless of the monastic lineage to which he or she is attached. A monk ordained in the Theravāda lineage, or a layperson associated with it, can also be a Mahāyāna Buddhist simply by taking the Bodhisattva vow, even in private, and there are numerous cases of this happening both in the present and distant past. Indeed, Mahāyāna monks and nuns are ordained in monastic traditions closely related to the Theravādin lineage: that of the Mūlasarvāstivādin Vinaya in Tibet, and the Dharmaguptaka Vinaya in East Asia.

The major difference between Theravāda and Mahāyāna is textual, since the Theravādin tradition does not accept Mahāyāna sūtras as authoritative teachings of the Buddha. But this distinction is again not so simple, for para-canonical texts in Pali have sometimes been accepted as authoritative teachings of the Buddha within Theravādin cultures; the Chinese and Tibetan canons also contain a significant amount of canonical or non-Mahāyāna literature derived from various Indian traditions. All Buddhist traditions were free to compose, redact and define their own textual collections, and the variety of literary activities and practices which resulted from this cannot easily be reduced to a simple dichotomy between Theravāda and Mahāyāna.

Beyond these limited textual differences, all forms of Asian Buddhism have similar aesthetic, devotional and ethical norms, and all are based on the same basic ideology. More importantly, a shared mythic heritage has laid the foundations for similar forms of apotropaic, karmic and gnostic Buddhism within Theravāda and Mahāyāna cultures. Although the imagined destinies of Mahāyāna and Theravāda Buddhists often differ – Mahāyānists in the Far East aspire to be reborn in the Pure Land of the Buddha Amitābha, for example, whereas Theravādins might wish to be reborn in a heaven of the Pali canon – there are virtually no differences between either the basic aspiration or the pietistic means of fulfilling it. At the level of the gnostic virtuoso, the Tibetan Vajrayānist, Zen monk, and Theravādin forest meditator might all imagine that they can achieve liberation from rebirth in a single life, even if this is imagined somewhat differently.

Just as was the case in India, Buddhism in Central Asia and China was widely spread by missionaries and their lay supporters, often merchants, before extensive royal patronage was received. This resulted in an extensive network of semi-autonomous monastic guilds, in which Buddhist monasteries occupied a cultural sphere of their own, around the edges of the state's jurisdiction. Chinese Buddhism, and to a lesser extent the Buddhist traditions of Central Asia, were therefore similar to Indian Buddhism and dissimilar to other forms of Buddhism in Asia, by virtue of their relative autonomy from the royal court.

Buddhism along the Silk Road

The Aśokan support of Buddhism enabled its missionaries to travel beyond north India, arriving first in Sri Lanka and the Greek-ruled kingdoms to the northwest. From these regions Buddhism eventually spread to Central Asia, the Far East, and at a later date Southeast Asia (from Sri Lanka via South India). The cultural heart of the northwest frontier region, whether ruled by Indians, Greeks or various Iranian tribes, was the kingdom of Gandhāra (more or less equivalent to the Swat valley of modern Pakistan). It was local forms of Gandhāran Buddhism, with texts translated into and composed in the local Gāndhārī dialect, using the Kharoṣṭhī script (first used in an Indian context in Aśoka's inscription at Kandahar), and with Greek-influenced art and iconography, that were taken along the Silk Road to Central Asia, eventually reaching China in the first century AD.

Gandhāra was connected to the Central Asian kingdom of Bactria by a South Asian extension of the Silk Road trade route, one which ran northwest through the Khyber Pass; the road from Bactria then led east to China along the northern route of the Silk Road. But another trade route ran northeast from the Gandhāran capital of Taxila, passing through Gilgit in northern Pakistan on a route through the Karakorum mountains before reaching the edge of the Takla Makan desert. At this point the Silk Road splits into a northern and southern branch: the former travels northwest to Kashgar, joining up with the northern Silk Road, and heading northeast towards China, through the towns of Kucha and Turfan; but at the Takla Makan desert the southern branch of the Silk Road travels directly East to Khotan, Yarkand, Niya and Loulan, on a route skirting northwest Tibet. Both branches of the Silk Road met at Dunhuang, an old trading town which in the first century BC was the most westerly point of the Chinese Han dynasty.

It is likely that Buddhists had already reached Bactria in the third century BC, when it was still ruled by the Greeks, for the Pali sources claim that a Greek called Yonadhammarakkhita took part in the Aśokan missions. Further Buddhist missionaries probably travelled west from here, within the Eastern Greek empire that stretched all the way to the Mediterranean, for early Manichean texts from the neighbouring Iranian country of Parthia show a few traces of Indian Buddhist terminology. A Buddhist influence on Pythagoras and the stoics is also likely, and a later influence on Christian monasticism is possible; the claims of the Persian scholar Al Bīrunī (973–1048), that the 'samaniyya' religion existed in Iraq and Syria before imperial Persia extended its support to Zoroastrianism, must therefore be taken seriously. But however far west Buddhism spread, without any state support and with major powers favouring other religions, it ultimately came to nothing.

More enduring traditions were established in the oasis towns along the Silk Road. These early Buddhist centres were dominated by the

Buddhist traditions of Gandhāra, as can be seen in the artistic and architectural styles at the old sites, most famously the giant Buddhist statues of Bamiyan (destroyed by the Taleban in 2001), which portrayed the Buddha in a distinctly Hellenistic style. A Gandhāran influence can also be seen in the numerous documents recovered from the arid remains of the Silk Road kingdoms. The earliest of these use the Kharoṣṭhī script, both for Buddhist texts in Gāndhārī and for local Iranian dialects; after around 400 AD, Kharoṣṭhī was replaced by the Brāhmī script used by Buddhist communities in Gupta India (the use of Sanskrit increased throughout this time). The oldest surviving Buddhist documents have been found in sites near to Gandhāra (including Bamiyan): these are generally not older than the first century AD, although a more recent find can perhaps be dated to the first century BC. Kharoṣṭhī documents from the Silk Road date from around 200 AD onwards, indicating that even if Buddhists moved through the region as early as the first century AD (on their way to Han China), a significant presence only occurred much later due to immigration from Gandhāra.

The Silk Road presence of documents relating to Buddhism, and of Buddhist architectural sites, in the third century AD, occurs not long after the decline of the Kuṣāṇa empire, which stretched from northwest India to the kingdom of Bactria, the western terminus of the Silk Roads leading from Central Asia. The level of Buddhist support provided by this dynasty and its greatest emperor, Kaniṣka, who ruled in the early second century AD, is not clear. Although Buddhist texts from the northwest claim that Kaniṣka was a Buddhist convert, it is more likely that the dynasty followed some sort of Iranian religion, probably Mazdeanism, at the same time extending some support to the Buddhists. The fact that a fourth century AD Buddhist manuscript from Bamiyan states that Huviṣka, Kaniṣka's successor, had 'set forth in the Mahāyāna', is tantalizing, but might only indicate a Buddhist belief that some Kuṣāṇas were Buddhist converts. But the fact that Indian, Greek and Iranian deities are present in Buddhist art of the northwest frontier and Silk Road suggests a typically Buddhist absorption of foreign thought-worlds, and so it is possible that Kuṣāṇa culture had been more or less Buddhicized.

Surviving remains indicate that the forms of Buddhism established along the Silk Road followed the Indian mainstream closely, although documents from the southern town of Niya, capital of the Kroraina kingdom, show that its Buddhists were lay priests who only donned monastic clothing on Uposatha days. Besides the Dharmaguptakas of Gandhāra, the major schools of Buddhism established included the (Mūla-)Sarvāstivādins and Mahāsāṃghikas, both of which were prominent in Kashmir and the northwest. The donors to these schools established *stūpas* and art which followed the mythic themes of the Indian sites, and supported monasteries in which traditional teachings and texts were initially transmitted through Indian languages and scripts; local vernaculars were eventually used in the medieval period. Monastic Buddhism flourished at the major Silk Road towns: Khotan on the southern Silk Road, and Kucha and Turfan along the northern Silk Road. Khotan and Kucha could perhaps be called Buddhist kingdoms, but the religious pluralism of the Silk Road, and small size of even the most important city states, suggest a religious pluralism similar to that of pre-Gupta India, meaning that there was probably no such thing as the symbiosis of Sangha and royal court achieved elsewhere in Asia.

Silk Road evidence for Mahāyāna is limited. The earliest evidence consists of Chinese records which state that the Buddhist monks of Khotan attempted to suppress a Mahāyāna sūtra being sent to China in 260 AD, in the belief that it was heterodox. And when Faxian passed through the region in 401, he noted a mainstream (Hīnayāna) presence in most Silk Road towns. Other evidence shows a slight Mahāyāna presence: Faxian noted Mahāyānists in Khotan in 401, and a mid-third century Buddhist document from Niya records that the local governor of the town had 'gone forth in the Mahāyāna'. The book of Zambasta, composed in Old Khotanese and dating to the early medieval period, shows a local form of mythic Buddhism with a strong Mahāyāna orientation. But there is less evidence for Mahāyāna in the towns of the northern Silk Road: Kucha was dominated by the (Mūla-)Sarvāstivādin school, and Kumārajīva (*c.*344–413), the most famous Buddhist from Kucha, was trained in Sarvāstivāda thought, in Kucha and then Gandhāra, before converting to Mahāyāna in Kashgar.

The fifth century was a period of instability along both the southern and northern branches of the Silk Road, a period in which Gandhāran influence declined, and the Kroraina kingdom disappeared. During the sixth and seventh centuries Turkish tribes from the north competed with the Tibetan and Chinese empires for overall control of the region. The Tang dynasty of China exerted its influence through its garrisons during the seventh century, although control was lost to the Tibetan empire towards the end of the century, which lasted until after the An Lushan rebellion of the mid-eighth century. From the ninth until the thirteenth centuries, the Turkic Uighurs gained control of Kucha and Turfan along the northern Silk Road towns, and offered significant support to the Buddhists. But Khotan fell to the Karakhanid Turks in 1006, at which point Islam was imposed and Buddhism disappeared. The entire region was controlled in the thirteenth century by the Mongol empire, which tolerated all religions, although the Turko-Mongol rulers of the fourteenth century, such as Tamerlane (1336–1405), supported Islam. At this point Buddhism more or less disappeared from the Silk Road, surviving only in Turfan until the mid-fifteenth century, and in Dunhuang until the twentieth century. The entire region is now inhabited by Turkic-speaking Muslims.

Immigrant Buddhists in China

Buddhism was brought to China during the first century AD, around the mid-point of the Han dynasty (221 BC–207 AD), by Buddhist monks travelling along the Silk Road. The early Buddhist communities were situated in the capital cities of Luoyang and Chang'an, and were made up almost entirely of Central Asian immigrants. Scriptures and teachings were initially transmitted orally, but the process of translating into Chinese had begun by the second half of the second century: first by the Parthian An Shigao in the mid-second century, then by the Gandhāran Lokakṣema between 178 and 189, and then by the Kuṣāṇa Dharmarakṣa in the second half of the third century. The texts translated were either in the Gāndhārī language or partially Sanskritized versions of it.

The records from this period indicate that only a single ordained Chinese monk belonged to An Shigao's translation team, whereas both he and Lokakṣema were aided by a number of Chinese laymen. This does not imply any great Han interest in Buddhism, and if so it would seem that the translations were made for the benefit of immigrant communities, as they gradually lost their old knowledge of Gāndhārī and related Indian dialects. Indeed, one of the surviving works of An Shigao is a highly technical exegetical text, which assumes a reasonably advanced knowledge of Buddhist thought. This suggests that An Shigao was not so much a missionary trying to win a new audience, but was more concerned to cater to the needs of the converted: his efforts seem directed towards a small, dedicated community under the instruction of a traditional master.

This is not to say that Buddhism was without impact in Han China. There is limited evidence that it was known at court and in scholarly circles, and some Daoist texts of the late Han period describe visualizations that are absent before the arrival of Buddhism in China. Such practices show that some Daoists were aware of Buddhist texts and were perhaps even directly in contact with Buddhist meditators. This suggestion is confirmed by the fact that some of Lokakṣema's lay supporters were also devotees of a Daoist cult; these Buddhists were no doubt aware of the mainstream Buddhist texts on meditation contained in An Shigao's corpus of translations. Similarities between the Buddhist practice of observing the breath and the Daoist practice of breath-control probably stimulated this initial Chinese interest in Buddhist meditation.

Events moved in favour of the small Buddhist communities with the collapse of the Han dynasty in 220 AD. At this point, the Confucian ideology endorsed by the royal court declined in prestige, and a more open and enquiring intellectual climate emerged. In particular, the 'dark-learning' (*xuanzue*) of the Neo-Daoist school gained in prominence, and its interest in such things as the emotional detachment of the sage who lives in accord with the 'Way' (*dao*), and the original non-being of the world, furthered an interest in similar Buddhist ideas. With a growing corpus of texts translated into Chinese, and ongoing contact with Buddhist communities to the west, by the end of the third century Buddhism was well placed to assume a more prominent position in the religious and intellectual life of China.

During the 'Three kingdom' period (*c.*220–80), learned Buddhists from immigrant families thus began to attract the interest of elite circles. The third generation Indo-Scythian Zhi Qian, a Buddhist layman from Lokakṣema's centre in Luoyang, exerted great influence at the Wu capital of Jianye after his arrival there in 229; his contemporary Kang Senghui (d. 280), a Sogdian originally ordained in Jiaozhi (modern Hanoi), was also an important translator and influential figure at the Wu court. Both were educated in the Chinese classics, and so were able to translate mainstream and Mahāyāna texts into elegant Chinese. In order to communicate Buddhist ideas to the local intelligentsia, these thinkers drew upon the 'dark-learning' of the Neo-Daoists to present the teachings on emptiness in a Sinitic guise.

Although Buddhism widened its appeal beyond its immigrant base during the third century, it still lacked a solid institutional base. Before Dharmarakṣa's translation of some Vinaya works, monastic rules were probably transmitted orally and perhaps only partially observed, with ordination consisting of the simple act of tonsure. It would take another century for a complete translation of a Vinaya to be made (the lack of an authoritative monastic tradition impelled the monk Faxian to travel to India in 399). But at the beginning of the fifth century a number of Indian Vinayas were finally translated: initially the Mahāsāṃghika Vinaya was followed in the north and the Sarvāstivādin Vinaya (translated by Kumārajīva) flourished in the south, but both were replaced by the Dharmaguptaka Vinaya in the seventh century.

The Formation of Chinese Buddhism

To the neo-Daoists, the Mahāyāna speculation on emptiness must have appeared a novel way of approaching the indigenous mystical tradition. But for the Buddhists, Daoist speculation was a useful means of opening up the Dharma to native minds, a good example being the monk Zhih Dun (314–366), who wrote a commentary on the book of Zhuangzi, a Daoist classic. The neo-Daoist sort of Buddhism which emerged in the third century, based on pioneering works of earlier figures such as Zhi Qian and Kang Sengui, did not endure. But the synthesis with neo-Daoism allowed the perfection of understanding to gain a foothold in Chinese intellectual life, and this enabled a distinctly Chinese form of Mahāyāna Buddhism to emerge.

The turning point in the Chinese assimilation of Buddhism thus took place around the beginning of the fourth century, in the form of a 'gentry Buddhism' that flourished around Jianye (renamed Jiankang in 313 AD), the royal capital of the Eastern Jin dynasty. This fusion of neo-Daoist and Buddhist speculation was a form of gnostic Buddhism: a virtuoso appreciation of Buddhist thought more or less devoid of apotropaic or karmic elements, and without any apparent attempt to grasp the idea at a meditative or mystical level. The emerging gnostic

Buddhism of Jianye was the key factor in the eventual emergence of Buddhist schools that were more Chinese than Indian.

A more traditional course of development was followed in the north and west, where connections with Central Asia were maintained through trading contacts between the Western Jin dynasty (265–316) and Central Asia: forms of Buddhism in this region were much closer to Indian and Central Asian norms. Indeed, in the early fourth century, the growing Buddhist community of Dunhuang, at the eastern end of the Silk Road, expanded its sphere of influence to the royal court and elite circles in the cities of Chang'an and Luoyang, especially through the efforts of Dharmarakṣa (active *c.*266–308). An Indo-Scythian from a wealthy immigrant family of Dunhuang, and educated in the Chinese classics, Dharmarakṣa built up a large following in the two major cities of the north. His translations of more than 150 Buddhist works, almost entirely Mahāyāna, laid foundations for the cross-over into mainstream Chinese culture that would take place during the course of the fourth century.

Dharmarakṣa's influence was furthered in the fourth century by the Kuchean monk Fotudeng. After arriving in Luoyang in 310, Fotudeng forged a close relationship with the Later Zhou dynasty (319–351) before his death in 349, offering diplomatic advice as well as apotropaic services such as prognostication, rainmaking and healing. Beyond the court he built up a large following of Central Asian and local disciples; although the focus and activities of his school is unclear, it is likely that Fotudeng built upon the mixture of mainstream and Mahāyāna practices long present through the work of such figures as An Shigao, Lokakṣema and Dharmarakṣa.

Fotudeng's brand of northern Buddhism was subsequently spread throughout China by his disciples, the most prominent of whom was Dao'an. After travelling south in 349, Dao'an established a centre in Xiangyang in 365, where he taught an eclectic mix of Buddhist teachings based on his former interest in An Shigao's texts on meditation and his developing interest in the *prajñā-pāramitā* (which he understood according to the neo-Daoist interpretation of the gentry Buddhists). From 379 until 385 Dao'an was an important figure at the Former Qin court of Fu Jian, in Chang'an, under whom a further influx of missions and translation projects were inaugurated, and then continued by his successor Yao Xing between 393 and 416.

Initially a marginal concern of immigrant minorities, Buddhism prospered in the more speculative environment that opened up with the fall of the Han dynasty. The socio-political changes which allowed China to become increasingly Buddhicized required, in turn, that Buddhism become increasingly sinified. This was aided by the fact that by this time Buddhism had developed into a highly diverse movement. In particular, Mahāyāna ideas and the Mahāyāna elaboration of mythic themes endowed the movement with the capacity to adapt to, and flourish in, the well-established cultural and intellectual norms of China: a fully Chinese Buddhism was probably only possible in a Mahāyāna guise.

By the end of the fourth century the Buddhist movement was well established in China: in the north and west, more traditional Indian forms of Buddhism from Central Asia predominated, whereas at the court of the Eastern Jin towards the south and east, an indigenous interpretation of traditional Buddhist thought resulted in a nascent form of gnostic Buddhism. Somewhere between these two poles were the Buddhist centres of Xiangyang and Lu Shan, established by Dao'an and his disciple Huiyuan. The new schools that emerged from the sixth century onwards drew upon these different currents to create uniquely Chinese forms of Buddhism.

Kumārajīva

Born in Kucha of Kuchean and Indian parents in 344 AD, as a boy Kumārajīva studied the Sarvāstivādin system in Kashmir. After further study in a Sarvāstivādin centre at Kashgar, he was converted to Mahāyāna by Sūryasoma, a monk from the royal house of Yarkand, close to the Mahāyāna-influenced Buddhist centres of Khotan. This was a philosophical conversion to the perfection of understanding: Kumārajīva embraced the notion of emptiness at the expense of his former Sarvāstivādin realism. But in 383, at the age of 39, Kumārajīva was captured in Kucha by Chinese invaders and taken to Chang'an, then under the rule of the Later Qin dynasty (384–417). Here he was supported by Yao Xing and put in charge of a large translation team, this work continuing until his death in 413.

Kumārajīva's scholarly output in Chang'an was a major moment in the emergence of Chinese Buddhism: his prolific and sophisticated translations included canonical Vinaya texts, Mahāyāna Sūtras and important Madhyamaka treatises. Based on his translation of three important works (Nāgārjuna's *Mūlamadhyamaka-kārikā* and *Dvādaśanikāya-śāstra* plus Āryadeva's *Śataka-śāstra*), as well as his important *Mahā-prajñāpāramitā-śāstra*, supported by the contributions of his disciples, the perfection of understanding tradition and Madhyamaka thought were promoted more or less in line with their Indian formulation, rather than the neo-Daoist explorations of the fourth century. In all his writings, Kumārajīva faithfully transmitted Nāgārjuna's Madhyamaka, criticizing the Abhidharma reductionism and taking the canonical discourses in an anti-realistic sense.

Kumārajīva thus argued that notions of existence and non-existence are mere 'fantasy conceptions', and that cause and effect in the phenomenal world are unreal. Nāgārjuna's negations of causality, stated in the first chapter of his *Mūlamadhyamaka-kārikā*, and his arguments about the logical impossibility of existence or existents, were therefore made known in China for the first time. The neo-Daoist interpretation of the perfection of understanding was thus challenged by the nominalistic understanding that language does not denote really existent, mind-independent objects; Nāgārjuna's understanding of the true nature of all things as an ineffable suchness (*tathatā*), the real state of all *dharma*s (*dharmatā*) beyond conceptual duality, was also significantly different from the substantialist interpretation of emptiness proposed by the neo-Daoist Buddhists.

These ideas were assimilated differently by Kumārajīva's pupils, for example Sengrui (352–436) and Sengzhao (374–414). Sengrui had studied the perfection of understanding before joining Kumārajīva in Chang'an in 402, and despite the neo-Daoist influence of his former master Dao'an, his grasp of Madhyamaka is made clear in his rejection of conceptual dualities, such as existence/non-existence and *saṃsāra*/Nirvana. Sengrui thus avoided the substantialistic interpretation of emptiness as a cosmic absolute, and replaced it with a negation of philosophical realism, in line with the understanding of his teacher.

A more advanced degree of assimilation is evident in the works of Sengzhao, a widely read scribe from a poor family in Chang'an who converted to Buddhism from neo-Daoism after reading the *Vimalakīrti Sūtra*. After becoming a monk and working on Kumārajīva's translation of the *Pañcaviṃśati-prajñāpāramitā Sūtra*, in his essay 'Prajñā has no knowing' (*c.*404–408 AD) Seng Chao expounded an anti-realistic analysis of the cognitive difference between an ordinary person and the holy man: he pointed out that through his empty, thoughtless mind a holy man apprehends neither that which exists nor does not, with *prajñā* instead functioning like a mirror and so enabling an intuition of emptiness, this being understood not as a cosmic 'void' but rather as the ineffable, non-objective truth of phenomena.

Kumārajīva appears to have been little interested in establishing a school, and the transmission of Madhyamaka beyond the third generation of his pupils is unclear. Although some Madhyamaka influence can be seen in the early Chan writings, philosophical realism ultimately prevailed in China, aided not only by the neo-Daoist influence, but also by the influence of Abhidharma and other mainstream Buddhist traditions. The failure of Madhyamaka to break the substantialistic interpretations of the perfection of understanding can be seen in the case of Huiyuan, whose neo-Daoist understanding of *śūnyatā* as a cosmic absolute remained intact despite an extensive correspondence with Kumārajīva.

Pure Land Buddhism

Apart from the philosophical Mahāyāna of the perfection of understanding, Mahāyāna texts belonging to the mythic tradition were translated at an early date and exerted a significant influence in China. Such texts were known in China as early as Lokakṣema's translation of the *Pratyutpannabuddha-saṃmukhāvasthita-samādhi Sūtra*, but by the time Kumārajīva had translated the shorter *Sukhāvatī-vyūha Sūtra* in 402 AD, numerous mythic texts as well as other translations of the longer and shorter *Sukhāvatī-vyūha Sūtra*s had been circulated. These formed the basis for the emergence of a broad sort of Chinese Buddhist spirituality, comprising simple faith and prayer as well as more complex sorts of contemplation and visualization. Sustained contemplation on the name of the Buddha Amitāyus (also known as Amitābha) is described thus in the shorter *Sukhāvatī-vyūha Sūtra*:

> Moreover, Śāriputra, beings ought to resolve for a Buddha-field. Why is this? Because it is where they will meet that class of good men. But they are not reborn in the Buddha-field of the Tathāgata Amitāyus merely through an inferior mass of merit. Whichever son or daughter of good family hears the name of the Tathāgata Amitāyus, and pays close attention to it, for one, two, three, four,

> five six, or seven nights with a focused mind, when they die the Tathāgata Amitāyus will appear in front of them, surrounded by his community of disciples and retinue of Bodhisattvas. The person who dies thus with an unswerving mind will be reborn in the cosmic realm of Sukhāvatī, the Buddha-field of that Tathāgata Amitāyus.

The same text describes a simpler spiritual method, by which faith in the Buddhas invokes their 'grace' and thus leads to rebirth in Sukhāvatī and eventually Buddhahood:

> What do you think, Śāriputra, why is that Dharma discourse called the 'grace of all Buddhas'? Every son or daughter of a good family who shall hear the name of this Dharma discourse and treasure the names of the Buddhas, the Blessed Ones, will receive the grace of these Buddhas and be irreversibly set on the path to the unsurpassed, supreme awakening. Therefore, Śāriputra, have faith and believe, but do not doubt me or those blessed Buddhas! For all those sons and daughters of good family who make the mental resolve for the Buddha-field of that Blessed Tathāgata Amitāyus, as well as those who have acted thus or are acting thus, will be irreversibly set on the path to the unsurpassed, supreme awakening. They will be born in that Buddha-field, or have been born there and are being born there now. Therefore, Śāriputra, faithful sons and daughters of a good family ought to arouse the resolve, in their thoughts, for that Buddha-field.

Other Mahāyāna sūtras which describe the practices leading to rebirth in a Buddha-field (or 'Pure Land') present the Bodhisattva path as a visionary quest, one focused on the visualization of Buddhas of the present, such as Amitābha, and requiring the resolution to be reborn in their paradisiacal realms, where rapid progress to awakening is possible. According to the *Pratyutpanna-buddhasaṃmukhāvasthita-samādhi Sūtra*, after settling down to meditate in a secluded place, a devotee should reflect on the fact that Amitābha is surrounded by a host of Bodhisattvas in Sukhāvatī, 'a thousand million myriad Buddha-fields away'. They should then practise the recollection of Amitābha in the western quarter, for up to seven days, after which they will see him (perhaps in a dream), and so hear his teachings (which should be preserved). In this text the Buddha also teaches that the visualization

Fig. 12. Mid-seventh century Amitābha statue at Buddhist caves near Xian, the old capital city of Chang'an

of Amitābha's supernatural body leads to rebirth in his Buddha-field (Sukhāvatī):

> Because of this calling to mind of the Buddha, these bodhisattvas will succeed in being born in the realm of the Buddha Amitābha. They should always call him to mind in this way: The Buddha's body is endowed with all the thirty-two marks, he radiates light, he is fine and upstanding beyond compare, in the midst of the assembly of monks he preaches the sutras, and the sutras he preaches are of indestructible form.

Through figures such as Dao'an and Huiyuan in the fourth century, this visionary tradition developed into an influential aspect of Chinese Buddhism. In around 372, along with eight of his followers at his centre in Xiangyang, Dao'an held a ceremony in which he and his followers gathered in front of a statue of Maitreya and resolved to be reborn in his celestial abode (the Tuṣita heaven in which all Bodhisattvas spend their penultimate existence). Kumārajīva's pupil Sengrui was also a participant in Dao'an's Maitreya cult, although he later went on to develop a keen interest in the visualization of Amitābha as practised by Huiyuan at his centre on Mt. Lushan.

The devotional practices which flourished among Huiyuan's community, in the form of a cult focused on the Buddha Amitābha, had a greater impact on the formation of the mythic tradition in East Asia. Huiyuan's biography states that in 402, along with 102 monastic and lay members of his community, he made the vow to be reborn in Amitābha's western paradise of Sukhāvatī; this took place before an image of Amitābha, in a ceremony that required offerings of flowers and incense. It is probably a later exaggeration that this occasion marked the formation of a 'White Lotus Society', for no such group continued beyond Huiyuan's death: an institution to maintain and promote the practice was not formed.

It would therefore seem as if Dao'an and others, who belonged to a lineage going back to Fotudeng, transmitted important aspects of northern Buddhism to central China: such things as devotional activities focused on Buddha images, making offerings, the prostration before the icon and circumambulation of the altar thus began to spread through China. From these beginnings Pure Land devotionalism was so thoroughly disseminated that it came to define Buddhism in China and East Asia as a whole, forming a sinified version of the old religious aesthetic of Magadha, and in the process establishing a common religious culture for East Asian Buddhism. It was against this general aesthetic and pietistic background that different orientations and schools began to emerge.

Since it promoted a wide range of practices at different levels, the Pure Land tradition was eminently suitable as a common vehicle for Chinese Buddhism as a whole. At its higher reaches, Pure Land practice might involve visualization over extended periods of time, perhaps up to a week or more, as seems to have been the case at Huiyuan's mountain retreat. But recollecting the Buddha's qualities through chanting and recitation, or cultivating a pious state of mind through simple devotional acts, opened up this form of religiosity to those less interested in more advanced forms of meditation. All the different Pure Land practices belonged within a broad and flexible tradition of karmic Buddhism, their common goal being to gain sufficient merit to be reborn in Sukhāvatī.

A diversity of Pure Land practices were spread by proselytizers such as Tan-luan (476–542), Daochuo (562–645) and his disciple Shandao (613–681). According to Daochuo, taking refuge in Amitābha and reciting his name is sufficient to attain rebirth in his realm; Shandao, on the other hand, focused primarily on the visualization of Amitābha, and the recollection of him through recitation. This influential practice is termed *nien-fo*: the uttering of the phrase *namo amituo fo*, 'homage to the Buddha Amitābha'. The term *nien-fo* signifies more than just recitation, however, for it is a translation of the Sanskrit term *buddhānusmṛti*, 'recollection of the Buddha', and so denotes a range of practices such as contemplation, visualization, invocation and so on. Through recitation, Shandao presented Buddha-recollection in a simple form in which it could be easily grasped and practised.

Only one aspect of the Pure Land tradition, as it developed first in India and then East Asia, was significantly different from the mainstream background: the idea of grace. The shorter *Sukhāvatī-vyūha* states that even hearing it guarantees the grace (or more simply, 'assistance', S: *parigraha*) of the Buddhas named therein, and that merely aspiring for Buddhahood leads to rebirth in Amitābha's Pure Land, where full awakening is assured. In other words a devotee need not expend any serious effort to follow the path, but can instead rely on an external agency for salvation. A related idea is embodied in the figure of the celestial Bodhisattva Avalokiteśvara, who in the Lotus Sūtra is said to look in all directions, adopting diverse manifestations in order to help needy devotees. These ideas became increasingly important in East Asian Buddhism, in such manifestations as the Pure Land societies of medieval Song China and later popular forms of Buddhist pietism which emerged in Japan.

Chan: the Meditation School

Buddhist meditation had been known in China since An Shigao's translations of mainstream texts on the subject. But there is little else to say about it, and certainly no emergent meditative traditions as such, until the writings of Dao'an in the fourth century. Meditation was apparently practised on Mt. Lushan, for eminent teachers such as the Kashmirian Buddhabhadra, disciple of the meditation master Buddhasena, visited this centre in 410 at the invitation of Huiyuan. At roughly the same time, however, Sengrui lamented the lack of meditative expertise in China.

A thoroughly sinified tradition of meditation eventually emerged during the sixth century, and by the late seventh century this rudimentary school was known as *chan-zhong*: the 'meditation lineage', the word *chan* being an adaptation of the Prakrit *jhāna* (or Sanskrit *dhyāna*). The Chan tradition traced its roots to the obscure figure of Bodhidharma, an immigrant monk who arrived in China in the early sixth century. According to the mid-sixth century account of Tanlin, a pupil of Bodhidharma's disciple Huike, as well as the seventh century biography of Daoxuan, Bodhidharma was a South Indian who arrived in China 'after crossing distant mountains and seas'. A rather different picture is presented by the 'Record of Buddhist Monasteries in Luoyang', a text of 547 AD which notes the presence in Luoyang of an Iranian Buddhist monk called Bodhidharma in 527 AD, who had evidently reached China via the Silk Road.

Given the impressive historical records of Chinese Buddhism, it is curious that the traditions about Bodhidharma are so limited and contradictory. This can only mean that he was a minor figure in his lifetime, probably a quietist with few disciples and little direct impact; Tanlin's claim that he had only two disciples – Daoyu and Huike – should thus be taken seriously. These humble beginnings created issues of authenticity and legitimacy, problems which were eventually resolved through the creation of complex Chan lineages going back to the Buddha himself, via a line of 28 patriarchs culminating in Bodhidharma. The Chan claim of a direct transmission of Buddhist truth beyond the texts, through a communication of the 'Buddha mind' from master to pupil, was a useful fiction in establishing the school's credentials in the early eighth century.

This lack of information prevents a clear appraisal of Bodhidharma's teachings. According to Tanlin, Bodhidharma taught two means of entering the 'Way' (*dao*): that through 'principle' (*li*) and that through 'practice' (*xing*). But the latter is not really a practice at all, since it consists of an outline of the correct attitude to be adopted in daily life: acceptance and quietude with regard to karmic retribution, impermanence and craving; and then 'according with Dharma', through practising the six Bodhisattva perfections with a correct understanding of Buddhist truths. The entrance through principle also lacks what could be described as a meditation method, since in describing how a person should awaken 'by means of the teaching', it sets out no practice whereby meditative states could be cultivated. This account instead focuses on comprehending the Buddha-nature idea of an ultimately real identity within, which is identical with the true nature of things hidden by 'the unreal covering of adventitious dust'.

The only suggestion of anything like a method in this incomplete record is that the entrance through principle concludes with the advice to practise 'wall-gazing' (*biguan*), although the exact meaning of this term is unclear. The basic orientation of the entrance through principle is thus to understand Mahāyāna ideas about the ultimate nature of reality, before somehow deepening this understanding through meditation. If so, it would seem that early Chan meditation involved first a deep contemplation of the way things really are, followed by a quietist attempt to cultivate this understanding at a more intuitive level. In the language of Indian Buddhism, this approach to spiritual practice is equivalent to the cultivation of insight (*vipaśyanā*) before calm (*śamatha*). Daoxuan thus believed that Bodhidharma's approach was a sort of 'methodless method', in which the negation of preconceived notions is followed by 'wall-gazing'.

Such an approach would seem to explain why most early Chan documents focus not on meditation *per se*, but rather on ideas, especially those of the perfection of understanding, the Buddha-nature tradition and Yogācāra thought. The two latter traditions were known at a relatively early date, as the *Laṅkāvatāra Sūtra*, an important source of Yogācāra and Buddha-nature ideas, was translated into Chinese by Dharmarakṣa in the third century AD. Also important for the synthesis of these two streams of thought was the 'Awakening of faith in the Mahāyāna', possibly an apocryphal text composed by Paramārtha in 553, which follows the tradition of the *Ratnagotravibhāga*, or *Uttaratantra*, an obscure Mahāyāna text according to which the liberated reality of the Buddha (called both *tathāgata-garbha* and *dharmakāya*) is a purified mind-essence. Since the *Ratnagotravibhāga* is not a Yogācāra text, its formulation of the *tathāgata-garbha* as a sort of purified consciousness should perhaps be regarded as a later formulation of meditative realism.

These different streams of thought combined to form the following philosophy of meditation in the nascent Chan tradition: Mind or Buddha-nature is a person's true identity and also an eternally pure, cosmic absolute, a nondual state of consciousness empty of all conceptualization and the dualities created by thought, which a Bodhisattva can realize and so become a Buddha. Exactly this understanding can be seen in the *Xin Xin Ming*, a work attributed to Sengcan, the third

Chan 'patriarch' (of the late sixth century), but which was composed posthumously, like all early Chan texts, in the mid-eighth century, probably among the school of Shenxiu, disciple of the fifth Chan patriarch, Hongren:

> 10. Abide not with dualism, carefully avoid pursuing it; As soon as you have right and wrong, confusion ensues, and Mind is lost.
>
> 22. When the deep mystery of one Suchness is fathomed, all of a sudden we forget the external entanglements; When the ten thousand things are viewed in their oneness, we return to the origin and remain where we ever have been.
>
> 25. In the higher realm of true Suchness there is neither 'self' nor 'other': when direct identification is sought, We can only say, 'Not two'.
>
> 27. This Absolute Reason is beyond quickening [time] and extending [space], for it one instant is ten thousand years; Whether we see it or not, It is manifest everywhere in all the ten quarters.
>
> 31. Where Mind and each believing mind are not divided, and undivided are each believing mind and Mind, This is where words fail; for it is not of the past, present, and future.

Regardless of the authorship of this text, its lack of anything that could be called a meditation method, and focus on key Mahāyāna ideas, agrees with the limited evidence for Bodhidharma, and illustrates well the major speculative concerns of the early Chan tradition.

Sudden Awakenings

The circle of meditators that developed around Bodhidharma and his followers remained obscure until Hongren (601–674), reckoned by later tradition as the fourth-generation successor of Bodhidharma, that is to say, the fifth Chan patriarch. By the time of Hongren and his teacher Daoxin (580–651), the supposed fourth Chan patriarch, the loose meditative movement was located at a monastic complex in Huangmei, well to the south of the imperial capitals of the Tang dynasty. The beginning of a distinct school suggested by this institutional base is mirrored by the early Chan manuscripts recovered from Dunhuang. These contain a plurality of ideas and practices, and suggest a movement which in the seventh century was in the process of forming a distinct identity. Although still relatively obscure in this period, the movement moved into the mainstream when Shenxiu (*c.*606–706), pupil of Hongren, was invited by Empress Wu to the capital city of Luoyang in 701.

This entrance into the centre of Chinese Buddhism opened up new possibilities as well as posing new challenges. Within the sophisticated Buddhist culture of Luoyang and Chang'an, two aspects of the Chan lineage were potential sources of suspicion and doubt: the lack of any literary heritage, and the shadowy beginnings of the tradition in an obscure meditator. The fact that most of the early Chan literature was composed in this period of recognition and success, including the fictitious Chan lineage reaching from Bodhidharma to the Indian 'patriarchs', shows that the followers of Shenxiu went to great lengths to address these issues.

A distinct identity among the established traditions of the North was thus created for the meditation school, which had previously consisted of nothing more than a loose network of teacher–pupil affiliations. This form of mythic authentication allowed for patronage on a greater scale, and set the stage for the school's eventual dominance of Buddhist monasticism in China. But it was not without problems: in particular, the notion of a patriarchal succession did not give equal prominence to other branches of the Chan lineage emanating from Hongren. This was pointed out in polemical form by Shenhui (670–762), a second-generation successor of Hongren via his teacher Huineng (639–713).

Between 730 and 745, Shenhui launched attacks on what he called the 'Northern school', claiming that Huineng was Hongren's rightful heir and, more destructively, criticizing its gradualist theory of meditation. This attack drew theoretical support from the *prajñā-pāramitā* critique of conceptual dualism: Shenhui effectively applied the ultimate truth statements of this literature to the conventional realm, and so claimed that the very idea of meditation and spiritual progress is an illusion. But this critique of gradualism was also a consequence of his lack of interest in meditation: since he was a polemicist rather than a meditator, Shenhui's so-called 'Heze' lineage made little impact, and had disappeared by the early ninth century.

Despite Shenhui's failure as a teacher and founder of a lineage, his critique of any gradualist method had a profound impact on all subsequent Chan speculation. Henceforth there was a general tendency to avoid any talk of meditative gradualism, so that any Chan teachings tended towards Shenhui's 'subitist' rhetoric. This can be seen in the Platform Sūtra, a text probably composed by the Oxhead school in the latter half of the eighth century (the oldest extant example is a Dunhuang manuscript of 780 AD), and which soon became the most important text of the Chan tradition. Although entirely fictitious, the text reports the supposed teachings of Huineng, a figure introduced in dramatic fashion with the account of the patriarchal succession from Hongren. The story states that in order to determine a successor, Hongren asked his pupils to compose a stanza encapsulating their understanding of Chan. The verse ascribed to Shenxiu, Hongren's most important and successful pupil, is stated as follows:

> The body is the bodhi-tree,
> the mind is like a bright mirror's stand.
> At all times we must strive to polish it
> and must not let dust collect.

In response to this Buddha-nature formulation, a verse expressing a more radical *prajñā-pāramitā* understanding is ascribed to Huineng, romantically depicted as an uneducated temple worker:

> Bodhi originally has no tree.
> The bright mirror also has no stand.
> Fundamentally there is not a single thing.
> Where could dust arise?

These two verses differ only with regard to the means of achieving realization: whereas Shenxiu affirms the need for spiritual progress over time, Huineng denies this. The juxtaposition of these different perspectives should perhaps be understood as an attempt to realign the relationship between Buddha-nature themes and perfection of understanding aspects of the Chan tradition, with the latter being prioritized above the former. Unlike the earlier predominance of the Buddha-nature, as indicated by the priority of the *Laṅkāvatāra Sūtra* among the pupils of Shenxiu (and possibly Hongren), the Platform Sūtra promoted the perfection of understanding, in particular the *Vajracchedikā-prajñāpāramitā Sūtra* ('Diamond Sūtra'), and this redirected the course of subsequent Chan speculation: the negation of any form of conceptual dualism was henceforth preferred to the idea of spiritual cultivation and the gradual emergence of the mind's immanent suchness.

As a consequence of political factors such as the An Lushan rebellion (755–763), and religious developments such as the rise of Buddhist Tantra at the Tang court, the lineages stemming from Shenxiu had all but disappeared by the second half of the eighth century. In this period the Hongzhou school of Mazu Daoyi (709–788, a second-generation heir of Hongren, via Zhishen, 609–672) flourished and dominated Chan until the Huichang persecution of Buddhism in 845. After the polemics of Shenhui, the Hongzhou school played an important role in unifying the Chan movement: Mazu's disciples achieved a wide distribution throughout the entire Tang empire, and for the first time a single Chan lineage achieved a pan-imperial institutional presence. The Hongzhou school thus laid the foundations for the monastic dominance of Chan during the Song period that followed.

The records of the Mazu and his followers suggest a fairly orthodox and even elitist school, with the teachings of the Mahāyāna sūtras presented through striking maxims such as 'mind is Buddha' and 'ordinary mind is the way'. This articulation of Buddhist truths in an innovative and appealing fashion does not resemble the Chan writings of the Song period (960–1279): these depict Mazu as a spiritual iconoclast, who used unconventional teaching methods such as shouting, violence and posing absurd questions as an aid to arrest the process of thinking and so stimulate a sudden awakening to religious truth. The depiction of Mazu as an anti-authoritarian Chan rebel was probably a pious fiction, a romanticized account of the great teachers of the Tang created by the Song Buddhist establishment (although it could also be based on a private tradition of Chan teaching).

By the eleventh century, it was believed that five lineages (or 'houses') of Chan had derived from Huairang (677–744) and Xingsi (d. 740), the two successors of Huineng; however, the fivefold scheme – Guiyang, Linji, Caodong, Yunmen and Fayan – is a simplification which obscures much greater diversity in the tenth and early eleventh centuries. Eventually only two transmission lineages survived, mainly because it was these that produced the largest number of influential Chan masters who attained elite support: the Caodong, stemming from Dongshan (807–869) and his disciple Caoshan (840–901), heirs of Huineng's lineage via Shitou (700–790); and the school of Linji (d. 866), derived from Mazu's Hongzhou lineage via Baizhang

(720–814) and Huangbo (d. 850). These schools can be understood in simplistic terms as a further formulation of the two polarities within the Chan tradition: that tending towards Buddha-nature ideology (Caodong), and that tending towards the perfection of understanding (Linji). These two orientations are illustrated by the approaches to spiritual practice of their two most famous representatives during the Song period: the 'silent illumination' meditation of Hongzhi (1091–1157), and the *kànhuà* meditation of Dahui (1089–1163).

Whereas silent illumination meditation focuses on the innate purity and freedom of the mind, which only has to be attended to in order to let thoughts disappear naturally, revealing the luminosity within, Dahui utilized the encounter dialogues (or 'precedents': *gong'an*) between Chan master and pupil as aids to meditation. These dialogues typically revolve around the enigmatic questions of Chan masters ('What is the sound of one hand clapping?', or 'Why has Bodhidharma left for the East?') and the varying responses from their students. For example, one story states that a student asked Zhaozhou (778–897) 'Does a dog have the Buddha-nature, or not?', to which Zhaozhou simply answered, 'No!'. This entire exchange constitutes the gong'an, and in Dahui's method the Chan pupil would focus its 'keyword' (or huatou), in this case Zhaozhou's answer 'No!', as a means of focusing the mind in a non-conceptual state.

The Caodong and Linji schools were transmitted to Japan in the late twelfth and thirteenth centuries respectively, where they survive in the form of Sōtō and Rinzai Zen; at the same time, Dahui's kànhuà meditation reached the Korean peninsula where it was appropriated enthusiastically by Jinul. But in China itself, after the extensive patronage in the Song period, when Chan became the dominant school of Buddhism, the meditation tradition, like Buddhism itself, was increasingly marginalized in Chinese society.

Tiantai, Huayan and Other Schools of Chinese Buddhism

Apart from the various wisdom, visionary and devotional sorts of Mahāyāna transmitted to the East, the scope of Chinese Buddhism was expanded by other Buddhist traditions which made the same journey, and by new traditions which developed from them. The most important Abhidharma text, the *Abhidharmakośa-bhāṣya* of

Vasubandhu, was translated into Chinese by the Indian missionary Paramārtha between 563 and 567. The study of this text has been an important aspect of East Asian Buddhism ever since, but since Paramārtha also translated numerous Mahāyāna works, including some of Asaṅga's Yogācāra treatises, the study of Abhidharma in East Asia has mainly been pursued as an adjunct to Yogācāra studies.

The intellectual tradition established by Paramārtha was superseded by that of Xuanzhang (600–664), who established a more orthodox Yogācāra school. But for the subsequent history of Chinese Buddhism, Paramārtha remained important for his contribution to the synthesis of Yogācāra and Tathāgata-garbha, in particular the identity of the Buddha-nature with a ninth state of consciousness, a sort of purified substratum consciousness beyond the traditional eight levels of consciousness taught by the Yogācāra school. The synthesis of these ideas, especially as articulated in his 'Awakening of Faith in Mahāyāna', laid theoretical foundations for Chan, but was also an important influence on two further traditions in the Tang period: Tiantai and Huayan.

These two schools were based on two large Mahāyāna Sūtras of the mythic sort, the 'Lotus' (*Saddharma-puṇḍarīka*) and 'Flower Garland' (*Avataṃsaka*) *Sūtra*s. The former had probably been composed by the second century AD, and was translated into Chinese by Dharmarakṣa in 286 and then again by Kumārajīva in 406. The general focus of the text is supernatural events of the most remarkable kind: in terms of mythic creativity, the Lotus Sūtra is only surpassed by the Flower Garland Sūtra. The authors of the Lotus Sūtra were apparently aware that its mythicism was too much for some, for it often sets out a defensive strategy to deal with those who ridicule it. Thus the text extols the benefits of worshipping it (with perfume, incense, flowers and so on), both for its apotropaic rewards (such as gaining the protection of supernatural beings) and even gnostic ends (the mere recitation of one of its verses being said to guarantee the attainment of Nirvana).

The devotional forms of Buddhism that arose around the Lotus Sūtra in China resembled the Pure Land tradition, but differed in focusing on Śākyamuni rather than Amitābha. This difference in the ultimate figure of devotion was not of serious consequence, however, since the text inspired a similar form of piety; the Lotus Sūtra claims that the Buddha did not really die in Kuśinagara, but will live until the end of the aeon, and so is able to respond to pious Buddhists out of compassion, just like Amitābha. Apart from its radical understanding of the historical Buddha, the Lotus Sūtra extended the concept of skill in means by teaching that Śākyamuni can utilize any teaching as long as he judges it will benefit the recipient. On this basis the text teaches that the goals of the Indian Buddhist mainstream – becoming a Buddhist saint (*arhat*) or a 'solitary Buddha' (*pratyeka-buddha*) – are not really liberating, but were invented by the Buddha in order to advance his disciples towards the only true spiritual goal of complete awakening. There is therefore only one path (*eka-yāna*), that which culminates in Buddhahood.

These ideas were taken up in the Tiantai school, so named after the mountain residence of its third patriarch, Zhiyi (538–597). Although not considered the founder of the tradition Zhiyi was its most influential thinker, and organized the Lotus Sūtra's ideas on skill in means and the single path into a comprehensive classification of Buddhist teachings (*panjiao*). According to Zhiyi's scheme, the *Avataṃsaka Sūtra* was the first teaching of the Buddha, delivered immediately after the awakening, but as an expression of the Buddha's awakened understanding it was too advanced, and so not understood. The Buddha thus reverted to revealing the canonical teachings, only turning his attention to the higher teachings of the *prajñā-pāramitā*/Madhyamaka and Yogācāra traditions much later, before finally revealing the teachings of the *Saddharma-puṇḍarīka* and *Mahā-parinirvāṇa Sūtra*s, just before he (apparently) died.

This classification shows that Zhiyi held the *Avataṃsaka Sūtra* in high regard. This text was translated into Chinese by Bodhibhadra in the early fifth century, with another, larger version made by Śikṣānanda towards the end of the seventh century. Both translations are heterogeneous, incorporating other sūtras (such as the *Daśabhūmika* and *Gaṇḍavyūha Sūtras*) as well as other material (possibly authored in the Central Asian kingdom of Khotan). Although certain parts of the text betray an awareness of philosophical Mahāyāna (e.g. the *Gaṇḍavyūha Sūtra*, which mentions Madhyamaka and Yogācāra ideas), the text is emphatically a mythic work focused on the majestic nature and supernatural abilities of the Buddha, and the ultimate realm of phenomena fully mastered by him (the *dharma-dhātu*). Its mythic elevation of the Buddha goes to the extreme length of identifying him with the cosmos, or else with a primordial Buddha named Vairocana, of whom he is apparently an emanation.

Possibly even more than the *Saddharma-puṇḍarīka Sūtra*, the *Avataṃsaka Sūtra* represents the pinnacle of mythic speculation within the Buddhist tradition. This, along with its huge length, varied contents, and marginal philosophical contents made it a rich source for Chinese thinkers, in particular Fazang (643–712) and Zongmi (780–841), the third and fifth patriarchs of the 'Huayan' school respectively. Fazang constructed a classificatory scheme (*panjiao*) similar to that of Zhiyi, albeit culminating in the *Avataṃsaka Sūtra* rather than the *Saddharma-puṇḍarīka Sūtra*. But he also worked the *Avataṃsaka*'s idea of the essential identity of all with the cosmic Buddha into a doctrine of 'interpenetration' or 'interdependence'. This philosophy is not explicitly stated in the text, but was instead teased out by interpreting its supernatural and miraculous happenings according to the old Chinese distinction between absolute reality (*li*) and phenomena (*shih*). The hyperbolic descriptions of the Buddha's ability to enter phenomena at will thus allowed for the creation of a uniquely Sinitic Buddhist philosophy.

The philosophy of interpenetration is most clearly stated in Fazang's teaching to Empress Wu, as recorded in his 'Treatise on the Golden Lion'. Fazang here points out that the shape of a golden lion cannot be separated from the gold itself, which means that the absolute reality of the Buddha-nature (or ultimate realm of phenomena, the *dharma-dhātu*) is in fact identical with mundane phenomena: *dharma*s are not emanations of the absolute, but are consubstantial with it, and yet the two realities are also in some sense distinct. The analogy of Indra's net of jewels was used to illustrate this notion of interdependence: in a cosmic net with jewels at each node, every jewel thus reflects every other jewel, just as the cosmic totality is contained within any particular point in the cosmos.

Other Indian traditions were influential in Tang China. Daoxuan (596–667), who worked for a while in Xuanzhang's translation centre, made an important summary of the Dharmaguptaka Vinaya which became a handbook for monastic life in China, and laid the foundations for all subsequent Buddhist monasticism in East Asia. Esoteric Buddhism was also influential at the Tang court, after being introduced by Śubhākarasiṃha (637–735) in 716, and then promoted by Vajrabodhi (671–741) shortly afterwards. These Indian Tantrists transmitted to China the esoteric Buddhism practised in and around the monastic universities of northeast India, a tradition continued by the Central Asian Amoghavajra (705–774, Vajrabodhi's disciple), who won the patronage of the Tang court (at the expense of the northern Chan school). Numerous Tantras were translated by these scholars, and although the school did not survive the Wuzong persecution of 845, its textual corpus laid the foundations for the Shingon school in Japan.

Buddhism in the Song and Beyond

By the beginning of the seventh century, and after several hundred years of dissemination and formulation, Buddhism had been thoroughly sinified and attained a prominent position in Chinese society. By the early ninth century, a minor movement of immigrant monks had grown into a major monastic and temple culture that exerted a considerable influence in Chinese society. The strength of the movement is shown by the fact that the imperial census of 845 recorded the existence of 4,600 monasteries, 40,000 shrines and over 260,000 monks and nuns.

This influence was not confined to the monastic cloisters and temple courtyards. Throughout the Tang dynasty (618–907) the Buddhist Sangha was active in Chinese society, engaging in a variety of social and economic endeavours: looking after the sick, poor and old; building roads, digging wells, and supporting local businesses (mills, presses, pawn-broking, agriculture and so on); and providing financial services such as holding deposits and lending money at interest. This worldly expression of spiritual virtue flowed out from local traditions and societies, and especially the multiplicity of monastic guilds, whose varying spiritual orientations were constructed around different texts and practices, and headed by a learned class of monks. The institutional autonomy on which these endeavours depended is well illustrated by Huiyuan's insistence, in 404, that since Buddhist monks have left society they do not have to pay the normal respect given to the emperor.

Given the posture of Huiyuan, and the growing influence and power of the Sangha, for example at the court of Empress Wu at the beginning of the eighth century, it is not surprising that the Buddhist rise was periodically checked, such as by the persecutions of Emperor Taiwu of the Northern Wei dynasty in 446 (and lasting until 452), and that of Emperor Wu of the northern Zhou dynasty in 574 (and lasting until 577). These anti-Buddhist measures were instigated by Daoist and Confucian traditionalists opposed to the foreign religion. Unlike the pluralistic culture of pre- and post-Mauryan India, in China the Buddhists existed in a Confucian environment, where the culture of filial piety provided no obvious function for bald renouncers, and in which the emperor ruled over all aspects of society as the 'son of heaven'. The Sangha was therefore hard pressed to win acceptance and freedom, and periodic setbacks were only to be expected.

Apart from the Confucian suspicion of an alien culture, a further motivation is revealed in the persecution undertaken by the Tang emperor Wuzong in 845. Over the course of two years, monasteries were destroyed, their wealth confiscated and all monks and nuns forced to return to lay life. This was not just a case of cultural xenophobia, with traditional elements at the Chinese court reacting to a successful immigrant creed: it was also an attempt to curtail the socio-economic power of the Buddhist Sangha, by dismantling its semi-autonomous guild culture.

Wuzong's persecution turned out to be just one of many temporary setbacks from which the Buddhists soon recovered. More importantly, the persecution proved to be an important moment in the gradual increase in state supervision of the Sangha, which had been building over the course of the Tang dynasty. This was a reaction not only to the missionary success of the Buddhists, but also to the close ties which had developed between the Sangha and elite circles. Thus the minimal supervision of the Northern Wei Dynasty, achieved through establishing a clerical 'Chief of Monks' in 396, was superseded by direct state regulation of the Sangha during the Tang period, implemented through various government departments, such as the 'Court of State Ceremonial' and 'Ministry of Rites'. After the Wuzong persecution the Sangha's prominent cultural position was easily restored, and maintained for several hundred years, but the Buddhists never again achieved the same cultural freedom.

The position of Buddhism within Chinese society reached its peak in the Song period (960–1279). Official statistics compiled in 1221 indicate that the Buddhist presence had increased from the Tang period, there being 40,000 monasteries and temples, and a large body of ordained monks and nuns (around 400,000 and 60,000 respectively). Buddhism was widely supported by all classes, with the

Sangha claiming the allegiance of many influential supporters in and around the imperial court, and having a pervasive influence on art and literature. The Song period was therefore one of consolidation, of maintaining the traditions received from the Tang, and reflecting on the long history of Buddhism in China. There was no little romance in the Song depiction of the Buddhist past: the Chan authors of this time imagined the meditation masters of the Tang as crazy-wisdom teachers of great ingenuity, wisdom and wit.

This does not mean that Buddhism in the Song was, by comparison, sterile and devoid of spiritual inspiration. Buddhist hagiography in the Song rather suggests that the Chinese involvement in Buddhism had now reached its culmination, with uniquely Sinitic schools and institutions developed, and an important position in Chinese society well established. Since the spiritual and cultural adventure required to reach this elevated position was now over, the Sangha was inevitably a more static, but no less creative or engaged institution. Indeed, the general configuration of Chinese Buddhism achieved in the Song set the general trends for all forms of Buddhism in East Asia thereafter, with Chan Buddhism institutionally and intellectually dominant, in the form of the Linji and Caodong schools.

Although Buddhism gradually assumed a more peripheral position in Chinese society after the Song dynasty, it would be incorrect to view the post-Song history of Chinese Buddhism in terms of a narrative of decline. While the general predominance of Confucianism at the imperial court pushed the Sangha to the margins during the Ming period (1368–1644), once there the Buddhists occupied their own cultural sphere. The Sangha thus reverted to its position as a semi-autonomous spiritual guild, and so remained until the early twentieth century, when it still functioned as a vital feature of Chinese culture: there was still a sizeable and dedicated body of monks, nuns and laypeople maintaining the old meditations and rituals, with monasteries still performing funerary rites and taking part in various socio-economic endeavours. The fact that Chinese Buddhists of this period believed that their tradition was undergoing a major revival should not be taken at face value, since the statistics do not show any significant growth or change. This common belief instead indicates an attempt to square the fact of a dynamic Buddhist tradition with the received idea of a post-Tang Buddhist decline.

Chinese Buddhism was closely controlled by the communist state in the 1950s and 1960s, and then almost completely destroyed by the Cultural Revolution between 1966 and 1976. But traditions have been revived as a result of the policy of religious liberalization since 1978: major temples and shrines have been rebuilt, and private religious observance permitted. Chinese Buddhism has remained an important cultural force in independent Taiwan throughout this period, and has grown significantly since restrictions on civil organizations were relaxed in 1989: organizations such as Ciji Gongde Hui, Foguashan and Fagushan have a dynamic lay membership, and manage numerous socially engaged projects.

These and other Chinese Buddhist groups generally promote a modernist agenda, the major inspiration for which was Ven. Taixu (1890–1947): Chinese Buddhist modernism is defined by its focus on ethical and spiritual engagement in the present, for example through establishing a 'pure land' in this world, rather than striving for it as something to be realized in the next life. This agenda stands alongside more traditional forms, in particular the old apotropaic and karmic traditions focused on the hereafter, which still dominate the Buddhist mainstream, and which have taken on a new significance in China as Buddhist traditions are recovered and rediscovered after the losses of the Cultural Revolution.

Chapter VIII
State Buddhism in Asia

> For the great enterprise of our country, it is necessary to procure the protective power of all the Buddhas. Therefore we have established Sŏn and Kyo monasteries and sent out abbots to practise and manage their respective doctrines.
>
> King Taejo of Goryeo, 943 AD

Buddhism and the Royal Court

Unlike its expansion in India or transmission to China, Buddhism was not established throughout the rest of Asia by individual missionary endeavour. This was instead achieved as a consequence of state patronage: Buddhists gained access to new lands through direct contact with kings and emperors, sometimes by attaching themselves to diplomatic envoys between royal courts. The presence of Buddhism at the royal court occurred as early as the mid-third century BC, when Buddhist missionaries accompanied Aśoka's envoys to the Sri Lankan kingdom of Devānampiya Tissa in Anurādhapura. But the same pattern was repeated as Buddhism spread from China to East Asia, and from Sri Lanka to Southeast Asia (via South India).

An unintended consequence of this highly successful missionary strategy was that Buddhism became involved in affairs of state: a symbiotic relationship between Sangha and the royal court was created, one not unlike that between Brahmin and monarch in ancient India. This was made possible by an aspect of mythic Buddhism that was largely overlooked in Buddhist India (excepting Tantric Buddhism) but which existed from the very beginning of the Buddha-legend. Canonical discourses of the Pali tradition state that if a person endowed with the 32 supernatural marks chooses to remain in the world (rather then a renounce it and so become a Buddha), he will instead become a 'wheel-turning righteous king' (*cakka-vattin dhamma-rāja*). The Cakravartin Dharmarāja is therefore a secular equivalent of a Buddha, and is thus responsible for instilling Buddhist ideals throughout his realm.

While the Dharmarāja ideal is not explicitly stated in Aśoka's edicts, it can perhaps be read in between the lines, such is the majesty with which Aśoka regards his own exalted position in furthering a thoroughly Buddhist Dhamma. Indeed, Aśoka's insistence on providing impartial religious patronage echoes the Dharmarāja ideal of the Pali *Cakkavatti-sīhanāda Sutta*, as a text which also articulates renunciant ideals in a thoroughly Buddhist guise (just like the Aśokan edicts). But unlike the mythical king of this text, or the edicts of later Buddhist monarchs, Aśoka's edicts do not announce him as a Dharmarāja. This ideal was perhaps too explicitly Buddhist, and if so, it would seem that Aśoka was effectively a Buddhist Dharmarāja who could not say so, or act so, at least not too conspicuously.

In the pre-Aśokan polities of northern India, in a religious culture dominated by autonomous groups of outsiders striving for release, there was no such thing as a state religion. The expansion of the Mauryan imperium institutionalized this distinction between religion and state, for the urban civilization it promoted had its own, entirely secular, bureaucratic norms, and avoided the priestly advice of the Brahmins (whose version of kingship required the political implementation of their sacred rites and social vision). At the forefront of this cultural order were the various Buddhist fraternities, which functioned independently, according to their own rules, much like the guilds of merchants and craftsmen that supported them.

For Aśoka, and hence other, weaker, Buddhist kings of India, the political potential of the Dharmarāja ideal could therefore not be fully realized, at least not before the advent of Tantra: Buddhist-supporting kings were bound by the renunciant separation of religion and worldly affairs, which prevented a more thorough integration of Buddhism in the political realm, and by the Vinaya model of acephalous monastic guilds which assumed institutional and legal autonomy. Although there was little possibility of the Buddhist Sangha becoming involved in the affairs of state, this was not the case in other Asian polities in which renunciant culture was unknown, and in which there were no serious religious rivals to the Buddhists. In such lands the Dharmarāja's association with the cosmic lustre of a Buddha was exploited, allowing the old boundaries between the Sangha and state to be dissolved.

The principal political function served by Buddhism in Asia was legitimation: by conferring its sanctity on the king, the Sangha came to play a vital role in supporting royal authority, for monarchs and emperors were able to claim that their rule was an intrinsic aspect of the cosmic order (as presented by Buddhists). Thus situated within the sacred time and space of Buddhist cosmology, rulers imagined themselves as official patrons and protectors of the Dharma, styling themselves Cakravartins, Bodhisattvas and even Buddhas, and expecting in turn that the Buddhists would use their apotropaic prowess to protect the realm. This was not just a show of power and prestige, however, for the Buddhist kings of Asia were often pious devotees, whose patronage was necessary if the Sangha was to achieve social acceptance in alien cultures, and so enable the Dhamma to establish deep local roots and endure.

Regardless of even the most well-intentioned royal support, state Buddhism in Asia was bound to differ from the acephalous and apolitical institution founded by the Buddha. Closely connected to courtly circles, or at least not easily distinguished from them, the Sangha played an important role in state administration, the making of laws and the creation of national cultures. Quite apart from their spiritual and ethical function in society, Buddhist monks and nuns became a learned elite through whom socio-political norms and a Buddhist-inspired courtly culture were disseminated. As guardians of national culture, the Sangha played a vital role in maintaining the ideological structure on which local identity and royal authority rested. Buddhism thus became involved in the forces of patriotism and nationalism, often at the expense of such basic ideals as compassion and non-violence. Deeply involved in affairs of state, Buddhist attention was focused within rather than without, so that over the course of the medieval period the missionary ethos more or less disappeared.

While the position of the Sangha in society altered as Buddhism spread beyond India and China, its essential religious functions did not. State support could not alter the fact that the guild model was embedded in the monastic rules and procedures of the Vinaya. Even when the royal court defied the explicit advice of the Buddha by appointing a leader of the Sangha – a 'Sangha-rāja' within the religious realm – it was virtually impossible to enforce complete control over all monastic fraternities and lineages. Royal patronage did not, therefore, result in monolithic forms of Buddhism in Asia. Power flowed out from the centre, but there was always scope for legitimately ordained monks to set out alone and start their own monastic communities, perhaps in the forest where they might generate an ascetic prestige that the royal and ecclesiastic powers could not oppose; individuals were always free to adapt ideas and practices to suit their own needs and agendas. Forms of Asian Buddhism are therefore more diverse than might be expected for a religion with an official position at the royal court: state support could not completely undo the decentralized institution anticipated by the Buddha's advice to 'be a light unto yourselves'.

The difference between guild and state Buddhism was not absolute, therefore, but was rather a matter of historical circumstance, and the dichotomy between the two models should thus be seen in terms of the Weberian notion of ideal types. Since the two were never distinguished in canonical texts, in practice the boundaries between them were blurred: Buddhist rituals were held at royal courts for state purposes in both India and China, whereas semi-autonomous guilds reappear throughout the history of Buddhism in the rest of Asia. But the initial spread of Buddhism in India and China, which was not sponsored by the state, created a much greater level of institutional autonomy than elsewhere in Asia. From the very beginning guild monasticism positioned the Sangha at the social periphery, a vantage point from which royal connections could be cultivated, whereas elsewhere monastic fraternities were initially positioned at the socio-political centre, even if this still allowed for the creation of relatively autonomous monastic guilds throughout the kingdom.

The lack of an absolute distinction between the two models of cultural transmission cannot disguise the fact that the reception of Buddhists at the royal court added new dimensions to the Buddhist mission. This means that although similar kinds of apotropaic, karmic and gnostic Buddhism are found throughout Buddhist Asia, this apparent cultural unity conceals fundamentally different perceptions of religious purpose: the differing sorts of patronage and institution building involved in the transmission of guild or state forms of Buddhism established distinct cultural paradigms, within which the meaning of the Dhamma was bound to change. The difference between guild and state Buddhism is hence more significant than the distinction between Theravāda and Mahāyāna. For whereas the latter obscures a vast body of shared ideas and practices, the former touches on underlying cultural structures which explain how Buddhism has actually functioned in society, throughout the course of its long history in India and Asia as a whole.

The Theravāda Tradition in Sri Lanka

The Pali chronicles state that Buddhism arrived in Sri Lanka in the mid-third century BC with envoys that travelled between the courts of Aśoka and King Devānampiya Tissa of Anurādhapura. The Buddhist mission was apparently led by Mahinda, son of Aśoka, who was soon followed by his sister, the nun Saṅghamittā. Texts, relics and other sacred symbols, such as cuttings from the Bodhi tree, and of course the ordination lineage of monks and nuns, were all transmitted from the Kukkuṭārāma (or Asokārāma), the main monastery of Aśoka's capital Pāṭaliputta, via the Buddhist centre of Vedisa in central north India (Sanchi in Madhya Pradesh).

Of the different scholastic approaches which had emerged in northern India, the emergent Sri Lankan tradition was associated with the *vibhajja-vāda*: the 'analytical teaching', identified as much by its opposition to Sarvāstivāda and Pudgalavāda ideas than by any distinct metaphysic. Over the coming centuries the Sri Lankan fraternities maintained close connections with other Vibhajjavādin schools in India, such as the Mahīśāsakas, Dharmaguptakas and Kāśyapīyas. Notwithstanding the value of this scholastic affiliation, the fact that Mahinda had introduced a monastic lineage that could be traced back to the Buddha was more important to the emergent Sri Lankan Buddhism: monastic lineage and practice, rather than intellectual or spiritual affiliation, was a more fundamental means of identification in Buddhist South Asia.

In the Sri Lankan tradition the lineage introduced by Mahinda was referred to as that of the *thera*s or *theriya*s ('elders'), the authoritative teachings of whom was termed *thera/theriya-vāda* ('teaching' of the 'elders'). It is from the terms *thera*, *theriya* and *theravāda* that the modern terms 'Theravada' and 'Theravadin' are derived, although both were rare before the twentieth century. For the scholar-monks of medieval Sri Lanka, the most important term of identification

Fig. 13. Buddha statue on Mihintale mountain where the Indian Buddhist missionary Mahinda met Devānampiya Tissa of Anurādhapura

was *thera*, for it referred to the elders who gathered the canonical teachings at the First Council of Rājagaha; the 'teachings of the elders' were understood to be the Sutta and Vinaya portions of the Tipiṭaka. Although all Buddhist lineages claimed exactly the same origin, the Sanskrit equivalent of *thera/theriya-vāda* (*sthavira/sthāvira-vāda*) was not, apparently, an important factor in the identity of other Buddhist fraternities in India. It would seem that only the Buddhist tradition in Sri Lanka maintained this link to the First Council as a primary form of identification; for the other Buddhist groups in India, this shared heritage was probably presumed, meaning that more specific terms of identification were required.

After the establishment of the Mahāvihāra monastery in Anurādhapura by Devānampiya Tissa, Buddhism was more or less adopted as the official religion of state. Henceforth the Mahāvihāra was the central institution of Sinhalese Buddhism, and although other traditions emerged from it, only this lineage has endured to the present. The surviving Pali literature of Sri Lanka is therefore that of the Mahāvihāra, meaning that the history of Sri Lankan Buddhism is a story told from the Mahāvihārin perspective. Had other lineages achieved supremacy instead of the Mahāvihāra, different intellectual and spiritual orientations, possibly including the alleged Mahāyāna inclinations of the Abhayagiri fraternity, would probably have received more support. But the institutional history would not have been very different: a close relationship between the Sangha and the royal court of Anurādhapura would not have been affected by any variation in monastic lineage.

Apart from the foundational efforts of Devānampiya Tissa, a close connection with the royal court is made clear in the Pali chronicles' account of the war waged war against the Tamil king Eḷāra by Duṭṭhagāmaṇi (r. *c.*161–137 BC). The *Mahāvaṃsa* describes Buddhists as being deeply involved in this conflict, by placing a sacred relic in Duṭṭhagāmaṇi's standard and offering his army moral support. This chronicle also shows how Buddhist ethics could be violated by a close relationship with the state, for it states that no bad karma was created from killing Duṭṭhagāmaṇi's non-Buddhist Tamil enemies, since they are the moral equivalent of cattle.

Royal support played a significant role in the next important development in Sinhalese Buddhism: in the late first century BC, during the reign of Vaṭṭagāmaṇi, the *Mahāvaṃsa* records that civil war, invasions from India and famine left the Sangha in a precarious position, as a result of which a decision was taken to commit the sacred texts of the Tipiṭaka to writing. Although writing had been known in South Asia since the time of Aśoka, this was the first attempt to write down the entire canon, and the endeavour laid the foundations for a highly learned scholastic tradition within the Mahāvihāra.

By this time the Sangha was probably in receipt of extensive patronage, in the form of agricultural estates, villages, water tanks and canals; the main donors were, of course, the royal court and members of local elites. Probably before the same development in India, Buddhist monasteries thus came to be feudal landlords, managing the labour of the inhabitants and sometimes taxing them. The Sangha even came to own slaves, for whom more convenient designations were found (such as *ārāmika* and *kappiya-kāraka*, terms normally associated with voluntary monastic attendants). Being in control of considerable resources, and generally exempt from tax, the Sangha was able to derive a large income from its lands, and even sell estates where necessary. By about the fourth century AD, donations to the Sangha included permanent endowments, which ensured a steady stream of income.

The reign of Vaṭṭagāmaṇi was historically important in one other major respect: his gift of the Abhayagiri monastery to Mahā Tissa, which eventually led to the emergence of separate monastic fraternities in Anurādhapura, and thus the island as a whole. This cannot have happened immediately: a gradual distinction of lineages resulting in different fraternities in the early first millennium AD is the most likely scenario. By the fourth century AD a third lineage located in the Jetavana *vihāra* had split off from Abhayagiri, and until the twelfth century the history of Sinhalese Buddhism was essentially the history of relations between these three fraternities and the state. Situated in the capital of Anurādhapura, all three were at the centre of overlapping monastic networks that spread throughout the island; although the post-canonical Pali literature mentions other groupings – such as the Dhammarucikas, Sāgalikas and more general groups such as *āraññavāsins* and *gāmavāsins* – it is not clear if these were monastic lineages independent of the three major fraternities.

Early Buddhism in Southeast Asia

The Pāli chronicles which record Mahinda's arrival in Sri Lanka also state that a Buddhist mission was sent to *suvaṇṇa-bhūmi*, the 'Land of Gold', the location of which is unknown. Buddhist traditions in Southeast Asia claim that it refers to some place there, and this possibility is supported by the fact that trade between India and Southeast Asia is mentioned in early Pali works (such as some Jātaka commentaries). But there is no material evidence for a Buddhist presence in the region until much later: the earliest Buddhist remains in Southeast Asia date to the fourth or fifth century AD, or even later, in the form of Buddha statues in the Amaravati style of South India, and pillars topped with Aśokan-style wheels (*dharma-cakras*).

Epigraphic remains indicate that the early forms of Buddhism in Southeast Asia were dominated by a Pali Theriya tradition arriving from South India rather than Sri Lanka: an abundance of Pali inscriptions, dating from roughly the fifth to eighth centuries AD, in a version of the South Indian Pallava script, have been recovered from the ancient Mon kingdom of Dvāravatī (of the Chao-Phraya basin in central Thailand) and the Pyu kingdom of Śrī Kṣetra (in upper Burma). Little is known of the South Indian Theravādins. The fact that Parakkama Bāhu II restored the Sinhalese Sangha in the thirteenth

Fig. 14. Schwedagon pagoda, Yangon, an old Mon stūpa *which possibly goes back to the early influx of the South India Theravāda in the fifth century* AD

century with the help of Tamil monks suggests that the South India Theriyas existed until the late medieval period. But the fifth century migration of Buddhaghosa to Sri Lanka, and of other South Indian Theriyas to Śrī Kṣetra, along with the general demise of South Indian Buddhist sites at this time, suggests the tradition was in decline for most of the early medieval period.

The variety of Southeast Asian inscriptions, which cite canonical and non-canonical Pali texts – often remarkably close to modern printed editions – suggest that the South Indian Theriyas had an extensive literary collection, more or less an exact copy of the canonical Pali literature which has been transmitted to the present. The so-called 'Golden Pali Text', an early fifth century inscription recovered from an ornate Pyu reliquary, suggests that the local Theriya tradition was in receipt of royal patronage, and if so it would seem that the transmission of Pali Buddhism to Southeast Asia was achieved through association with ruling elites.

Other inscriptional evidence, in different Prakrits and in Sanskrit, and from kingdoms to the east (Funan and Chenla, more or less equivalent to the area of modern Cambodia, and Champa, roughly equivalent to Vietnam) and south (Śrivijaya, roughly equivalent to Sumatra and adjacent areas in Java and the Malaysian peninsula), suggest that there was a plurality of Buddhist traditions, and also a Brahminic presence, in Southeast Asia during the second half of the first millennium AD. Images of Brahminic deities and Mahāyāna Bodhisattvas, found at ancient Dvāravatī sites and the Pyu city of Śri Kṣetra, thus show that Mahāyāna and Brahminism were supported even in regions where the Theriya school flourished.

The Theravādin tradition in Southeast Asia has therefore never existed in isolation from other Buddhist and non-Buddhist traditions. But Brahminism in Southeast Asia was never a serious competitor, at least after the demise of Angkor, for it was not a popular movement and was generally confined to a ceremonial function at the royal court. Mahāyāna traditions were more serious rivals for much of the first millennium AD: material remains from upper Burma indicate extensive contact with northern India, especially during the Pāla and Sena periods, and it would seem that Mahāyāna and Tantric Buddhism flourished throughout the region in the medieval period.

The greatest sphere of Sanskritic influence in mainland Southeast Asia, both Buddhist and Brahminic, came from the Khmer kingdom of Angkor. Indian art, literature, philosophy and political thought arrived in the pre-Angkorian kingdoms of Funan and Chenla in the same period as Buddhism was transmitted there. Soon after 800 AD this appropriation of Brahminic culture enabled the creation of a major state in the region of Angkor, a kingdom based on the *maṇḍala* ideology of medieval Brahminic political thought, as described in the Brahminic *Arthaśāstra* ('Treatise on Political Aims'). According to this ideology, a central dominion is surrounded by gradually diminishing spheres of influence among its vassal kingdoms, there being no distinct borders between neighbouring polities, with authority and control determined by the distance of any locality from the major power situated at the political centre.

At the heart of the Angkorian state, from the very beginning with the reign of Jayavarman II (r. 802–854), was the Tantric identity of king and deity: Tantric Hinduism, with its cosmic symbolism and ritual paraphernalia, was a potent force for the creation of a royal personality cult and a strong state based on it. Inscriptions thus identify Jayavarman II with the Hindu God Śiva and refer to him as a 'divine king' (*deva-rāja*). During this period, when the Tantric cults of Śiva and Viṣṇu were strongly supported by the royal court, Buddhist groups received moderate patronage. The material remains suggest that Mahāyāna cults were maintained from the period of Yaśovarman (r. 889–900), and that these were strongly promoted by Jayavarman VII (r. 1181–1218), the last of the great Angkorian god-kings.

There is little evidence for Theriyas within the Angkorian polity: the fact that hardly any Pali inscriptions have been found in the region as a whole indicates that the Theravādins had little influence there. But support for Brahminic and Mahāyāna cults dwindled with the demise of Angkor, and in their aftermath the Theriyas established themselves as the dominant religious tradition. But the form of Theravāda which rose to predominance in the post-Angkorian period retained elements from the region's diverse religious past, and is best considered a Southeast Asian sort of Buddhism rooted in, but not completely defined by, the Pali tradition.

Pali Civilization in Medieval Asia

The rise to prominence of Theravāda Buddhism throughout mainland Southeast Asia began early in the second millennium AD. The old Theriya tradition which had survived in the Mon city states of lower Burma, such as Thaton, was appropriated by the Burmese king of Pagan, Aniruddha (r. 1044–1077), and similar royal support was received by related Theriya lineages further east in the following centuries: support in Angkor is shown by the fact that in the late twelfth century, a son of Jayavarman VII was among a group of Southeast Asian monks who travelled to Sri Lanka. In the following centuries, the old Theriya traditions of Dvāravatī received official patronage from the emerging Thai kingdoms of northern and central Thailand, particularly in Chiang Mai and Sukhothai, after they broke away from the Angkorian *maṇḍala* in the thirteenth century.

A well supported Theriya tradition in Southeast Asia was good news for the old Theravāda tradition of Sri Lanka. For by the late eleventh century, after roughly 200 years of intermittent war between the Sinhalese and Tamil Cholas, Anurādhapura had been sacked and the capital moved to Polonnaruwa in the east. During this period many Buddhist traditions were lost: the order of nuns disappeared, and the order of monks survived only when the Theriya lineage was

Fig. 15. Thirteenth-century Buddhist remains at Wat Mahathat, Sukhothai

imported from lower Burma by King Vijayabāhu (r. 1070–1110). There had probably been some contact between Southeast Asia and Sri Lanka before this, but the absence of any such information in the Sri Lankan chronicles suggests that no meaningful relationship had yet been forged.

These developments coincided with the more or less complete disappearance of Buddhism from India. After the demise of the Pāla dynasty in the twelfth century, the focus of cultural exchange in Southeast Asia thus shifted away from India and towards Sri Lanka. For much of the second millennium AD, traditions of Theravāda learning and culture were exchanged across the Indian Ocean, drawing disparate realms together in a shared ideology and identity, communicated through the medium of the Pali language. When the Southeast Asian party including the son of Jayavarman VII returned from Sri Lanka in 1181, the Mahāvihārin lineage was established in Pagan – the sole lineage remaining in Sri Lanka after Parakkama Bāhu I had abolished the Abhayagiri and Jetavana lineages (or 'unified' them into a single tradition) in 1164. The scholarly tradition of the Mahāvihāra thus became established in Southeast Asia.

Fig. 16. Medieval Theravāda civilization: seated Buddha statue from Gal, Polonnaruwa, twelfth century

The same pattern of decline and foreign missions marks the history of Sri Lankan Buddhism in more recent times. The Theravāda lineage was re-established in the Sri Lankan court of Kandy in the late sixteenth century and then again in 1753, by missions from Burma and Thailand respectively. This history of monastic decline and revival illustrates the problems involved in the state patronage of Buddhism. Kings endowed the Sangha with wealth and land because they wished to harness the spiritual eminence of Buddhist monasticism: Buddhist rituals were sought to legitimize the royal court through their sacred symbols and paraphernalia, while Buddhist doctrine was drawn upon to emphasize the king's official position in the Buddhist cosmos. Underlying these motives was the general pre-modern belief in magic: eminent Buddhist monks were believed to possess supernatural powers, as a result of their monastic purity, and it was this holy lustre that kings wished to access, if not actually then at least symbolically.

However reasonable it seemed to kings, state support for Buddhism had unintended consequences. For by safeguarding their own rule through material donations to the Sangha, kings provided the Sangha with the means of excess and decline. The loss of purity this caused subsequently jeopardized royal authority, thus necessitating royal intervention and the re-establishment of monastic standards. Apart from the political necessity of reviving lax traditions in decline, sometimes with help from abroad, the motif of monastic purification could also be used by kings to reconfigure political allegiances to their benefit: the general pattern was that when a new reign was established, a king would typically take steps to buttress his power through aligning the court with favourable factions in the Sangha.

The ideology of purity and power is the deep reason behind royal patronage of Buddhism in all times and places. But it has never been the sole reason for state support: besides the cosmic legitimation provided by the perceived holy purity of the Sangha, kings promoted Buddhism across the Theravāda world for its civilizing effects. With an extensive network of village temples and monastic estates, the Buddhist Sangha was situated at the heart of local communities. Quite apart from Buddhism's legitimizing role at the royal court, Theravāda monastics acted as intermediaries between the populace and the elite, and thus enabled the spread of literacy and a Pali-based culture.

The Practice of Theravāda Buddhism

In a world of village temples and monasteries, in which state and Sangha supported and maintained each other's prestige and interests, popular practice in Theravāda Buddhism has always been focused on making merit. The primary means of achieving this was through donations to the Sangha, the purest 'field of merit', in return for which Buddhist monks were obliged to perform rituals and ceremonies (especially of death), and function as educators and preachers. To carry out these roles has always required a knowledge of the narrative canon (dominated by Jātaka tales), a medium which provided ideological support for the simple act of making merit, and which established the ethical ideals of the Dhamma in Theravāda cultures.

An important means of making merit in Theravāda is chanting Pali formulas. These centre on devotion towards the Buddha, especially through recalling his unique virtues and qualities, but also include protectional chants and formulas (*paritta*, *rakṣā*), the recitation of which is regarded as a sort of white magic that wards off bad luck and effects good fortune. In such practices there is generally no distinction between karmic and apotropaic Buddhism: what counts as merit-making is a magical means of procuring worldly success, and icons and shrines at which rituals are performed, both within and beyond the temple, are the abode of powerful supernatural beings, from the Buddha himself to various classes of spirit. These supernatural beings are generally derived from the canonical literature, but also include various ghosts, nature spirits, national guardian deities and Hindu gods. Such figures function as protectors of the Buddha's Dhamma, but can also be propitiated by devotees for their own purposes.

Many of these apotropaic and karmic practices also feature in the form of gnostic Theravāda sometimes termed 'Esoteric Southern Buddhism' or Tantric Theravāda, but which is better referred to by indigenous terms such as 'Yogāvacara' ('practice of yoga') and *boran* ('ancient'). This practice, which is structured around visualization, includes such elements as initiation by a skilled adept, the recitation of magical formulae, rituals performed around a sacred space demarcated by a mystical diagram (*yantra*), and the invocation of various deities and supernatural beings. While there are clear similarities between Yogāvacara and Buddhist Tantra, its underlying ideology is unique to the Theravāda world: the practice focuses on the visualization of the Buddha as a crystal sphere within, to be used as a means of fashioning a spiritual body which can be made to exit the body at death in a final attainment of liberation.

The origins of this tradition are obscure. It is possible that systems of Buddhist Tantra were transmitted from East Bengal to Burma in the Pāla period, and there is no reason to suppose that these did not continue to flourish among Ari monastic lineages even after the extension of the Pagan kingdom towards lower Burma in 1057 AD, and the extensive patronage of the Pali tradition thereafter. Indeed, the lay esoteric practitioners (*weizkado*) of modern Burma resemble the ascetic sorcerers (*vidyādhara*) and Siddhas of medieval Bengal: their overriding aim is to become semi-immortal, remaining in the world helping others until the appearance of the future Buddha Maitreya, at which point the religious goal becomes that of attaining Nirvana or the full awakening of a Buddha.

These ideas are not clearly related to the Yogāvacara tradition, however, the historical evidence for which is generally confined to Thailand, Cambodia and Laos; this suggests an origin in the Tantric-influenced Buddhist communities of Angkor, followed by their absorption within Theriya traditions during the late medieval period. But a Sri Lankan origin cannot be ruled out, however, even if the practice was transmitted there relatively recently (by means of a Siamese mission in 1753), for aspects of Mahāyāna and Tantra are known to have flourished within the Abhayagiri lineage during the first millennium AD; even Buddhaghosa's *Visuddhimagga*, the dominant text of Theravāda scholasticism, mentions 'secret books' in its discussion of meditation. The lack of any pre-modern Sri Lankan evidence for Yogāvacara can possibly be explained by a medieval disappearance of the tradition, perhaps during the troubled period between the ninth and eleventh centuries.

Non-esoteric Theravāda meditation is nowadays based on the canonical dyad of calm (*samatha*) and insight (*vipassanā*), especially the latter, which has a strong basis in the Abhidhamma. Although this practice is a modern expression of the ancient, contemplative school of Indian Buddhism, only vague connections with the early period can be discerned. It would seem that *vipassanā* was revived afresh in both Burma and Sri Lanka during the eighteenth and nineteenth centuries, when barely any connection to the past remained, thus requiring a careful use of the canonical texts and the scholastic works of Buddhaghosa to restore the tradition. In general, the modern *vipassanā* traditions do not see much value in meditative absorption or 'calming' meditation (*samatha*, assigned to which are the four *jhāna*s and the formless meditations). Where this is the case, *samatha* is generally used as a preliminary to insight meditation, the latter being instead directed towards the contemplation of conditioned experience and its transience, usually by means of the four applications of mindfulness.

Theravāda and Modernity

The Theravāda nations of South and Southeast Asia have faced and survived serious challenges in recent centuries, in particular colonialism (the British in Burma and Sri Lanka, the Portuguese and Dutch in Sri Lanka, and the French in Cambodia, Laos and Vietnam) and

Fig. 17. Devotional offerings at Maha Brahma shrine, Ratchaprosong, central Bangkok

communism. But both have been avoided in Thailand, which since 1932 has been a democracy with a constitutional monarchy. The challenges of modernity in Thai Theravāda have therefore been faced from a position of relative cultural strength, despite frequent political instability. The spirit houses found outside houses, hotels and shopping malls show that Thai Theravāda has maintained its identity and vitality on its own terms, in a space alongside the manifestations of modernity, and without apparently suffering any seriously deleterious effects. The general cultural ambience of Thai Theravāda – with its Pali tradition and liturgies, its forest meditators and scholars, and old Buddhist conceptions of the king as a Dhammarāja – has thus survived.

None of this means that Thai Theravāda has remained static in the face of rapid social change. The conditions of modernity have instead allowed for a plurality of responses to the changing world, encouraging new institutions, cults and apparently endless reformulations of received practices and ideas at a level below institutionally sanctioned norms. New movements such as the Dhammakaya Foundation and Santi Asoke, in their very different responses to modernity, draw attention to the intrinsic diversity within Thai Theravāda. Whereas the Dhammakaya Foundation has adapted to social change, by promoting a modified form of Yogāvacara meditation within a generally

Fig. 18. Magha Puja celebrations at the Maha Cetiya, Wat Phra Dhammakaya

conservative form of Theravāda, Santi Asoke has instead styled itself as an ascetically oriented purification movement, with a nationalist edge, the focus being not so much on accommodating modernity, but rather in criticizing its manifestations – such as globalization, capitalism, consumerism – and retreating from the world.

This vibrancy at both the institutional and individual levels has tended to dilute the increasing centralization since the transformation of the Siamese *maṇḍala*-kingdom into the nation state of Thailand. A major step in this centralization was the Sangha Act of 1902, which set up a centrally imposed power structure and system of monastic education. This built upon the earlier attempts of King Mongkut (Rāma IV, r. 1851–1866, previously Vajirañāṇa bhikkhu) to purify the Sangha by establishing the new Dhammayuttika lineage, with a focus on promoting textual orthodoxy along with a more strict observance of the Vinaya. But this emphasis on canonical Buddhism and Theravāda rationalism was not simply a Western-influenced attempt to modernize, for Mongkut's 'textualism' occurred before any serious Orientalist work on the Pali canon. Just like the promotion of canonical Buddhism by King Mindon of Burma (1808–1878), at whose 'Fifth Council' of 1871 a new edition of the Pali canon was prepared – and subsequently inscribed onto

Figs. 19 & 20. The world's largest book: Some of the 729 pagodas at Kuthodaw temple, Mandalay, which house stone slabs containing the edition of the Pali canon prepared under King Mindon in 1871

729 stone slabs at the Kuthodaw Pagoda in Mandalay – Mongkut's Buddhist activities fit the traditional pattern of monastic purification by a powerful Dhammarāja at the beginning of his reign, even if in this case the king was keenly aware of the rapidly changing world outside Siam.

The similarity between indigenous Buddhist modernism in Thailand and Burma ceases with King Mindon. For early in the reign of Mindon's successor, King Thibaw (r. 1878–1885), British forces advanced on Mandalay bringing to an end the last Buddhist kingdom of Burma. With the British refusing to take on the traditional role of Buddhist patron, the late nineteenth century was a period during which the Burmese confronted the disenchanting forces of imperialism. New, reformist, monastic lineages arose, such as the Schwegyin Nikāya, as well as millennial movements led by charismatic holy men protesting against colonial rule; other modernizers promoted rationalism, social engagement and an increased level of lay practice, both for the sake of spiritual renewal and re-asserting national identity. The lay meditation movements which emerged in the early twentieth century, in particular those of Ledi Sayadaw and Mahasi Sayadaw, arose in this context, and were subsequently promoted by U Nu, first Prime Minister of independent Burma in the post-colonial period.

Ever since Burmese independence, and in spite of the dictatorships that have ruled since, versions of the old symbiosis between Sangha and state have been restored. The regime of Ne Win and those that followed – the BSPP (Burma Socialist Programme Party), SLORC (State Law and Order Resurrection Council) and SPDC (State Peace and Development Council) – revived the tradition of state patronage by Buddhist rulers. Various ritual, charitable and educational endeavours have thus been sponsored: the military regimes continued the traditional role of U Nu, whose most notable act of patronage was to sponsor the 'Sixth Council' of Rangoon (1954–1956), at which a new edition of the Pali canon was prepared. The need for such state support was not merely to uphold tradition: control of the largest non-state institution was also an important factor, as shown by the prominent role of monks in the uprisings of 1988 and 2007. The release of Aung San Suu Kyi in 2011, and free elections of March 2011, may indicate a permanent change in the Burmese state, but its future relation with the Sangha is as yet unclear.

Communism posed a more destructive challenge to Theravāda

Buddhism in Cambodia, where between 1975 and 1979 all monks were defrocked and many killed during the Khmer Rouge genocide. Cambodian Buddhism was virtually destroyed during this time, although there has been a gradual restoration since 1979, which gained pace after the departure of the Vietnamese in 1989. The Mahānikāya lineage was restored soon afterwards, and the Dhammayuttika, originally introduced from Thailand in the late nineteenth century, was re-established in the 1990s. Many temples and monasteries have been reconstructed, although most of the literary heritage of Cambodian Buddhism has been lost. There was no such violence in neighbouring Laos after the introduction of communism and fall of the monarchy in 1975, but the Sangha's influence in society has been carefully limited, and patronage minimized.

Sri Lankan responses to modernity have largely come about in response to colonialism, through figures such as the lay Buddhist Anagarika Dharmapala (1864–1933). Drawing especially upon Orientalist writings, Dharmapala presented rational aspects of the Pali canon as the pure, original form of Buddhism, and hence the ideal resource for a spiritual and social revival in Sri Lanka. This response to modernity has been termed 'Protestant Buddhism', for like the reformation in Europe it has generally focused on rationalism and bypassed traditional forms of authority (especially by emphasizing a layperson's private practice of the Dhamma). The religious individualism of the protestant reformers has more recently been surpassed by a general diffusion of authority: modern media and technology have allowed for a proliferation of lay movements, particularly those focusing on social reform and meditation among the educated middle class. Beyond these modern developments, spirit cults and village shamanism have found a new and larger audience among the diverse social classes of the cities.

A further aspect of Sri Lankan responses to modernity has been the emergence of Buddhist nationalism. Reformers such as Dharmapala presented their rational vision of Theravāda as part of the movement against colonialism, and this vehicle for Buddhist nationalism has continued to grow since independence was achieved in 1948. But just as the lay meditation movement is not a new development, so too is Sinhalese Buddhist nationalism a contemporary expression of old tradition. The aim to restore Buddhism as a state religion is a continuation of the Sinhalese Buddhist story, as traced in ancient times by the chronicles of the Mahāvihāra (in particular the *Mahāvaṃsa*). Now the civil war is over (since 2009), the future of this modern articulation of the ancient symbiosis between Sangha and state remains to be seen.

Perhaps the most important issue in contemporary Theravāda concerns the status of nuns. The *bhikkhunī* lineage died out some time in the medieval period, and the lack of an ordained nun – required to officiate at the ordination ceremony of any other nun – has prevented a revival of the order. This conservative position was challenged in the 1990s, when ordination ceremonies for *bhikkhunīs* were held in India, Sri Lanka, Australia and the United States, with the ceremonial lack of Theravādin nuns being compensated by the officiation of Taiwanese nuns (from the Dharmaguptaka lineage). The conservative Theravāda response to this has been to claim that such ordinations are legally invalid. But the Dharmaguptaka and Theravādin lineages are closely related, and there is no precept in the Pali Vinaya against the co-operation of different Vinaya traditions in official ceremonies. There being no decisive argument for or against the re-institution of the *bhikkhunī* order, their validation thus depends upon the attitudes of authorities within the different Theravāda traditions.

Buddhism on the Korean Peninsula

The introduction of Buddhism to Korea was achieved through state patronage in the late fourth and early fifth centuries AD. Although some Buddhists may have arrived earlier, the first documented Buddhist monk to reach the Korean peninsula was the Chinese monk Sundo, who in 372 arrived at the court of King Sosurim (r. 371–383) of the northern Goguryeo dynasty, having travelled from the court of King Fujian (r. 357–385) of the Former Qin dynasty of northern China (351–394). Buddhism then reached the court of Geungusu (r. 375–384) in the Baekje kingdom of the southwest in 384, through a mission sent from the Eastern Jin dynasty (317–420) of China. The final Korean kingdom to receive Buddhism was Silla, of the southeast, in the early fifth century AD during the reign of King Nulji (417–447).

This period of Buddhist transmission was one in which the three tribal kingdoms of Korea were expanding into larger polities, with more extensive administrative and bureaucratic powers. It is not difficult to see that in this process of state formation, the ruling families valued the social benefits of Buddhism. Apart from the use of Buddhist universalism as a means of creating a unified culture, Buddhists were sought for the magical protection provided by its cosmic pantheon of Buddhas and Bodhisattvas. Apotropaic Buddhism also made for a relatively easy assimilation of old animistic beliefs: shamanic practices and the worship of nature deities and ancestral spirits were all infused into emerging Korean versions of the Dharma. An enduring element from this period of Buddhist assimilation was the placement of Buddhist centres atop mountains and hills, in order to pacify the old local spirits and incorporate their protective power.

The Buddhicization of Korea was not without problems: an initial resistance to deviate from old tribal ways probably explains the relatively late acceptance of the religion in the Silla kingdom. It would seem that some noble houses were resistant to the socio-political power to be gained by rivals who appropriated Buddhism as a means of legitimization. But Buddhism was finally sanctioned by King Beopheung in 527, after the execution of Ichadon, a court noble and Buddhist monk whose martyrdom hastened official support. The quick spread of Buddhism afterwards suggests a wider dissemination since its arrival in the mid-fifth century. Beopheung was ordained a monk shortly before his death in 540, and more freedom was granted to Buddhist monks under the Silla king Jinheung (r. 540–576). The increasing prevalence of Buddhism during Jinheung's rule was decisive in the prominent place in Korean society it attained thereafter.

Despite its initial resistance, the Silla kingdom gained much from its patronage of Buddhism. Originally an isolated and weak kingdom in the southeast, after endorsing Buddhism its power and status increased until in 668 the entire Korean peninsula was united under its rule. The promotion of Buddhism by the Silla court thus helped both in creating a general culture and identity, and in legitimizing royal authority throughout the Unified Silla Period (688–935). For the rest of the Silla period, and the entirety of the Goryeo period which followed, the Buddhist Sangha was a unifying cultural force, whose presence was believed to guarantee national security through ritual appropriation of the cosmic pantheon of Buddhas (including Amitābha, Bhaiṣajyaguru and Śākyamuni) and Bodhisattvas (including Maitreya and Avalokiteśvara).

Early Buddhist Schools in Korea

During the fifth and sixth centuries Buddhist monks travelled from Korea to China to receive instruction and training from Chinese masters. This in turn allowed early schools of thought to be transmitted to Korea, including Abhidharma, Tiantai (Cheontae), Madhyamaka (Samnon) and Vinaya (Gyeyul). The study of the *Mahā-parinirvāṇa Sūtra* and Buddha-nature ideas were also important formative influences on Korean Buddhism, as was Pure Land Buddhism and Tantra, the arrival of which introduced a wide range of contemplative, devotional and ritual practices. But Korea was not just a passive recipient of Chinese Buddhism during this early period, for Korean monks also played an important role in Chinese Buddhist developments: in the late fifth and early sixth century Seungnang was a prominent Sanlun figure and influence on Jizang (549–623); the exegetical system of Wonhyo (617–686) was an important influence on the Huayan patriarch Fazang (643–712); and Wonchuk (631–696) was a prominent disciple of the translator and Yogācāra scholar Xuanzang (596–664).

Towards the end of this early infusion of Chinese Buddhist schools and texts, the study of Huayan was introduced by Uisang (625–702). Uisang had studied in China under Zhiyan (602–668), the second Huayan patriarch, and upon returning to Korea introduced the study of the *Avataṃsaka Sūtra*; the Hwaeom school which he founded at Pusok temple soon became prominent. Besides his importance in the intellectual history of Korean Buddhism, Uisang enjoyed close relations with the royal court and was a pivotal figure in the promotion of monasticism. Closely related to Hwaeom was the exegetical system created by Uisang's friend Wonhyo (617–686), whose massive output included more than 80 individual works of exegesis, and was a major influence on the emergence of a specifically Korean sort of Buddhist scholasticism – one in which different doctrinal perspectives are harmonized rather than distinguished, as in the Indian schools inherited by the Chinese.

After his ordination at the age of 15, Wonhyo decided not to travel to Tang China with Uisang, choosing instead to follow his own scholarly studies as a layman. These he pursued while leading an unconventional lifestyle, although this did not prevent a prodigious scholarly output. Only 22 of his works have survived, but these are notable both for their impartiality and scope, which extends over all the major Mahāyāna traditions known in East Asia. Unusually among Buddhist scholars, Wonhyo was not affiliated to any particular school, and this freedom from doctrinal prejudice allowed him to integrate the different strands of the highly varied Chinese canon into a single vision of the Dharma.

Two analytical themes underpin this synthetic approach: the 'harmonization of disputes' (*hwajaeng*), which involves showing that the exact points of doctrinal divergence depend upon viewing ideas from particular perspectives; and the idea of what has been termed 'interpenetrated Buddhism' (*tong bulgyo*), the viewing of intellectual diversity as aspects of a larger doctrinal whole rather than dogmatic rivals. The purpose of *hwajaeng* is therefore to explain away differences, whereas the point of *tong bulgyo* is to show how different perspectives form complementary aspects of a much greater doctrinal vision. Underpinning this organic whole is the idea of 'One Mind', the ultimate point of convergence for the various systems studied by Wonhyo.

The Meditative Tradition in Korea

Korean monks had travelled to China to study Chan before the Unified Silla Period, for example Beomnang, who in the mid-seventh century had studied under Daoxin (580–651), the so-called fourth patriarch of the Chan school. But it was not until the eighth century that a lasting Chan lineage was established in Korea. By the early ninth century nine schools of 'Seon' had been founded, each located at a different mountain monastery; eight of these were based on the Chan tradition of Mazu (709–788), the sole exception being the school founded by Ieom (869–936), which had roots in the Caodong rather than Linji Chan lineage.

The rise of Seon in the eighth and ninth centuries coincided with a period of political instability and the decline of the Silla dynasty. Mazu's Chan was therefore promoted in difficult times: by rejecting doctrinal study and adopting a brand of Chan dominated by subitist rhetoric, the early Seon schools moved beyond the structure of state-sponsored Buddhist learning. Unsurprisingly, the doctrinal schools (Gyo, primarily Hwaeom) and their state patrons were opposed to the new meditative traditions, forcing the meditators to retreat to the hills and establish their monasteries away from the Silla court in Gyeongju. Support for the meditators thus came from regional clans, whose opposition to the central Silla state made them natural allies of non-conformist meditators.

Despite the official opposition of the Silla court and the central Sangha authorities, the Seon schools gradually gained state patronage during the rule of the Goryeo dynasty (918–1392). By the end of this period, they therefore wielded significant socio-political influence, being renowned for both their meditative skills and their apotropaic services. But this more prominent position did not resolve the discord between Seon and Gyo: Gyo was opposed to the anti-intellectualism of Seon, whereas the Seon schools claimed superiority through the Chan myth that Bodhidharma had received direct transmission of the Dharma in an unbroken lineage stretching back to the Buddha.

An early but unsuccessful attempt to synthesize the two traditions was made by the Cheontae scholar Uicheon (1055–1101), a royal prince who studied various Buddhist systems in Song China. His learning in a wide variety of systems, including Chan, Huayan, Vinaya, Pure Land and Tiantai, allowed him to present Tiantai as a means of integrating diverse Buddhist perspectives. But his early death ruled out the possibility of making a lasting impression on Seon practitioners, who did not take up his system. The chances of any Gyo-authored synthesis diminished with the general decline of scholarship after the mid-Goryeo period. But by this time Hwaeom works were increasingly authored by Seon monks, and this prepared the way for the dichotomy between meditation and scholarship to be resolved not by Gyo theoreticians, but by Seon contemplatives.

A more enduring synthesis, when it eventually arrived, was thus devised from within the Seon tradition by Jinul (1158–1210). Ordained at Kulsansa, in a Seon lineage derived from Mazu's Hongzhou school, Jinul failed to establish a close relationship with any teacher throughout his career. His eventual synthesis of Seon and Gyo was therefore a consequence, at least in part, of a lack of personal instruction, for in turning to the Buddhist texts for inspiration from an early age, Jinul came to fashion an approach to Seon meditation grounded in scriptural study, unlike other meditators of his age. Textualism thus played an important role in Jinul's spiritual path: his first 'awakening' experience, which occurred in 1182 (at Chongwonsa, in the southwest of the Korean peninsula) shortly after he had passed his official Sangha examinations at the capital city of Kaesong, was inspired by his reading of the Platform Sūtra.

Based on the Platform Sūtra's focus on the innate purity of the mind, Jinul formulated the idea of a 'concurrent development of samādhi and prajñā'. According to this approach to meditation, the alertness of understanding (*prajñā*) prevents faults associated with absorption (*samādhi*), such as lethargy and inner abstraction, whereas the tranquillity of *samādhi* prevents faults associated with *prajñā*, chiefly excessive ratiocination. During his stay in Chongwonsa, Jinul was also influenced by Zongmi, a Huayan theoretician as well as a Chan meditator (of the Heze lineage). According to Zongmi's formulation of practice, maintaining the state of 'no thought' allows the mind's innate suchness to unfold, but this process of development begins in earnest with an initial awakening to the true nature of the mind. Meditation is thus a means of habituating the awakened state in everyday life, after first intuiting the true nature of the mind.

The next important step in Jinul's spiritual development took place in 1185, after three years of intense scriptural study focused particularly on the problem of the differing notions of enlightenment taught in the Gyo and Seon schools. Jinul resolved this problem by identifying the transconceptual enlightenment of Chan with the Huayan idea of realizing the interpenetration of all phenomena at the ultimate level (*dharma-dhātu*). This idea was influenced by his reading of the Huayan thinker Li Tongxuan (635–730), who proposed a version of the path in which awakening takes places at the very beginning of the ten levels of 'faith' according to the Huayan system. This idea was easily synthesized with the similar ideas of Zongmi, whose understanding that deluded states of mind are expressions of its innate suchness, and so not substantially different from it, allowed for a synthesis of the Seon notion of suchness with the Huayan notion of interpenetration.

Jinul presented this more developed understanding of the spiritual path as the 'faith and understanding' approach, according to the 'sudden' teaching: through faith a person grasps the teaching that the mind, in all its various forms and states, is identical with the state of Buddhahood: 'awakening' to this truth it is possible, through gradual cultivation, to trace the mind's movements back to its intrinsic radiance. Since Jinul claimed a Huayan source for the predominantly Chan idea of sudden enlightenment, he was able to argue that the Gyo idea of a long and arduous path – imagined according to the general mythic idea – was suitable for students of inferior capacity, whereas Seon teachings are for more advanced students. But this was not the final conclusion of Jinul's exegetical endeavours.

In 1190 Jinul finally established a Samādhi and Prajñā Society in Kojosā, nine years after devising the plan with like-minded monks during his Buddhist examinations in Kaesong. After seven years the community moved to Songgwang mountain, but on the way Jinul entered a three-year retreat, during which he studied the records of Dahui. The final stage of Jinul's Seon exploration of Buddhist thought thus consisted in his appropriation of Dahui's *ganhwa* meditation. The three stages of Jinul's career hence form successive levels of practice in his soteriological system, starting with the union of *samādhi* and *prajñā* for beginners, continuing with the faith and understanding approach for average students and culminating in *ganhwa* meditation for more advanced gnostics. Although Chan ideas, values and practices dominate this system, its theoretical foundations are provided by Huayan thought.

From Jinul's death in 1210 until the fourteenth century, the monastery at Songgwangsa/Chogyesan developed into the major centre of Korean Buddhism, one that attracted both Gyo and Seon devotees. And through the influence of Jinul and his successors, especially Hyesim (1178–1234), Dahui's *ganhwa* meditation came to dominate contemplative practice in the Seon tradition.

Buddhism and the State under the Goryeo and Joseon Dynasties

As the Korean peninsula became mired in turmoil towards the end of the Silla period, the house of Goryeo (918–1392) emerged to establish a new dynasty. This change in the political configuration of Korea did not affect the prestigious position of Buddhism at court and in society. Indeed, the relationship between state and Sangha was only strengthened: the first Goryeo emperor Taejo (r. 918–943) was a pious patron, building hundreds of temples and having elaborate rituals continuously carried out for the state. The ten principles of kingship he issued to guide his successors – beginning with the statement 'For the great enterprises of our country, it is necessary to procure the protective power of all the Buddhas' – indicate the prominent position of Buddhism in the realm.

In the Goryeo period Buddhism was therefore closely involved in state affairs; when a system of monastic examinations was created to run parallel to the civil service examinations, during the reign of King Kwangjong (949–975), the Sangha was effectively turned into a branch of the state bureaucracy. Monks thus became advisors at the royal court, the highest honour bestowed on these monastic officials being that of 'royal preceptor' (*wangsa*). The Sangha also became a major economic power, with large monastic estates worked by feudal tenants; since these estates were exempt from taxation, by the second half of the Goryeo period the Sangha had become a considerable drain on state resources. The excessive involvement in secular affairs, and inevitable monastic corruption this induced, led to attempts to purify the Sangha from within. Jinul's attempt to establish a pure community of knowledgeable meditators in the mountains, finally achieved with the foundation of Songgwangsa monastery in 1190, was as much a reaction to declining religious standards as it was to Seon and Gyo factionalism.

By the end of the Goryeo period, the symbiotic relationship between Sangha and state had begun to work against the long-term prospects of both: there were too many temples staffed by incumbents of dubious purity; state expenditure on them and their elaborate rituals was excessive; and the government was corrupt, and unsure of itself after the decline of the Mongol Yuan dynasty in China (replaced by the Ming dynasty in 1368). In these circumstances, the neo-Confucianism imported from Song China towards the end of the thirteenth century was an attractive alternative for those critical of the royal court and the state religion. The Goryeo dynasty was eventually replaced by the Joseon dynasty (1392–1910), and with strong neo-Confucian support it quickly eradicated the dominant position of Buddhism in the Korean state.

The anti-Buddhist reprisals began in earnest in the early fifteenth century, and were vigorously enforced for the next 200 years. During this time the deleterious effects on Buddhism were much worse than those of any of the relatively short-lived Chinese persecutions: hundreds of temples and monasteries were vacated, Buddhist funerals and begging were outlawed, ordination was often prohibited, monks were forcibly returned to lay life, and those remaining were not allowed to enter the capital city. Buddhism was effectively banned and its remaining practitioners marginalized. In the fifteenth century the number of monasteries dropped to less than 250; by the sixteenth century there were less than 100. Only the Seon school maintained its traditions with some vigour, its meditators and quietists perhaps better suited to the loss of patronage and a hermetic existence in the mountains.

This perhaps explains the fact that Seon teachers and thinkers appeared throughout these difficult times: figures such as Jacho (1327–1405), his student Giwha (1376–1433) and Bou (1515–1565) maintained a strong monastic tradition of meditation and scholarship. The fortunes of the Sangha were marginally revived by Queen Munjeong, a Buddhist who repealed some of the repressive measures in the mid-fifteenth century. The standing of the Sangha revived further when Seosan Hyujeong (1520–1604) created a militia of monks that played an important role in repelling the Japanese invasions of 1592–1598. Before this Seosan was a widely regarded scholar-meditator, his work having the aim of unifying study and practice, and so standing in the tradition of Jinul. But this did not prevent the continued marginalization of the Sangha until the twentieth century, even though Buddhist monks were held in high regard after Seosan, with some receiving honorific titles from the state.

The Colonial Period and Afterwards

Having existed in relative isolation and with no official patronage for almost all of the Joseon period, the Buddhist Sangha was well placed to survive the political troubles in East Asia during the early twentieth century. It is, indeed, probably because of the extended period of persecution that very old traditions were maintained: the monastic culture in the Jogye centres at present, with a curriculum based on *ganhwa* meditation and scriptural study, differs little from those known since the time of Jinul. The custom of travelling between different monasteries to further individual study has also been maintained, an itinerant pattern that persisted also in China until the twentieth century.

During the Japanese colonization of Korea (1910–1945) the prohibition on Buddhist monks entering cities was lifted. While this and other forms of institutional support were welcomed, they entailed further interference in Buddhist affairs, including attempts to affiliate Korean monasticism with the Japanese Sōtō Zen school. The most controversial measure introduced by the Japanese was the culture of married clerics: by 1926 the requirement of celibacy was abolished, and a class of married priests came to dominate the Korean Sangha, with long established traditions disappearing in the process. The Japanese influence was therefore mixed, and divided opinion among Korean Buddhists; the modernizer Han Yong-un (1879–1944) initially supported a married clergy, but came to oppose the level of Japanese interference in the Korean Sangha, and thus became involved in the nationalist resistance.

The period since the end of World War II has seen a protracted dispute between the married and celibate factions of the Korean Sangha. After numerous lawsuits and occasionally violent conflict between the two groups, the dispute was finally resolved in 1970 when the married clerics formed the T'aego order, and thus split off from the celibates, who formed the Jogye order. With the subsequent decline of the T'aego order, Buddhist disputes have been focused within the different groupings of the Jogye order, a recurring theme being the struggle between centralization and localization. Despite these problems, and the emergence of Christianity in the post-war period, the Korean Sangha has grown rapidly in recent decades, thanks to a proliferation of modernizing initiatives, involving various forms of social engagement (such as welfare and counselling programmes), and the increased involvement of the laity (evident especially in the popularization of meditation).

Buddhism now has a significant presence in the major cities of South Korea, with the population engaged in Buddhist practice estimated at about 20 per cent (around 10 million); the numbers of monks and nuns in the mid-1980s were about 12,000. While the Korean Buddhist tradition has developed a strong position from which to deal with modernization and democracy, especially since the 1980s, there has been virtually no Buddhist activity in the North since the Korean peninsula was divided in 1948. The communist regime in Pyongyang does not permit freedom of thought or conscience, and there have been reports of imprisonment and torture for unauthorized Buddhist practice.

Buddhism and the Royal Court in Early Medieval Japan

Buddhism was introduced to Japan from the Baekje kingdom of Korea in 538, when Prince Shōtoku (593–628) established a centralized

Figs. 21 & 22. Shrine at the Haeinsa temple (above), one of the major centres of the Jogye order. Its old library (below), houses the 81,350 wooden printing blocks which contain the Korean Tripiṭaka and date to the late fourteenth century

system of government which officially recognized Buddhism, and gave it preference over traditional Japanese animism (*shintō*). This allowed for the transmission of a number of schools from Tang China during the seventh century, including Madhyamaka (Sanron) in 625, Yogācāra (Hossō) in 653 and Abhidharmakośa (Kusha) in 658 (by pupils of Xuanzang). In the subsequent Nara period (710–784), two further schools were introduced: Huayan (Kegon) in 740 and Vinaya (Ritsu) in 754. With the establishment of the royal court in Nara, Buddhist ideology, ritual and monasticism became a major feature of the emerging Japanese state.

The Japanese assimilation of Buddhism was thus an important aspect in the creation of a unified socio-political order; the transmission of various other aspects of Chinese culture, such as writing and Confucian learning, aided this transformation. Buddhism was primarily valued for its apotropaic aspects: through Buddhist rituals and worship, and the purity of its monastic clerics, the royal court gained legitimation and strengthened its political position. The emperor, traditionally claimed to be a descendant of the sun, was thus identified with Buddha Vairocana (whose name means 'of the sun'), whose position at the centre of the interpenetrated Huayan cosmos provided symbolic power and a strong mandate for centralization. The royal court furthered its actual power by establishing and supporting a large number of monasteries around Nara, closely controlling monastic ordination and requiring monks and nuns to register at a single monastery. With an extensive network of temples devoted to the ritual protection of the state, and official ranks conferred upon individual monks, Nara Buddhism was effectively subsumed within the state bureaucracy.

As in the Goryeo period in Korea, a close relationship with the state was a cause both of Buddhist strength and tension; the situation was complicated by the close ties between powerful lay patrons and the monastic estates they supported, and from which they derived income. Positioned so close to the machinery of state, powerful monks were able to advance their own political agendas. The most outstanding example of this was the monk Dōkyō (d. 772), who towards the end of the Nara period used his close relationship with Empress Kōken in an attempt to claim the throne. Partly because of such problems, the royal capital was eventually moved to Heian-kyō (modern Kyōto), away from the Buddhist power base; this change allowed for the rise of new Buddhist traditions in the Heian Period (794–1185). Tiantai (Tendai) teachings had been known in the Nara period, but emerged as a separate school under Saichō (767–822) on Mt. Hiei in 805, and shortly afterwards, in 806, Kūkai (774–835) returned from China to establish Tantric Buddhism, based on Chinese translations of Yoga Tantras, in the form of the Shingon school.

As a disciplinarian keen on maintaining monastic law and Mahāyāna ideals, Saichō attracted prominent lay support, although ordination rights at his temple were allowed only after his death in 827. The Tendai school he established integrated elements from other Buddhist schools, as well as many aspects of the indigenous Shintō animism. It was also more heavily ritualized than its Chinese source: from the beginning Tendai incorporated many aspects of esoteric Buddhism, including rituals, *mantras* and *maṇḍalas* of the sort valued by lay patrons ever since the inception of Tantric Buddhism in India. Such ritualism prepared the way for a more general shift towards esoteric Buddhism proper, which was achieved by Kūkai, who established Tantric practice in Nara before Shingon temples eventually flourished on Mt. Kōya (near Osaka). Shingon became increasingly important at the Japanese court during the ninth century: already in 810 Kūkai had established rites for the sake of the kingdom, and by 834 a Shingon temple had been constructed inside the royal palace at Heian-kyō.

The apotropaic focus of Japanese Buddhism therefore intensified in the Heian period. Beyond its magical aspects, Japanese Tantra was useful for its ability to manipulate cultural power and prestige. With ritual techniques controlling an expansive pantheon of supernatural forces, expressed in an exaggerated version of the old religious aesthetic of Magadha, Buddhist Tantra was eminently suitable for creating an aura of magical sanctity and so legitimizing a ruler's political power. Tantric ideology effectively placed the Japanese emperor and his court within a national *maṇḍala*, especially since the Yoga Tantras were focused on Mahāvairocana, a deity easily integrated with the imperial sun cult (the connection goes back to the Nara period). The royal court was therefore bound by esoteric connections to a pantheon of Buddhist and indigenous deities; in the East Asian context, the prominence of *tathāgata-garbha* thought allowed for an even firmer establishment of the king in the sacred order, for this idea situated the ritual and social order within the cosmic principle of the Buddha-nature.

This esoteric order did not disappear even when, towards the end of the Heian Period, the influence of both the imperial court and the different Buddhist schools declined, and power shifted towards military warlords (*shōguns*) and their samurai warriors. In the Kamakura period (1192–1338) regional clans wielded power, leaving the imperial court and the emperor in Heian-kyō with little more than a symbolic function. But the conflict and fragmentation at the beginning of this period also allowed for new forms of religious expression, for it lent credence to a general belief that the Dharma had entered a period of irreversible decline (*mappō*). Along with the increased religious freedom that prevailed without the centralizing influence of the imperial court, the idea of *mappō* led to the emergence of new schools beyond the old networks of patronage: as power drained from the imperial court at Heian-kyō, and as pious Buddhists responded to socio-political disorder, popular regional movements arose focusing on different aspects of East Asian Buddhism.

Mappō and Popular Devotionalism

Even if the Kamakura period was a watershed in Japanese Buddhism, too much emphasis should not be placed on *mappō* as a determining factor in the formation of new schools. The older traditions of Nara and Heian did not disappear or suffer any major decline: the new populist movements did not replace the old elite, but rather added new dimensions to a religious world dominated by esoteric and ritual concerns. Nor were the Kamakura movements entirely new creations, for devotional practices, such as chanting and making offerings to images of Buddhas and Bodhisattvas, had already formed an integral aspect of temple practice in Nara and Heian. Local traditions beyond the royal court had also emerged before the Kamakura period: as was the case elsewhere in Asia, no matter how close the connections between Sangha and state, it was impossible to check the formation of autonomous groupings in an acephalous religious institution.

Popular devotionalism had existed in Japan since the ninth century, for example through the teachings of the Tendai priest Ennin (794–864); certain elements of Tendai ritualism had also been derived from Pure Land Buddhism, such as the *nembutsu,* the formula of homage to Buddha Amitābha (*namu amida butsu*). But pietistic practices based solely on it did not achieve any prominence until the twelfth century, when the devotional rather than contemplative aspects of the tradition found an increasing number of supporters. A devotional sort of Pure Land was popularized by Hōnen (1133–1212), who turned away from his Tendai training to promote the practice of reciting the *nembutsu*, in order to ensure rebirth in the pure land of Sukhāvatī.

Hōnen's Pure Land (Jōdo) school was based on the notion that liberation is not possible in the age of religious decline (*mappō*), when the pious Buddhist is entirely dependent upon the grace of Amitābha, the *nembutsu* being both a way of strengthening faith and of petitioning the deity. This idea was controversial: Sangha authorities reasonably concluded that it implied the bypassing of traditional practices such as merit-making and meditation, and could even sanction moral laxity, through the idea that all karmic sins can be eradicated by chanting the *nembutsu*. These fears were well founded, as some of Hōnen's followers were morally compromised, and hence were executed, with Hōnen himself exiled. Even 15 years after his death, Hōnen's writings were being burned as a threat to the Dharma.

Despite the problems faced by Hōnen and his followers, his pietistic ideas were further radicalized by Shinran (1173–1263), one of the pupils who had been exiled along with Hōnen in 1207. Shinran promulgated a more extreme doctrine of grace, according to which the *nembutsu* is not a formulaic means of propitiating Amitābha, but is instead a means of intensifying a person's faith in him, this being the determining factor in receiving his grace and so effecting a spiritual transformation before death. Shinran's innovations were not confined to Pure Land ideology, for he also inaugurated a new institution in East Asia by marrying (apparently motivated by a vision of the Bodhisattva Kuan-yin). This example was followed by his followers, who thus formed a class of married priests rather than celibate monastics.

A different direction in Japanese devotionalism was inaugurated by Nichiren (1222–1282). After studying Tendai on Mount Hiei, Nichiren developed his own pietistic brand of Buddhism based on the Lotus Sūtra, rather than the Pure Land traditions, to which he was violently opposed, believing them to be the primary cause of *mappō*. In the belief that only the Lotus Sūtra guarantees salvation, Nichiren advocated faith in the central figure of this text – Śākyamuni in his elevated cosmic form – and taught that salvation could be attained by reciting the formula *nam myōhō renge kyō* ('Homage to the Lotus of the True Dharma'). This devotional practice was inseparable from a nationalistic agenda, the aim of which was to save Japan in the age of decline; Nichiren believed that *mappō* was abetted by the deviant traditions promoted by other Buddhist schools.

With his fanatical insistence that true Buddhism is contained only in the Lotus Sūtra, and calls for the state suppression of other schools, Nichiren was a divisive figure, his ideas threatening the delicate harmony between Japanese Buddhist schools and their state connections. He was eventually exiled, first in 1261 and then again in 1271; in between these periods of exile, there were two unsuccessful attempts to assassinate him, in 1264 and 1271. Finally pardoned in 1274, after an attempted Mongol invasion was seen to vindicate his predictions of Japanese decline, Nichiren's return allowed his school to develop in less controversial circumstances, and ultimately adopt an important position within the Japanese Buddhist mainstream.

Nichiren's version of Buddhist devotionalism belongs at the extreme end of a common religious spectrum connecting all the devotionalistic schools in Japan. Hōnen, Shinran and Nichiren all preached Buddhist piety with a nationalistic edge: their fear of *mappō* was due as much to national disintegration as it was to the decline of Buddhism. Apart from these nationalistic elements, the religious culture promoted by the pietistic schools drew on Shigon ritualism – a Japanese elaboration of the Indian Buddhist aesthetic. Alongside the important contribution of the Zen schools and the ubiquitous Shingon, the flavour of popular Buddhism in Japan has been most defined by these devotional tendencies.

Zen Buddhism

Chan teachings were known in Japan as early as the Nara period, but did not make any impact until the Heian period (794–1185), at a time when the apotropaic concerns of the Japanese court favoured Tendai and Shingon. But with a sense of imperial decline looming, and a disintegration of the Dharma feared, numerous monks were inspired to travel to Song China to seek fresh sources of inspiration. This led to the transmission of various lines of Song Chan to Japan, and in the Kamakura period these developed into a specifically Japanese form of the meditative tradition, known by the term 'Zen' (a Japanese rendering of the Chinese *chan*).

One of the Tendai monks who travelled to China was Eisai (1141–1215), who returned in 1191 with a form of Chan transmitted in the Linji tradition (descended from Mazu's Hongzhou school). As in Korea, this school's subitist tendency towards sudden enlightenment was viewed with suspicion by state officials in the capital of Heian-kyō. This made it difficult for Eisai to establish a new school, but he was at least successful in gaining the support of the Shoguns and Samurai warriors of Kamakura, eventually establishing a Zen temple in 1202. With Japanese interest in Linji Chan roused, support from the Hōjō house enabled further connections with China, and this created the circumstances for the flourishing of the Linji lineage in the thirteenth century. The rise of Rinzai Zen was also aided by the departure of Linji masters from China during the rule of the Mongol Yuan dynasty (1271–1386), which did not favour this school.

As in the Chan tradition inspired by Mazu, Rinzai Zen is concerned with stimulating an instantaneous experience of enlightenment (*satori*) through unorthodox methods such as *kōans*, illogical utterances and physical shocks. These iconoclastic aspects of Chan do not mean that Rinzai Zen was a movement of personal liberty beyond the domain of the state – just as Mazu's Hongzhou school and Linji Chan were never antinomian in the sense made out by their hagiographers (and detractors). If anything, a closer relationship with the state was achieved than that forged by the Chan domination of monastic Buddhism in Song China. Starting with Eisai, who drew no boundary between meditative zeal and national aspiration, and continuing through the Kamakura period, Rinzai Zen was strongly connected to the ruling elite and the Samurai warriors who valued it for its disciplined, austere ethos (eventually leading to the 'way of the warrior', *bushidō*, in the seventeenth century). It is this meditative discipline, rather than the iconoclastic impulses that appear throughout the literature of the meditation school in East Asia, that has come to characterize Zen as a distinctly Japanese tradition.

A major step in the development of Japanese Zen occurred with the establishment of the Sōtō school by Dōgen (1200–1253). Born into the court nobility and then ordained as a Tendai monk, Dōgen studied at Eisai's Kenninji temple before spending a lengthy period studying under Caodong Chan masters in China (1223–27). After returning to Japan Dōgen founded the Eiheiji temple, which became the principal seat of the Sōtō Zen tradition after his death.

Although influenced by the Caodong school, and highly critical of the *kōan* practices of the Linji school, Dōgen was an original thinker and spiritual innovator, rather than a faithful transmitter of an authoritative Chan lineage. With some Huayan influence, he pushed the Buddha-nature speculation of the Chinese tradition towards a new formulation, by developing the notion of 'One Mind' into a form of pantheistic realism inspired by the Huayan notion of interpenetration:

> Therefore, mountains, rivers, and the great earth are all the sea of Buddha-nature. 'All is realised by virtue of [the sea of Buddha-nature]' means that the very time [all is] realised by virtue of it is none other than the mountains, rivers, and the great earth . . . Thus, to see mountains and rivers is tantamount to seeing Buddha-nature. To see Buddha-nature is to observe a donkey's jaw and a horse's mouth.

This understanding was based on a novel interpretation of a key passage from the Mahāyāna *Mahā-parinirvāṇa Sūtra*. According to Dōgen the statement that 'all sentient beings possess Buddha-nature' should be understood in the sense 'all existence is Buddha nature':

> We do not say 'all sentient beings are Buddha-nature', but instead 'all sentient-beings-the Buddha-nature-of existence'. This should be considered carefully. The 'existence' of 'the Buddha-nature of existence' should indeed be cast off. Casting off is all-pervasive and all-pervasive means [leaving no traces like] a bird's path in flight. Therefore, [it should be expressed] 'all Buddha-nature-existence-sentient-beings'.

This theory of the Buddha-nature forms the background to Dōgen's new understanding of meditation. Like the Huineng-inspired Chan idea of enlightenment first followed by meditative cultivation, Dōgen proposed the idea of practice based on enlightenment. This follows from his speculation on the Buddha-nature, for if all is simply Buddha, the notion of advancing towards liberation is an illusion. Practice and enlightenment must thus be the same. Just as in the Seon thought of Jinul, this means that faith in the teaching plays a crucial role, for only when inspired by faith can a person meditate without the idea that practice is prior to, and leads towards, enlightenment. For Dōgen, seated meditation thus expresses the very essence of Buddhism: it is equivalent to all Bodhisattva virtues, and is the culmination of all forms of Buddhist practice.

Dōgen's conceptualization of religious purpose marked a further step in the East Asian simplification of Buddhist meditation. For in his system meditation is not a means to an end, but is rather a matter of a letting the innate Buddha-nature unfold, without conscious direction, on the basis that this is all which is ultimately real: practice has no aim, there being no different state to strive for and realize. Meditation was rather re-imagined as an expression of Buddhahood, a simplification of individual religious purpose which goes some way towards explaining the popular appeal of Dōgen's Zen in Japan.

Both the Rinzai and Sōtō schools of Zen evolved into numerous lines of transmission and sub-sects that continued throughout late medieval Japan. In the fifteenth and sixteenth centuries, besides their close relationship with the ruling class, the two denominations enjoyed an increasing popularity beyond aristocratic circles and the world of feudal politics, a cultural legacy which has endured in such things as painting, landscape gardening and the tea ceremony.

Conflict and Modernity in Japan

Zen was a major cultural influence in the Muromachi period (1336–1603), but otherwise this was a time of conflict and division in Japanese Buddhism. The end of the fifteenth and early sixteenth century was a disastrous period of war, in which many Buddhist monks were killed and monasteries destroyed. Stability was achieved in the Tokugawa period (1603–1868), but this depended on an increased prevalence of Confucian ideology and an anti-Buddhist agenda. This eventually led to the dissolution of the close connection between Buddhism and the Japanese state in 1868, when the Meiji government embraced Shintō as the official religion of the imperial court, and condemned Buddhism as a foreign incursion. The state forces which had sustained Japanese Buddhism from the beginning were thus turned directly against it, in the form of a persecution in which temples were closed and destroyed, and monks forcibly returned to lay life. The 200-year-old temple registration system, which had been a means of integrating Buddhist organizations into the state bureaucracy – by requiring individual households to register at a local temple – was abolished and replaced by a system of civil registration.

Under attack from the imperial court and its Shintō allies, some Buddhists preserved a religious role through their ritual expertise, especially at funerary ceremonies, but others responded by promoting forms of Buddhist modernism, arguing that the forces emanating from the West could best be faced through rational elements in the Buddhist systems. The most common response, however, was to emphasize Buddhist patriotism and support for Japanese imperialism. The Buddhist Sangha was thus caught up in the militarization of Japanese society: Buddhists supported expansionist wars overseas, cheering Japanese successes against Russia, Korea and China, and with Zen priests among the most vocal supporters of the military effort in World War II. Despite the disestablishment of Buddhism, the symbiotic relationship between Sangha and state could not be so easily undone.

Since the end of World War II the Meiji separation of Buddhism and politics has worked in favour of the Sangha in Japan. With the temple network established in the Tokugawa period (1603–1868) still largely intact, and effectively free from the control of a central Sangha body (this was repealed in 1939), Buddhists have been able to respond to the aftermath of the war, and adapt to the rapidly changing modern world, more or less as a collection of individual guilds. There has thus been a proliferation of new religious societies, sometimes emerging within older denominations, but often entirely new creations. Some of these groups date back to the nineteenth century, but others arose shortly before and after World War II. Many have followed in the footsteps of the devotional and meditative schools which rose to prominence in the Kamakura period; a few, such as the notorious Aum Shirinkyo, have formulated new-age versions of Tantric ritualism and yoga, with a significant input from the animistic and spirit practices of Shintō.

Buddhism in post-war Japan has thus been re-energized by a peculiar mixture of apotropaic and gnostic cults. Many, if not most, of these cults have also assumed a more secular orientation, perhaps as an inevitable response to modern materialism, but perhaps also derived in part from Confucianism; a Confucian source is probably apparent in those sects which subsume individual fulfilment within the success of society as a whole, although this could also be explained as a contemporary manifestation of Buddhist nationalism. Such an interpretation helps explain the success of Sōka Gakkai, founded in 1938 and now one of the most well known of the new lay movements. Sōka Gakkai has re-channelled Nichiren's message of individual salvation towards this-worldly goals, with devotional practices such as chanting being presented as a means of achieving apotropaic goals in the present, and of improving society as a whole.

The success of Sōka Gakkai shows that when it is no longer required to serve its state patrons, Buddhism can very easily regain a universal purpose. But this example is not unique: contemporary Japanese Buddhism is defined by institutional independence, various sorts of social engagement, an important role for the laity, and universal aspirations often directed towards apotropaic goals.

The Early Rise, Fall and Rebirth of Buddhism in Tibet

Buddhism arrived in Tibet during the reign of its first emperor, Songtsen Gampo (*c.*604–650), under whom the Tibetan kingdom expanded into an empire stretching from the Silk Road to northwest China. Early Buddhist endeavours in Tibet are thus attributed to members of the royal court: two of Songtsen Gampo's wives, one from China and one from Nepal, are credited with constructing the important temples of Jo Khang and Ramoché, and a number of other temples were constructed through royal initiatives. Around the same time the Tibetan alphabet was created by one of Songtsen Gampo's ministers, on the basis of the Brāhmī script then used in northern India. This created the foundations for the emergence of classical Tibetan as a literary language, enabling Buddhist works in Sanskrit and Chinese to be translated into Tibetan. As in Korea and Japan, Buddhism was not simply appropriated to support royal power, but was part of an attempt to create a unifying national culture.

It was not until the patronage of emperor Tri Songdetsen (*c.*742–798), the first truly Buddhist ruler of Tibet, that Buddhism became the dominant force in Tibetan culture. In this period the first monastery was constructed in Samyé (*c.*780), and the translation of Buddhist texts – primarily Mahāyāna, transmitted by Indian missionaries such as Śāntarakṣita and his pupil Kamalaśīla – was undertaken on a grand scale. But unofficial Tantric works also circulated, and Tantric practitioners such as Padmasambhava – an obscure figure later credited with subduing the malevolent spirits opposed to

Śāntarakṣita's mission – played a mysterious role as Buddhism established itself in Tibet. The first Tibetan monks, drawn from aristocratic families, were ordained in the same period, and some enduring features of Tibetan Buddhism were established: a form of monasticism based on the Mūlasarvāstivādin Vinaya, a close relationship between the monasteries and nobility, and large-scale monastic feudalism.

Buddhist traditions from China and Central Asia were also influential during the eighth century, when the reach of imperial Tibet encompassed the Silk Road towns of Kucha, Khotan, Turfan and Dunhuang. In order to determine the official form of Buddhism, a series of debates were held at Samyé between roughly 792 and 794: the main protagonists were Kamalaśīla, a representative of Indian Mahāyāna and orthodox monasticism, and the Chinese master Mohoyen, a representative of the northern Chan school. At this decisive moment the royal court ruled in favour of the Indians, probably because the highly organized and hierarchical system of Indian monasticism better reflected the concerns of the royal court than Chan, which before the Song was still in the process of institutional evolution.

Not everyone was satisfied with the gradual Buddhicization of Tibet. In response to the lavish Buddhist patronage of the Tibetan emperor Relpachen (r. 817–836), his successor Lang Darma (r. 838–842) attempted to restrict the growing power of the monasteries. When this ended with his assassination at the hands of a Buddhist monk, the Tibetan empire was thrown into chaos and the imperial state disintegrated. During the century of conflict which followed Buddhist monasticism virtually disappeared, although lay forms of the religion survived, with some aristocratic families maintaining Buddhist rituals and even composing new texts in central Tibet. But a line of monastic ordination was maintained by monks who had fled to the far northeast, and when this lineage was brought back to central Tibet from Dunhuang in around 980, the work of re-establishing the monasteries began. A monastic lineage was also re-established in the west, in the early eleventh century, through a group of aristocratic Tibetans sent by Yeshe-od, ruler of the Guge kingdom, to receive ordination in Kashmir.

Different monastic lineages and lines of teaching thus became established during the eleventh century, despite opposition from those who had maintained non-monastic Buddhism in the period of imperial collapse. The lay Lama, an important feature of contemporary Tibetan Buddhism, emerged from this class of teachers who drew on the model provided by the Tantric gurus and *mahā-siddha*s of India. The lay teachers eventually coalesced into two separate traditions: the Nyingma and Bön schools, although the latter claimed an origin prior to the arrival of Buddhism, and so remained on the fringe of the Tibetan Buddhist world. The twelfth century was a vibrant period of institutional formation, during which many small lineages flourished but then failed to develop sufficient support, and so either disappeared or were absorbed into the monastic networks of the larger orders. Among the incipient orders of this period were the Kadampa tradition, established by Atiśa's disciple Dromtön (1005–1064), with a focus on monasticism and Mahāyāna philosophy; that of the Sakya monastery (founded in 1073); and the Kagyu, based on the Tantric teachings and lineage transmitted by Marpa (1012–1097).

Tibetan Buddhism and Political Power

The second wave of Buddhism in Tibet, which took shape in the eleventh and twelfth centuries, differed from the initial infusion of the imperial period by virtue of its esoteric inclinations. The Sakya tradition was based on the Tantric teachings of Drokmi, who studied at Vikramaśīla and received instruction in the Indian *mahā-siddha* tradition of Virūpa. It was Drokmi's disciple Könchok Gyelpo (1034–1102) who established Sakya monastery, in southern Tibet, in 1073. This emergent Tantric tradition was eventually rooted in more formal Mahāyāna studies by Sakya Paṇḍita (1182–1251) in the thirteenth century, who added the study of Madhyamaka philosophy (especially the works of the Indian scholar Candrakīrti) and the epistemological works of Dharmakīrti to the monastic curriculum.

A further lineage emanating from Vikramaśīla was derived from Atiśa (982–1054), an Indian monk who arrived in the western Tibetan kingdom of Guge in 1042. According to Atiśa's synthesis of Mahāyāna and Tantrism, observation of the monastic precepts and the Bodhisattva vow is followed by the higher ritual and yogic practices of the Tantras. Based on these teachings, the Kadampa tradition was established with the founding of Reting Monastery, in 1056, by Atiśa's disciple Dromtön, who had also received tantric transmission from Nāropa. This monastic tradition formed the background for the emergence of a different school, the Kagyu, through the figure of Gampopa (1079–1153), who had studied in the Kadampa school before receiving Tantric instruction from the hermit Milarepa (*c.*1052–1135). Milarepa had in turn received Tantric teachings from Marpa, a Tibetan who studied under Drokmi before spending a period of study in northeast India. Traditional accounts maintain that Marpa received instruction in Tantric *mahā-mudrā* meditation from the Indian Nāropa, a pupil of the *mahā-siddha* Tilopa. The Tantric lineage of Tilopa was thus transmitted to Milarepa and then institutionalized by Gampopa, with the founding of the Dagpo monastery in 1125.

The schools that emerged during the rebirth of Tibetan Buddhism in the eleventh and twelfth centuries thus incorporated Tantric practice within a general monastic and Mahāyāna framework, in obvious imitation of the monastic centres of late Pāla India. These new traditions were critical of the 'old school' (*nyingma*) traditions that survived the imperial period, which they believed had been adulterated both by indigenous 'Bön' practices and newly composed, inauthentic, texts. The old traditions which coalesced into the Nyingma school responded to this critique by defending their traditions in various ways: first by claiming to have received Tantric teachings from Padmasambhava, and second by claiming to be recipients of a special class of esoteric teachings called 'treasure' (*terma*) literature, this being received in meditative vision or else through actually discovering them hidden in the landscape. The Nyingma and Bön schools both taught Dzogchen meditation as the highest stage of the Tantric path, a development of *mahā-mudrā* meditation, similar to the Buddha-nature orientation of Chan speculation (and the Indian school in which the *Ratnagotravibhāga* was composed and circulated), according to which the inherent purity of awareness need only be realized in order for awakening to be achieved.

The post-imperial re-emergence of Buddhism played an important role in establishing cultural unity in chaotic circumstances. While it is peculiar that political stability was achieved through appropriating a partly transgressive religion, Tantra was strangely well-suited to this task. Esoteric Buddhism originally took root in the political disorder of medieval India, where it provided a metaphysical template that helped make sense of a world of multiple feudal states, and the shifting allegiances between them. Tantra thus provided a conceptual order which normalized, and even sacralized, a fragmented socio-political realm and so helped mitigate its conflict. Tantric ritualism was similarly used by the Tibetan aristocracy to sanctify the fragmented socio-political order left in the aftermath of imperial disintegration: esoteric Buddhism was, paradoxically, a cultural force that unified civilizational disorder by pulling conflicting political factions into a new, sacrally fragmented, paradigm.

Once cultural order had been achieved, the competition for political dominance was played out between the different monastic fraternities and their supporters among the nobility. With the Nyingma and Bön schools not developing monastic systems until the fourteenth and fifteenth centuries, and the Kadampa school declining in influence, the quest for political power was contested by the Sakya and Kagyu traditions. Initially the Sakyas prevailed: after the Mongol Yuan dynasty became imperial overlords of Tibet in the thirteenth century, Sakya Paṇḍita's influence at the Mongol court meant that suzerainty over Tibet was assigned to the Sakyas in 1247. The Sakya dominance of central Tibet lasted for around a century before the Yuan dynasty declined, after which the Phagmodru faction of the Kagyu school, under the leadership of Changchub Gyaltsen, successfully overturned Sakya rule in 1358.

The Kagyu dominance in turn lasted for about a century until Tibet regressed into a period of civil war lasting almost two centuries. Despite sectarian and political conflict, the period was also a time of scholarly consolidation, during which the bipartite Tibetan canon – of authoritative scriptures received from India (the Kangyur, first printed in Peking in 1411) and commentarial treatises (the Tengyur) – was formed, and of arranging the received Indian traditions into new, distinctly Tibetan scholastic and monastic systems which prevailed until the twentieth century. An early prominent figure in this Tibetanization of Indian Mahāyāna and Tantra had been Sakya Paṇḍita; the next major thinker and systematizer of Tibetan Buddhist was Tsongkhapa (1357–1419), whose Geluk school was to play a decisive role in the development of Tibetan Buddhism until contemporary times.

The Apotheosis of State Buddhism in Asia

Initially a reformist centre within the Sakya order – one that relied heavily on the old but now dissolute Kadampa tradition of

Atiśa – Ganden monastery, to the northeast of Lhasa, was founded by Tsongkhapa (1357–1419) in 1409. Starting off as just another monastic lineage within the ever-changing matrix of Tibetan schools, the Gandenpa order developed into a separate institution over the course of the fifteenth century. This success was due initially to Tsongkhapa's intellectual charisma, and his innovative reformulation of Sakya Paṇḍita's synthetic curriculum. According to this new system, Mahayānā ideology and philosophy were studied in a strictly disciplined monastic setting, for an extensive period of time, culminating in the Geshe degree, after which Tantric practice may be undertaken if so desired.

In response to the hostility of Sakya authorities, Tsongkhapa's followers termed themselves 'Gelukpas' (the 'virtuous ones'), a distinct identity furthered by the construction of a number of Geluk monasteries, including two in the vicinity of Lhasa (Drepung, founded in 1416 by Gendun Drup and Sera, founded in 1419), and Tashilhunpo, a monastery founded near Shigatse in 1445 (also by Gendun Drup), and eventually the home of the Panchen Lamas. With a monastic network stretching out from Lhasa, and with patronage from powerful aristocratic supporters, the Geluk order was well placed to assume a central role in the control of Tibet in the sixteenth century.

This finally came about through the Mongol support for the Geluk abbots of Drepung, and the Geluk appropriation of the peculiarly Tibetan office of reincarnated Lamas (*tulku*). The beginnings of the latter can be traced to Düsum Khyenpa (1110–1193), a disciple of Gampopa and first holder of the title 'Karmapa' within the Kagyu school, who is held to have foretold his rebirth as Karma Pakshi (1204–1283). The institution of reincarnated Lamas was gradually absorbed by other monastic lineages, but was not accepted at Ganden, whose abbots were chosen because of their scholarly and spiritual eminence. But other Geluk monasteries did absorb the tradition, in particular the lineage stemming from Gendun Drup (1391–1474, a pupil of Tsong khapa), whose successor Gendun Gyatso (1475–1542) was held to be his reincarnation.

Sonam Gyatso (1543–1588), the reincarnation of Gendun Gyatso, was given the title 'Dalai Lama' ('oceanic teacher') in 1578 by the Mongolian ruler Altan Khan, a title which was then applied retrospectively to his two prior incarnations. Sonam Gyatso's reincarnation, the fourth Dalai Lama, was Yonten Gyatso (1589–1616), the great-grandson of Altan Khan, who was succeeded by Ngawang Lobsang Gyatso, the fifth Dalai Lama (1617–1682). In the ongoing civil war between the southern region of Tsang and central Tibet – the former allied to the Karma Kagyu, the latter to the Geluks, especially its powerful monasteries in Lhasa – the support of the Mongols for the Geluks and their Dalai Lamas proved decisive. When the fifth Dalai Lama was installed as ruler of Tibet in 1642, the nexus of political power and monastic Buddhism reached its culmination: Ngawang Lobsang Gyatso (1617–1682) suppressed his enemies, built the Potala Palace as his residence and centre of the Tibetan government, and claimed to be an incarnation of Avalokiteśvara. Until the Chinese invasion in 1950, the ultimate source of power in Tibet resided in the reincarnated Dalai Lamas and their court at the Potala Palace, at least half of which was made up of monks.

Over the course of nearly 2,000 years and in a vast array of cultural forms, state Buddhism had served kings and polities in need of cultural stability; in return, the Sangha had been rewarded with the material means of preserving Buddhist institutions and teachings. But with the lineage of Dalai Lamas the symbiosis between Sangha and state reached its climax: Buddhists went beyond a position of support for the Cakravartin Dharmarāja by assuming leadership of the state itself.

The Collapse of Tibet in the Twentieth Century

The introversion of the Buddhist Sangha because of political demands is well illustrated in the case of Tibet. Until the Chinese invasion of the 1950s, Tibet had little contact with outsiders after the Mongolian influence in the sixteenth century. The country was officially closed to foreigners, although explorers occasionally gained access to Lhasa, such as Sven Hedin and Heinrich Harrer (who spent most of World War II in Lhasa and tutored the 14th Dalai Lama), and before them the expedition of Francis Younghusband in 1904, which resulted in the placement of a British consul in Lhasa. Perhaps Tibetan Tantra, with its adapted pantheon focused on local domains of power, was particularly susceptible to cultural introversion, but whatever the case, after centuries of isolation Tibet was unable to appreciate the threat from China and respond accordingly.

When monastic attempts to repel the Chinese invasion of 1950 failed, Tibetan independence was lost. The anti-Buddhist policies of the invading Chinese were not initially very extensive, but the 14th Dalai Lama, Tenzin Gyatso (b. 1935) was forced into exile in 1959, and was soon followed by more than 100,000 Tibetans, shortly after which the Tibetan disaster unfolded. The 'great leap ahead' of 1959–1961 was soon followed by Mao's cultural revolution from 1966 to 1976: monasteries were destroyed on a massive scale, thousands of monks and nuns were killed or else imprisoned and tortured, and much of the cultural heritage of Tibet was lost. The Chinese state's policy of cautious religious liberalization in the 1980s allowed some monasteries to be rebuilt, and permitted Tibetans to carry out religious practices in private. But despite this marginal liberalization, Tibetan monasteries remained under close Chinese supervision, especially after the uprising of 1987.

In 2011 the Dalai Lama stepped down as political head of the Tibetan government in exile. Although he remains the spiritual leader and national figurehead of the Tibetans, the Chinese still refuse to recognize him, no doubt because they fear the ability of Tibetan Buddhism to rouse nationalist sentiments. Quite apart from his political and spiritual roles, the Dalai Lama has established himself as one of the leading Buddhist modernizers, so exemplifying the pragmatism that has been an intrinsic aspect of the Dharma since the time of the Buddha.

Chapter IX
Why has Bodhidharma left for the West?

> But then I really believed in the reality of charity and kindness and humility and zeal and neutral tranquillity and wisdom and ecstasy, and I believed that I was an old time bhikku in modern clothes wandering the world (usually the immense triangular arc of New York to Mexico City to San Francisco) in order to turn the wheel of the True Meaning, or Dharma, and gain merit for myself as a future Buddha (Awakener) and as a future Hero in Paradise.
>
> Jack Kerouac, *The Dharma Bums*

The Indian Buddhist tradition preserved the first teaching of the Buddha as the 'Discourse on setting in motion the wheel of Dhamma' (*Dhammacakka-ppavattana Sutta*). The image of a wheel rolling forth suggests a mission that would continue from its own unstoppable momentum, and this was more or less the case as Buddhist monks travelled throughout pre-modern Asia. But the wheel ground to a halt in late medieval India, a disaster that was only prevented elsewhere through state patronage. Essential as the various alliances with the royal courts of Asia were, an unintended consequence was that Buddhism ceased to be a missionary religion over the course of the second millennium AD. Even if the Dhamma-wheel never stopped turning, the requirements to legitimize the state and establish national cultures turned the wheel on its side and sent it spinning around its axis.

This loss of an old and essential spiritual purpose did not affect Buddhist universalism, however, since the 'Sangha of the four quarters' retained an engaged role in all the cultures which supported them. The missionary imperative was thus preserved in a potential form, and was reactivated when circumstances began to turn in favour of the Buddhist mission in the modern period: after a long process of transformation and revival, Buddhist missionaries set out once more, resulting in the establishment of the Dhamma in the West in the twentieth century.

The story of this missionary revival begins with the European colonial presence in Asia during the sixteenth and seventeenth centuries, the ultimate starting point of which was Vasco de Gama's voyage to India in 1498. But a deeper occidental knowledge of Buddhism had to wait until the late eighteenth and early nineteenth centuries, when a number of Oriental institutes were founded, in both colonial Asia and the West. These included the Asiatick Society of Calcutta (established by the British High Court judge Sir William Jones in 1784), the Royal Asiatic Society of Great Britain and Ireland (established in 1823 by Henry Colebrooke) and the American Oriental Society (in 1842).

By the late nineteenth century the academic study of Buddhism had been firmly established. Although a minor scholarly pursuit in the West, this development marked a significant departure in the intellectual appreciation of the Buddha's Dhamma. Buddhist texts thus came to be edited, translated and published in the West, for example by the Pali Text Society, founded in 1881 by T.W. Rhys Davids, who had come into contact with Theravāda Buddhism while an administrator of the British Empire in Ceylon. This growing body of Orientalist scholarship was supplemented by popular writings on Buddhism, such as Sir Edwin Arnold's *The Light of Asia*, a poetic narrative of the Buddha's life first published in 1879. The Victorian reaction to this poem and other popular writings was mixed: while the Buddha's ethics and rationalism were praised by some (for example Colonel Henry Steel Olcott, who helped found the Theosophical Society in 1875), others believed the ideas of karma, rebirth, no self and Nirvana to be pessimistic. Buddhism was generally viewed as an exotic, beguiling curiosity, one that hardly seemed capable of having significant impact on the West.

But this is what gradually transpired, as numerous Western centres of Buddhism emerged over the course of the twentieth century. An important factor in this growth was Asian immigrants: beginning with Chinese immigration to the west coast of America in the mid-nineteenth century, more general patterns of immigration from

South, Southeast and East Asia since World War II, and from Tibet since 1959, have formed the basis of Buddhist communities in the West. The globalized and increasingly pluralistic world of the late twentieth and early twenty-first centuries has allowed these Asian traditions to endure and develop. But they have been supplemented by what is potentially a far more important development: the support of an increasing number of Western converts. It has become relatively easy for curious Westerners to learn about Buddhism, either by travelling East and seeking out traditional sources, or through contact with centres established by Asian immigrants or Western converts, or through visiting the local bookstore (and more recently, logging onto the internet).

Some of these cultural transformations can be seen in the transmission of Theravāda Buddhism to the United Kingdom. In 1954 William Purfurst (1906–1971), a British journalist and prominent member of the Buddhist Society of London (founded in 1924 by the high court judge Christmas Humphreys), became the first European to be ordained as a Buddhist monk in Thailand, when he went forth as Kapilavaddho Bhikkhu at Wat Paknam, Bangkok. After learning Dhammakaya meditation from the Thai master Phra Mongkolthepmuni (1884–1959), Kapilavaddho was instrumental in establishing the Theravāda monastic lineage at the London Buddhist Vihāra, earlier founded by the Sinhalese scholar monk, Ven. Nārada Mahāthera. This example illustrates the complex of factors and agents, from both the East and West, involved in the Western growth of Buddhism in the mid-twentieth century. But an increasingly decisive factor has been the Western converts, impelled by a wide variety of cultural factors.

Buddhism and Scientific Materialism

The Western interest in Buddhism can partly be explained as a response to the intellectual conditions of modernity. Since the transformation in values brought about by the European and American Enlightenment of the seventeenth and eighteenth centuries, rational objections to Christianity have eroded its support and cultural dominance; the rise of scientific materialism in the nineteenth century has led to an even more significant critique of traditional faith. While Buddhism is not immune to this critique, its rational dimensions have been promoted so as to avoid the major charges directed against Christianity: even if evolutionary theory and cosmology are advanced to rubbish the belief in God, such arguments carry much less force against a non-theistic religion.

It is true, of course, that the absence of a creator deity cannot hide non-rational aspects of Buddhism, such as the transfer of merit, the existence of supernatural beings and, to the scientific observer, karma and rebirth. But the Dhamma's non-theistic orientation has at least allowed modernizers to focus attention elsewhere, and thus sidestep the debate between theism and science. An important modernist tactic has been to present non-rational aspects of Buddhism as later additions to a purer form of the religion, which goes back to the Buddha himself, key elements of which are the Four Noble Truths and the discourse to the Kālāmas. While not exactly based in historical fact – karmic and even apotropaic aspects of the Dhamma cannot be extracted from any record of the Buddha's teachings – the modernizers have generally succeeded in presenting Buddhism as a rational solution to the religious predicament of the modern West.

This rationalist tactic has more recently developed into increasingly sophisticated explorations of the common ground between Buddhism and science. Many of these efforts have focused on meditation, which has been appropriated by psychoanalysts and therapists to expand the scope of mental healthcare. Mindfulness-based cognitive therapy, an adaptation of mindfulness now provided by the National Health Service in the United Kingdom, has achieved considerable success in the treatment of mental health problems. While overlooking the religious foundations of the practice, this secular adaptation of Buddhist meditation would not work unless the practice had a rational core. The basic Buddhist approach to spiritual practice, of observing experience as it actually is rather than avoiding empirical facts, fits fairly easily into the modern scientific approach, even if basic Buddhist values and the old religious orientation have been overlooked.

Buddhist ideas have also been applied to more theoretical aspects of modern scientific discourse. Apart from research into mental functioning based on measuring the effects of meditation on the brain, a growing number of publications have explored the common ground between cognitive science and the Buddhist understanding of the mind as a multi-layered nexus of causally related mental processes. The Buddhist refusal to posit an essential subject of experience makes good sense of neuroscientific models of cognitive functioning, much more so than the widespread materialistic adaptation of Cartesian mind–body dualism, according to which the brain is a subject of experience that functions rather like a computer. The relevance of Buddhist thought for other scientific disciplines has also been noted, in particular the possibility that Madhyamaka and Yogācāra arguments against materialism – based on the old idea that reality is changed through the act of cognition – cohere well with the basic assumptions of modern particle physics.

These various connections and explorations, while striking, do not imply that Buddhism might advance scientific knowledge, even if in certain cases Buddhist thought might suggest a better philosophical perspective from which to interpret the results of experiments, or propose new ways of exploring old philosophical problems in the Western tradition. From the Buddhist perspective their importance lies rather in the integration of the Dhamma into a scientific framework. As more Buddhist meditators take part in neuroscientific experiments on the brain, and as further common ground between Buddhist philosophy and science is explored, many more Westerners will be attracted to the Buddhist possibility of a rational approach to religion – one better suited to the intellectual and cultural concerns of the modern world.

Ritual and the Buddhist Aesthetic

The metaphysical shift from theism to materialism has profoundly affected the underlying presuppositions and approach to life in the modern West. But the effects go much deeper than the level of private belief, for public culture has also been transformed by the gradual decline of a shared ritual heritage and the material forms in which it is experienced. This cultural transformation follows a trajectory instigated by the Protestant reformation of the sixteenth century. The Protestant rejection of established ideas and practices, in particular the necessity of a priestly mediator between man and God, and the traditional emphasis on ritual and the sacraments, has helped foster a culture which is deeply rational and individualist.

The decline in ritual culture, especially evident in nations most deeply affected by the Protestant reformation, has opened up a new direction in Western civilization – one that has come to define the modern age. But these unprecedented developments have not been achieved without serious cultural loss: at the public level the disappearance of the shared rituals which bind communities together, and at the individual level the disappearance of an affective response to religious symbols. At the level of belief, the private sense of loss has been compounded by increasing rationalism ever since Protestantism was eclipsed by the more advanced discourse of modern science: in the Christian West, the gradual disappearance of religious aesthetics and the ritual experience has been complemented by a general loss of faith. The Western individual thus lives in a disenchanted and demythologized world, with no serious metaphysical rival to scientific materialism, with neither the private consolations nor shared communion of religious ritual.

The general situation is greatly different in the Buddhist societies of Asia, where the enchantments of traditional religion have been preserved, even in the face of rapid modernization. A protestant critique of tradition has never been properly formulated from within: while there have been occasional protests against ritualism, the ceremonial aspects of apotropaic and karmic Buddhism have not been seriously affected. Instead, the Buddha's idea that ritual serves a pragmatic purpose, and that religious ceremony inclines towards the higher ideals of the Buddhist path, have not been forgotten. The old religious aesthetic has thus remained intact, providing a general cultural background within which all Buddhist activity is conducted. Buddhist ritualism has not become a mere ornamental accompaniment to the Dhamma, therefore, but has remained an integral aspect of Buddhist practice in contemporary Asia.

Even if modernizers have generally avoided ritualism in favour of gnostic aspects of the Dhamma, Buddhist traditions have been transmitted to the West with their ceremonial aesthetics intact, and these have generally not been questioned by new converts. A good example is the Zen movement in America: although Chan iconoclasm played a major role in inspiring it, enthusiasts such as the Beats in the 1950s were also attracted by the tradition's mythological and material culture. The success of Tibetan Buddhism has also highlighted the appeal of Buddhist ritual: the vivid and elaborate ritualism of Tibetan Tantra has functioned as a seductive vehicle for the transmission of the entire tradition. To some extent the same is true of other forms of Buddhism: their appeal is partly based on a material culture derived from ancient Magadha, which stands in stark contrast to the largely deritualized and disenchanted cultures of the modern West.

This ritual appeal has been facilitated by Western romanticism. The romantic opposition to scientific materialism, and focus on direct experience, was an important influence on the American transcendentalists, who in turn were an important source for the Beats and the counter-culture which followed. Just as The Beatles were attracted to the devotional aesthetics of Hindu spirituality in the 1960s, many more were drawn towards the older Buddhist version of this uniquely Indian religious culture. A peculiar aspect of the romantic legacy has thus been to create a cultural space within Western society that has allowed Buddhism to take root. In that part of public life traditionally filled by the ceremonies, art and ornamentation of religion, Buddhists have begun the work of establishing a new material culture to promote the Dhamma.

Enchanted Individualism

In the popular imagination of the West, Buddhism is little more than a collection of peculiar material forms: colourfully clad monks and nuns chanting and meditating, pious laymen and women performing ceremonies at elaborate altars, burning incense, laying garlands of flowers before icons and so forth. While these material forms may be ridiculed by some, or bypassed by modernists interested in gnostic aspects of the Dhamma, for many other converts this cultural aesthetic is a source of enchantment. But resonating through both the rational and aesthetic dimensions of the Dhamma is a further, more subtle, reason for its appeal, one encapsulated in the religion's most potent symbol: that of a Buddha seated in meditation, an image of solitary spiritual perfection which offers a tantalizing glimpse into a different experiential world.

For most in the West, the image of the seated Buddha encapsulates the mystical essence of Buddhism as an exotic and profoundly world-negating religion. And yet for those who are attracted to the Dhamma, this image seems strangely natural, as if communicating an obvious truth, something of great importance but potentially within grasp. Why is this? The apparent paradox in the Western appreciation of the Buddha image – the sense of its aloofness and yet familiarity – is due to the fact that it sits at the intersection of two forms of individualism: the meditative, peripatetic kind followed throughout Buddhist Asia, and the socio-political kind found in the liberal democracies of the modern West.

The Buddhists of ancient India thrived in a culture of religious freedom unparalleled in the classical world. The emergence of settled monasticism did not change this, for the Buddhist Sangha in pre-modern Asia retained its peripatetic habits, and was supported by the ordinances of the Vinaya, which institutionalized the Buddha's spiritual individualism. The Sangha was a society of the free, and with a collective aim of complete freedom: within its own apolitical sphere, Indian Buddhists and their Asian successors were expected to think for themselves, take responsibility for their own deeds, and pursue their own salvific purpose.

An important factor in the spread of Buddhism to the West has been the appeal of this individualistic ethos. While the socio-political freedoms of the modern West lie in the secular rather than religious domain, it encourages a similar way of thinking: just as the ancient Indian Buddhist was theoretically free to follow the Dhamma according to his or her own conscience, the modern individual is theoretically free to make his or her own socio-political choices. In both cases individual choice is not diminished by a figure of absolute authority, but is rather tempered by the rule of law. Indeed, just as there is no Buddhist creator deity to supplicate, and generally no external agency to intervene and do one's spiritual work, in the liberal democracies of the West the individual is free from the authority imposed by a monarch or dictator.

The meeting of Buddhist and Western individualism is an underlying reason for the rapid rise of Buddhism beyond Asia in recent times. This is why a most famous statement of the Buddha is frequently cited in modernist works: the admonition given to his followers, just before he died, to be 'a light unto yourselves, taking refuge in only yourselves'. This dictum on personal responsibility encapsulates the individualistic and non-authoritarian approach of the Buddha, and is in general agreement with the reality of life in the liberal democracies of the West. For a modern individual enjoying the socio-political freedoms of a democratic state, the appeal of Buddhism lies not only in its ideas and practices, but also in the strangely modern place it imagines for a person in the world.

For converts to the Dhamma, Buddhist individualism is a sort of antidote to the metaphysical confusions of modern life – urbanization, industrialization and the materialistic discourses of science. Western individualism is therefore tied to a demythologized and disenchanted world-view, according to which a person is alone in a godless universe, consciousness nothing more than an emergent property of the brain, and individual existence ultimately reducible to a collection of biological processes. The void created by the loss of Christian faith has been occupied by science, which offers no higher values to guide society: in the emerging post-religious societies of the West, there is barely any sense of individual religious purpose and no such thing as shared ethos.

In contrast to this dearth of meaning, the doctrine of karma grounds Buddhist discourse in a spiritualized sort of individualism, one that runs counter to the materialistic narratives of science. A hidden aspect to the appeal of Buddhism is thus its ability to re-enchant the modern world: it is not simply the case that Buddhism provides rational religious ideas in a world dominated by science (the cognitive explanation), or that it presents its ideas and practices in the form of a ritual culture which has gradually disappeared from the West (the affective explanation), but also that it offers an ethos with the capacity to re-enchant the world, and perhaps mitigate some of the problems of modern liberalism (the metaphysical explanation).

A vivid depiction of this re-enchantment can be seen in Jack Kerouac's *The Dharma Bums*, a semi-fictitious portrayal of the Western encounter with Buddhism, in which the peripatetic Buddhist ethos is blended with the liberated world of post-war America. It is notable that rationalism plays little part in Kerouac's imaginary world, which is rooted in the Buddhist aesthetic and a romantic view of the meditative life: the enchanted Buddhist America of this book is the antithesis of modern scientific materialism. There is therefore a strange parallel with the past: just as the Tantric movement helped establish unity in the fractured Buddhist world of medieval India and post-imperial Tibet, through imagining a new, sacred order, so too is it reasonable to assume that the modern appropriation of Buddhism could be a means of re-enchanting the fragmented cosmos of the modern, demythologized West.

This perhaps seems unlikely at present, since the association of Buddhism with the counter-culture perhaps underestimates the strength of the growing movement. With the earlier Victorian appreciation of Buddhist ethics and rationalism long forgotten, the appropriation of Buddhist devotional aesthetics by hippies in the 1960s was assumed to be a passing fad. But this judgement is superficial. While some Beats dropped their interest in Buddhism when flares and long hair went out of fashion, many others have maintained their early motivation. It is entirely possible that amid the flowers and incense, a new religious ethos is in the process of creation, a modern adaptation of the old Buddhist individualism, one which provides an answer to the problems of scientific materialism and the atomized societies of the West.

Incipient Traditions

The wandering mendicants of the fifth century BC saw no point in existence, and so withdrew into their own world beyond the fringes of civilization. Although the Buddha promoted a positive ethos, which modified the ascetic aloofness of the age, neither he nor his followers questioned the renunciant separation of religion from the state. The Buddhist Sangha thus spread across India as a network of autonomous guilds, which promoted the values that allowed the urban civilization to flourish. Such favourable circumstances did not usually pertain at other times and in other places, however. Unless state patronage was secured the Buddhist Sangha was either marginalized (as in China) or else disappeared (as in India).

In contrast with the historical spread of Buddhism in Asia, the state has played no role in its recent transmission to the West. The democratic distinction between church and state has instead allowed Western Buddhists to function in their own cultural sphere, in a fashion not entirely different from their Indian ancestors. The major difference between ancient and modern Buddhists is therefore social rather than cultural: although both have promoted a culture of decentralized spiritual networks, modernizers have emerged within an already advanced civilization, and have played no role in its growth. In terms of its social function, therefore, the transmission of Buddhism to the West resembles its dissemination in ancient China.

There are further similarities with the Chinese precedent. Just as the laity played a prominent role in the transmission of Buddhism to China, the emerging Buddhist centres of the West have been predominantly lay-focused. And in both cases a significant contribution has come from an individualistic sub-culture: Daoist spirituality was an important starting point for the Chinese interest in Buddhism, whereas the post-romantic counter-culture has played more or less the same role in the West. These similarities suggest that contemporary Western Buddhism is in a similar phase to Chinese Buddhism prior to the emergence of schools in the early medieval period, and if so, it can be assumed that new Western traditions will emerge in due course.

Such schools will probably develop more rapidly than in China, because of the modern ease of communication, and will probably be more diverse, for a larger number of Buddhist traditions have been transmitted to a civilization of much greater intellectual scope. But even if so, it is probably too soon to expect new schools at present. While modernizers have begun to fashion distinct forms of Buddhism, nothing within the emerging blend of rationalism, ritual aesthetics and meditation could yet be called a new tradition, let alone school. A case in point is socially engaged Buddhism which, despite the claims of some, is not a new phenomenon within Buddhism, let alone a distinct path or movement: engaged Buddhists differ from the past only in their mode of expressing Buddhist ideals (for example through political activism), not in the fact of social expression itself.

Even emerging traditions fall below the threshold of being a school in the sense of a unified tradition of doctrine, practice and social function. A good example is the American Vipassana movement, which is innovative but limited in its sphere of Buddhist activities and interests, and without a clearly defined philosophical purpose. Modernist trends and strategies should thus be viewed as a formative phase in the emergence of a new, Western Buddhism, a preparatory step towards the emergence of mature traditions in the future. Thinkers such as Stephen Batchelor and Jon Kabat-Zinn could perhaps be considered modern counterparts to An Shigao, whose work prepared the way for a mature meditative tradition in China without having any decisive input into its exact nature. The ideas of contemporary Buddhist modernists, and the previous generations of innovators will most probably fade away once they have served the purpose of providing a platform for the Dhamma in the West.

New Metaphysical Horizons

One of the most distinct features of Buddhist modernism is its this-worldly orientation; that is to say, the preoccupation with meditation as a means of cultivating well-being in the present, without any serious concern for the hereafter. Although particularly obvious in the American Vipassana movement, this feature of contemporary Buddhism is indicative of Buddhist modernism in general, both East and West. But the modernist focus on the present moment is not exactly an innovation, as it has been an aspect of the Dhamma since the time of the Buddha. In the *Sāmaññaphala Sutta,* the primary canonical text on the path to Nirvana, the Buddha presents the different stages of the Buddhist path as 'fruits' to be enjoyed in the present; the *Kālāma Sutta* similarly points out that even if the karmic aim of Buddhist practices turns out to be misconceived, it at least leads to well-being in the present (p.9). The modernist focus on the present is only new to the extent that it inverts the traditional predominance of karmic aims over prosperity in the here and now.

An inversion of traditional concerns, rather than genuine innovation, would seem to confirm the suspicion that new Buddhist schools are still some way off. Indeed, it could be argued that Western modernizers have not yet looked very deeply into the traditional heritage, ignoring more theoretical aspects of Asian traditions in their focus on this-worldliness. A consequence of this modern preoccupation has been that the deep aspects of a world-view, upon which a coherent system and practice could be founded, have been downplayed. For Buddhism to establish deep roots and flourish in the West, this metaphysical problem must be addressed: broader systems are needed, and not just meditative therapy, as in the past when therapeutic aspects of the Dhamma were included within a larger religious vision.

This is not to say that tentative metaphysical steps have not been taken. But even when this has been the case, it has not usually been recognized as such: a good example is Stephen Batchelor's 'Buddhism without beliefs', which claims metaphysical agnosticism but in fact presupposes scientific materialism. The long-term appeal of this fascinating materialist contribution to the Dhamma is therefore doubtful: without properly acknowledging its metaphysical presuppositions, Buddhism without beliefs has thus far been denied the systematic treatment which might eventually result in a new school. But in this case it is perhaps misguided to expect a new Buddhist system anyway, for it is hard to imagine any kind of Dhammic materialism: if Nirvana and the karmic metaphysic are replaced by scientific materialism and empiricism, a humanist school of contemplation will perhaps be the more likely outcome.

The unusual prominence of this-worldliness, the lack of metaphysical innovation and the spectre of disenchanted Buddhism may raise doubts about the long-term influence of Buddhist modernism. But the success of Tantric Buddhism shows that the contemporary picture is not so one-sided. Different traditional and modernist influences are to be found even in movements closely associated with Buddhist secularism, such as the Vipassana movement in America, and in the future this will allow for greater levels of creative variation in the modern forms of Buddhist spirituality. Indeed, the mixture of traditional teachings and secular developments shows that the Western audience is not avowedly empiricist or materialist. In this formative phase of Buddhism in the West, there is much engagement with Asian tradition without any complete acceptance or denial of the old beliefs, a general approach that could be termed 'pro-belief' rather than the narrower categories of 'modernist' or 'secularist'.

The pro-belief approach could be considered a new manifestation of the 'middle way' – one which navigates a path between traditional articles of faith and modern empiricism, thereby creating the cultural space for Western Buddhists to find their feet in a new context. From another perspective, as a contemporary manifestation of Buddhist pragmatism, one which allows Buddhist values, ideas and meditations to be established in a new culture, it could be understood as a modern adaptation of the Buddha's skill in means. However it is interpreted, as an intuitive exploration of Buddhism rather than a conscious strategy of cultural navigation, the pro-belief approach has allowed for the easy circulation of traditional ideas alongside modernist innovation. If the pro-belief approach is more prevalent than the secularist innovations of recent times – which denude the Dhamma of its metaphysical foundations – a creative adaptation of tradition is a more likely Buddhist path into the future.

The formation of Western schools will thus depend on a deeper exploration of Buddhist metaphysics, which may occur in an Asian institutional setting (such as the now flourishing centres of Tibetan Buddhism), or in those centres in which modernist concerns are set

Fig. 23. Thich Nhat Hanh teaching at Plum Village

against a traditional background (such as Thich Nhat Hanh's 'Order of Interbeing', which blends *prajñā-pāramitā* and Huayan thought), or even in the more secular environment of the Vipassana centres. Everything is at least in place for this next step in the spiritual adventure to be taken: the resources available are much greater than at any time in the past, including a vast range of traditional texts and an increasing number of contemporary studies. Since most of these sources are more or less accessible at the touch of a button, the next phase in the turning of the Dhamma-wheel may even take place in private, as Asian and Western Buddhists alike take responsibility for the Buddha's mission from the more individualistic perspective of the modern world.

List of Maps and Figures

Further Reading

Introductions and Overviews

Bechert, Heinz and Gombrich, Richard. 1991. *The World of Buddhism: Buddhist Monks and Nuns in Society and Culture*. Thames and Hudson.

Buswell, Robert E (ed.). 2003. *Encyclopedia of Buddhism*. Gacl.

Gethin, Rupert. 1998. *The Foundations of Buddhism*. Oxford: Oxford University Press

Harvey, Peter. 2000. *An Introduction to Buddhist Ethics: Foundations, Values and Issues*. Cambridge: Cambridge University Press.

Keown, Damien and Prebish, Charles S. 2006. *Introducing Buddhism*. London, New York: Routledge.

Rahula, Walpola. *What the Buddha Taught: Revised and Expanded Edition with Texts from Suttas and Dhammapada*. Second and enlarged edition. New York: Grove Press.

Robinson, Richard H. and Johnson, Willard L. (assisted by Sandra A. Wawrytko and Thanissaro Bhikkhu). 1997. *The Buddhist Religion: A Historical Introduction*. Fourth edition. Belmont: Wadsworth Publishing Company (International Thomson Publishing).

Williams, Paul. 2008. *Mahāyāna Buddhism: The Doctrinal Foundations*. Second edition. London, New York: Routledge.

India

Bronkhorst, Johannes. 2009. *Buddhist Teaching in India (Studies in Indian and Tibetan Buddhism)*. Boston: Wisdom Publications.

Lamotte, E. 1998. *History of Indian Buddhism. From the Origins to the Śaka Era. Translated from the French by Sara Webb-Boin*. Louvaine: Université Catholique de Louvain (Institut Orientalist Louvain-la-Neuve).

Warder, A. K. 2008. *Indian Buddhism*. Third edition. New Delhi: Motilal Banarsidass.

Williams, Paul with Tribe, Anthony and Wynne, Alexander. 2012. *Buddhist Thought: A Complete Introduction to the Indian Tradition*. Second edition. London, New York: Routledge.

East Asia

Bowring, Richard John. 2005. *The Religious Traditions of Japan, 500–1600*. Cambridge: Cambridge University Press.

Ch'en, Kenneth. 1972. *Buddhism in China: A Historical Survey*. Princeton: Princeton University Press.

Dumoulin, Heinrich. 2005. *Zen Buddhism: A History, India & China (Volume 1)*. Revised and expanded edition. BloomingtonWorld Wisdom.

Matsuo, Kenji. 2007. *A History of Japanese Buddhism*. Folkestone: Global Oriental.

Theravāda

Crosby, Kate. 2013. *Theravada Buddhism: Continuity, Diversity, and Identity*. Chichester: Wiley-Blackwell.

Gombrich, Richard. 2006. *Theravāda Buddhism: A Social History from Ancient Benares to Modern Colombo*. Second edition. London and New York: Routledge.

Swearer, Donald K. 2009. *The Buddhist World of Southeast Asia*. Second edition. Chiang Mai: Silkworm Books.

Tilakaratne, Asanga. 2012. *Theravada Buddhism: The View of the Elders*. Honolulu: University of Hawai'i Press.

Tibet

Kapstein, Matthew T. 2006. *The Tibetans*. Malden: Blackwell.

Powers, John. 2007. *Introduction to Tibetan Buddhism*. Second edition. Ithaca: Snow Lion.

Index

I.B.TAURIS INTRODUCTIONS TO RELIGION

Daoism: An Introduction – Ronnie L Littlejohn
HB 9781845116385
PB 9781845116392

Jainism: An Introduction – Jeffery D Long
HB 9781845116255
PB 9781845116262

Judaism: An Introduction – Oliver Leaman
HB 9781848853942
PB 9781848853959

Zoroastrianism: An Introduction – Jenny Rose
HB 9781848850873
PB 9781848850880

Confucianism: An Introduction – Ronnie L Littlejohn
HB 9781848851733
PB 9781848851740

Sikhism: An Introduction – Nikky-Guninder Kaur Singh
HB 9781848853201
PB 9781848853218

Islam: An Introduction – Catharina Raudvere
HB 9781848850835
PB 9781848850842

Christianity: An Introduction – Philip Kennedy
HB 9781848853829
PB 9781848853836

Hinduism: An Introduction – Will Sweetman
HB 9781848853270
PB 9781848853287

Buddhism: An Introduction – Alexander Wynne
HB 9781848853966
PB 9781848853973

Mormonism: An Introduction – Malise Ruthven
HB 9781780760100
PB 9781780760117